Additional Praise for *Clearing the Bases*

"Barra's clear-eyed analysis makes *Clearing the Bases* one of the most thought-provoking books on the game to appear in some time."

—*Bookpage*

"Barra . . . worships at the altar of statistics, where he isn't afraid to sacrifice a sacred cow or two."

—*The Washington Post*

"Who is the 'greatest player' of the twentieth century? Barra provides a myriad of statistics and facts and his choice will take most readers by surprise."

—*Baltimore Sun*

"Barra . . . contributes some remarkable sleuthing and fine analysis."

—*Seattle Post-Intelligencer*

Clearing the Bases

The Greatest Baseball Debates
of the Last Century

Clearing the Bases

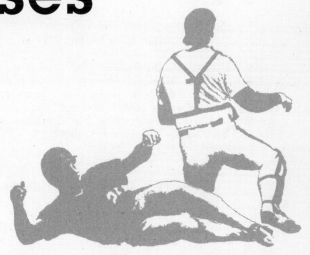

Allen Barra

Foreword by Bob Costas

Thomas Dunne Books   St. Martin's Griffin   ⚘   New York

Dedicated to the memories
of Ross Wetzsteon and Lee Lescaze

THOMAS DUNNE BOOKS.
An imprint of St. Martin's Press.

www.stmartins.com

Library of Congress Cataloging-in-Publication Data

Barra, Allen.
    Clearing the bases : the greatest baseball debates of the last century / Allen
Barra; foreword by Bob Costas.—1st ed.
        p. cm.
    ISBN 0-312-26556-5 (hc)
    ISBN 0-312-30253-3 (pbk)
    1. Baseball—United States—History—20th Century. 2. Baseball play-
ers—Rating of—United States. I. Title.

GV863 .B26 2002
796.357'0973'0904—dc21   2001048992

First St. Martin's Griffin Edition: May 2003

10 9 8 7 6 5 4 3 2 1

Contents

Contents

Foreword

It's impossible to watch or read about baseball these days without being bombarded with statistics and "achievements" that, in the context of the history of baseball, actually mean little.

Enter Allen Barra, part of a small but noble brigade that thinks, really thinks, about sports. For many years, Barra's thoughtfully researched and carefully considered articles and books have shed new light on sports debates great and small. He's never hesitated to question long-held assumptions—including his own—and often arrives at surprising conclusions, always presented in a lively and persuasive fashion. In a sports world saturated with uninformed grandstanding and "analysis" that is often as overheated as it is superficial, Barra's stuff stands out. His passionate but unsentimental interest in history is both rare and welcome.

In *Clearing the Bases*, Barra becomes possibly the first sports historian ever to delve deeply into the questions that many of us have been debating for much of our lives, for instance: Mays or Mantle? Case long since closed, you say? Not so fast. See what Barra has to say. If you believe, as I do, that no truly great player has ever been so unappreciated as Mike Schmidt, count on Barra to champion the cause and arm you with the arguments that build to the point where they're all but irrefutable. (Well, if not actually irrefutable, at least pretty darn strong.)

Has history ever really given Juan Marichal his due, particularly when he is compared to Bob Gibson and Sandy Koufax? If you believe that Marichal is owed something by baseball history, you'll get a kick higher than a Marichal windup from reading this chapter. As to the question of whether or not today's pitchers can hang with greats like Cy Young, Walter Johnson, and Lefty Grove, let Barra make a case for what Roger Clemens would have done against the old-timers. (This one might really surprise you.)

And, as a bonus for football fans who don't think statistical analysis can be revealing, watch Barra polish up Bart Starr's star in the pantheon of great NFL quarterbacks.

Sit. Read. You'll enjoy it. And best of all, you'll learn something. Trust me. It'll be good for you. But one thing: Next time you debate these questions with someone, make sure you've read this book first.

Bob Costas
NBC Sports

Introduction

My father used to tell me that as a boy all I ever wanted to argue about was who was stronger, Superman or the Hulk? Who was faster, the Flash or Green Lantern? From such a misspent youth has this book evolved. After all, such debates are kid stuff, but who would deny that such kid stuff is important to us? The typical adolescent male daydream is supposed to be about striking out the Yankees to win the World Series or of hitting the jump shot at the buzzer to beat the Celtics, but if there were any way of measuring such things, I'm fairly certain that most of us would have proved to have devoted more time and energy wondering and arguing about who was better than who than in fantasizing ourselves into the games.

To be completely honest, the reason I wrote this book is because I have been dying to read it for years, and no one else has gotten around to writing it. All my life I've wanted to know who, at their respective peaks, was better, Mickey Mantle or

Introduction

Willie Mays, or who the best pitcher in baseball history was. Now, I think I know, or at least I feel satisfied that I know as much as statistics can tell me. I currently write sports columns for *The Wall Street Journal* and for the internet magazine, Salon.com as well as occasional features for *Playboy* and *The New York Times*, and most of them deal with different aspects of the same questions: who's the best hitter? Who's the best pitcher? What's the best team of all time? Which are the best current players in each sport, and how do they stack up to the all-time greats? I get hundreds of letters and e-mails a year on these questions, many of them not mere reactions to what I've written but questions and speculations about things I haven't even thought about yet. Some of the essays presented here are extensions of the arguments made in the pages of those publications, while others were inspired by questions from interested readers. In writing all of them I've relied on fairly basic numbers, statistics that can be found and used by just about any fan. Occasionally I'll use information compiled by some random crack researcher whose word you'll just have to take unless you want to go back and watch hundreds of hours of footage on your own. Mostly, though, I've used what can be found in *Total Baseball*, the official encyclopedia of the game, and the Stats, Inc. *All-Time Major League Handbook*. I'm a big fan of the work done by baseball's great "S.A.B.R.-metric" researchers—i.e., researchers who are members of the Society of American Baseball Research—and I fully acknowledge the work they have done in pioneering baseball analysis and in creating a species of literate, intelligent fans. But my audience is much broader; I want to confine myself to numbers that the average fans are familiar with, or at least that I can make them easily familiar with.

Besides, most of the arguments I make in this book do not demand complex stats; they simply demand someone looking at something in a way they haven't looked at it before. If I can do that to you—if I can get you to think about any of the players presented here in a way you haven't thought about before—I'll have succeeded, whether I end up changing your mind or not.

The essays are in three groups. The second group are some brief "position papers" on the numbers used and why I have such faith in them; if you flip to them and they catch your fancy, I suggest you read them first before going ahead to the longer ones. If you're a hard-core baseball stat junkie, they might seem a bit basic to you, so jump right into the Mantle-Mays or Grove-Clemens-Koufax pieces. Part three is an attempt to apply some of the same types of analysis I use on baseball to the careers of Wilt Chamberlain and Bill Russell in basketball and some outstanding football figures, particularly Bart Starr. This book is being marketed to baseball fans, but I have an enlightened editor at St. Martin's Press, Pete Wolverton, who actually thinks that fans who watch baseball occasionally drop in on football and basketball as well and urged me to include these essays as "a little bonus."

I've tried to frame these arguments as a fan might, laying my own prejudices out at the beginning (for instance, I was raised a Willie Mays fan and always will be). But I've tried to construct them as a non-partisan fan would, someone who was more interested in discovering the answer than in pushing an agenda. Let me lay out one prejudice right here: I believe in statistics. I do not trust people who say they do not. Whether it was Benjamin Disraeli or Mark Twain or whoever who said, "There are two kinds of lies, damned lies and statistics," he was trying to pull the wool over someone's eyes. Well, no, I take that back; I can see how someone would feel that way, particularly in regard to the manipulation of statistics, but this is not an argument against damned statistics, it is an argument against damned liars. How in the world any baseball fan can say that he doesn't trust statistics is beyond me; stats are the life blood of the sport. No matter how many games you watch you can only see a tiny fraction of the games played; if you can't trust numbers to tell you what happened when you weren't there, then what can you trust? You may not have sufficient information to make a judgment, but that is not an argument against statistics, it's an argument for *more* statistics.

I must get ten or more e-mails a month from well-meaning fans who want to let me know that, because I didn't rank their favorite team or player as high as they think I should, I "shouldn't rely so heavily on statistics." What's odd is that they never tell me what, in lieu of statistics, I should be using. Funny, too, I never get hostile letters from people for using statistics when I rank their favorite team or player too high.

Then there is the fan who wants to let you know that "You shouldn't rely too heavily on statistics, statistics aren't everything." Again, they never get around to telling me what I should be using in my analysis besides statistics, but nevermind, they are essentially right. I've never been entirely sure how I feel about intangibles; on the whole, I suppose, I agree with Bill James's classic assessment that "Intangibles are a fan's word for talents that don't exist." But I'm aware that there are some talents that contribute to winning that we can't quantify—or at least that we haven't found a way to quantify—and that as analysts we should always leave a little room for skepticism. Simply put, I feel about intangibles the way an elderly Irish woman felt about the fairies when asked by Sean O'Faolain: "No, I don't believe in them. But they're there." I've tried in some essays, particularly the Joe DiMaggio-Ted Williams comparison, to allow for the contribution of what can't be measured on paper (except, perhaps, by results). But always, I want to exhaust the limits of the known before I delve into the unknown; I want to know just how far statistics can take me before I even consider what is in the realm beyond.

There is a limited amount of paper in this world and many people to thank. I'll start with two men, now dead, who had a big effect on my life and work, and to whom I dedicate this book. Please indulge me a moment while I talk about Ross Wetzsteon. Ross Wetzsteon was a great man and a great editor. Before I came to New York, more than twenty years ago, he took time to read my work (mostly in *The Chicago Reader*) and encouraged me to write for *The Village Voice*, for which, over the next ten years, I wrote nearly three hundred columns, features, and reviews, most of them for the sports section.

It still amazes me how many people read *The Voice* back then and still remember it. I was in a cab once in Santa Fe, New Mexico, headed for the airport when the driver saw my name on the ticket. "Hey," he said, "I used to read you in *The Voice* when I was at the University of New Mex." Two years ago when I was in Montana working on a story for *The New York Times*, a Crow Indian, a park guard at the Little Bighorn battlefield, recognized my name from the *Voice* sports section. I owe most of that to Ross, who established the *Voice* sports section, picked three or four writers he liked, gave us advice and guidance, and then pretty much let us run wild—sometimes, I admit, too wild, but he always took our part with management when we crossed the line. And cross the line we did in the mid and late '80s, building a big cult following and ruffling the feathers of the sports establishment to a point where we'd often get "secret" calls from editors at the established sports magazines and big daily sports sections saying how much they'd like to hire us but that we had really pissed off so-and-so high up on the masthead. After a couple of years I felt a little like Cleavon Little in *Blazing Saddles*, the black sheriff who nobody will admit to liking in public but who gets chocolate cakes slipped through his window as he becomes an "underground favorite." We didn't make much money, but we had a hell of a lot of fun.

Ross was "old" *Village Voice,* which is to say along with his friend, fellow journalist, and baseball enthusiast Geoffrey Stokes (for years, the *Voice*'s press critic and one of the quirkiest and most readable baseball writers anywhere), the last editors to believe that publications should be writer, not editor dominated—and he was a terrific writer himself, particularly on tennis, baseball, and theater, which was his first love. When he first came to New York from Montana in the mid-'60s, he immediately plunged into the arts scene and soon became one of the founders of the OBIE Awards for Off-Broadway theater. He was among the first to champion David Mamet, Wallace Shawn, and Sam Shepard (You can still read his astute assessment of Shepard's work in his introduction to *Fool for Love and Other Plays*). Ross was also a superb judge of literature. He introduced me to, among others, James Merrill, Grace Paley, James Purdy, and a baseball writer/analyst from Kansas named Bill James, whose books he was constantly buying and handing out to friends. Ross was one of those rare journalists who appreciated both logic and passion, and he sensed a kindred spirit in James, whose baseball analysis was, for him, an antidote to the "Us guys" baseball and sports writing that dominated New York papers in the early '80s. When you made a statement in any piece for Ross, particularly something on baseball, he'd say "What is your source? Is it credible?" or "Where is your evidence for that?" and ask politely to see your homework. Largely under the influence of Ross and Geoff Stokes there evolved a typical *Voice* style sports piece which usually began by taking some currently popular notion and turning it on its head based on a thorough re-reading of history.

Ross Wetzsteon died in 1998 and in a tribute piece I wrote for him I bowed to political pressure in favor of another *Voice* editor who had edited sports and mentioned him as "one of the inspirations" behind the *Voice* sports sections. That was a lie and I'm ashamed to have said it. I appreciate the chance to set the record straight.

The *Voice* sports section died before Ross. In 1991 the then managing editor (who was soon to be fired) hired a new sports editor with a loathing of all sports American. After a two-year diet of soccer and hockey the old readership bailed out, and the section was cut. Fortunately, I had a fan I never knew about at *The Wall Street Journal* named Lee Lescaze who asked me to lunch and said "You know, you really should be writing this weird stuff for a much bigger audience." Myself, I couldn't have agreed more, and Lee, who had been an award-winning reporter for nearly thirty years, took the time and trouble to help me shape the "By the Numbers" column in *The Wall Street Journal,* from which many of the best debates in this book were shaped. Lee died of cancer in 1996. Since then, Paul Steiger, a dream of a managing editor, has given me space and enough free reign to carry my "By the Numbers" column into previously uncharted territory.

Numerous others, both through their support and talent for arguing, have earned a mention here. Among them are: Howell Raines, currently the managing editor of *The New York Times*, who has been an inspiration since he was film critic for *The Birmingham News* in the late '60s and always found the time to advise, comment, and suggest when I was starting out in New York; Vic Ziegel, the sports editor of *The New York Daily News*, who has been supportive over the years and is always ready with a good argument during a lull in the press box; Kevin Baker, author of the great American novels *Sometimes You Can See It Coming* and *Dreamland* and one of the best telephone debaters in the world; Stephen Randall, executive editor of *Playboy*, a fine editor and, as of 2001, a fine novelist as well; David Talbot, executive editor of *Salon* who said upon hiring me that he wanted me to do "just what you used to do at *The Village Voice*," and both Gary Kamiya and King Kaufman at *Salon* who helped me to do that; Michael Anderson at *The New York Times Book Review*, a vigorous debater who argues the way I like to argue, not to win but to provoke thought and midwife insights; Kyle Chrichton at *The New York Times Sunday Magazine* who gave me a lot of good space for some pretty radical views; George Plimpton, who has always been there over the years with a good word or a much-appreciated note; David Denby of *The New Yorker*, who convinces me that I sometimes reach smart fans who don't live in sports pages; to Glen Waggoner of *ESPN Magazine*, who, in the early days of the publication let me go as far out on a limb as any editor ever; Miles Seligman of *The Village Voice*, who is waking up some echoes in the revived sports section; Allen St. John, sports columnist of *The Voice* who has an uncanny knack for knowing when to think like me and when not to; Mike Siano and Billy Sample of Radio MLB, masters of presenting the most complex argument to the widest audience in the shortest amount of time; to Mike Leary of *The Baltimore Sun* and formerly of *The Philadelphia Inquirer*, who put the bee in my bonnet for this book several years ago; Bert Randolph Sugar, who will argue about anything at the drop of a hat and have a contrary opinion ready before the hat hits the floor; Rob Neyer, an accomplished contrarian in his own right as a baseball columnist for ESPN-Online and a sometimes cowriter for special columns in the *Journal*; my cousin, Joseph Anello, who will argue about anything and everything and persist at it even when you have proven to him that he is wrong about Larry Bowa's fielding range, which he vastly overrates, but excuse me, I digress; to Joseph Casamento and Alan Nordstram, whose tough baseball card trading back in Old Bridge, New Jersey planted the seeds for some of these essays—by the way, Joe, I would appreciate that 1961 Mantle All Star card back anytime you're ready; Doug Pappas, editor of the S.A.B.R business newsletter and one of the last hopes of baseball journalism; Coach T. J. Troup of Tustin, California, a groundbreaker in football research; George Will, for his good wishes and gallantry in returning my occasional criticism with good will; Jesus Diaz, a fellow researcher and crack telephone debater since my days at *The Village Voice*; George Ignatin, an economics professor at the University of Alabama in Birmingham and early mentor in sports stats with whom I wrote two books, *Football by the Numbers, 1986* and *1987*, for the old Prentice Hall house; Roger Kahn, for years of encouragment and support; Bud Goode, the unfortunately now-forgotten mentor of football analysts who first got me to study the game; Marvin Miller, who never fails to stimulate brain waves; Bill James, the finest baseball historian, analyst, and writer of my generation, without whom none of us would be here; and Bob Costas, whose three-hour phone conversations every eight or nine months give me enough material for several weeks' columns.

Also, to my late father, Alfred Barra, who got me interested in kid's stuff like this in the first place. Dad, I did my best for Willie Mays, but we were wrong (you were right, though, about Flash and Green Lantern).

Clearing the Bases

1

Getting Tough with Babe Ruth

Four Myths About Babe Ruth

1. Babe Ruth as the Savior of Baseball

As every baseball fan knows, it's an article of faith that Babe Ruth "saved" baseball after the disgrace of the 1919 "Black Sox scandal" and the 1920 death of Ray Chapman from a fastball to the head by Carl Mays. While Ruth's power and flamboyance revitalized the game and in time brought out new fans, there is no evidence whatsoever that baseball in this period was in any danger of losing fans for any reason. Here are the American and National League attendance figures for 1917, '18, '19, '20, and '21:

	1917	1918	1919	1920	1921
American League	2,858,858	1,707,999	3,654,236	5,084,300	4,620,328
National League	2,361,136	1,372,127	2,878,203	4,036,575	3,986,984

Attendance in both leagues did take a sharp dip, but it was in 1918—probably due to the dip in the economy from the end of the war—but, in any event, well before either the Black Sox scandal or Chapman's death. The AL led by nearly half a million in 1917, just 335,000 or so in 1918, then, in 1919, it was back up to over 775,000. But 1920 was the first season that the Black Sox scandal could have hurt attendance and it was actually up substantially, by more than 1,400,000 in the AL, *but also* by nearly 1,160,000 in the National League, where Ruth did not play. In 1921, attendance in both leagues took a surprising dip, despite the fact that Ruth was having what many consider to be the greatest season of his career. The answer that would seem to make the most sense is that baseball went into a sharp one-year decline after World War I, after which interest rose sharply for the next two seasons before leveling off. Ruth no doubt helped to fuel the surge but he may very well have been carried along by it as well. In any event, there was no drop in attendance following the Black Sox scandal or the death of Ray Chapman, so there was nothing for Ruth to save baseball from.

2. Babe Ruth Begat the Lively Ball Era

Ruth was, apparently, the first player to stride up to the plate in just about any and all situations with the intention of hitting a home run. From 1919, when he led the American League with 29 home runs while still playing for Boston, through 1921, when he led the league with 59 while playing for the Yankees, no one else quite got the idea. In those three seasons, one George Kelly, first baseman for the New York Giants, is the only other player in either league to hit more than 19 (Kelly led the NL in 1921 with 23). Then, in 1922, Rogers Hornsby led the National League with the incredible total of 42, and Ken Williams of the

Browns passed up Ruth for the AL crown, 39 to 35. In fact, Curt Walker of the A's also surpassed Ruth with 37. But rather than surge forward, over the next five seasons power hitters fade into the background and leave the stage to Ruth. Cy Williams, playing for the lowly Phillies in 1923, is the only hitter in either league to hit as many as 41 until Gehrig burst on the scene with 47 in 1927.

What is the explanation for this? Why did it take everyone else so long to start catching up to the coming trend in baseball, the home run? And why, once the home run is established by Ruth, do both leagues then go into a home run lapse that lasts several seasons? Even assuming that Ruth was greater by far than any of his contemporaries, is it possible that from 1919 to 1927—in fact, to 1929—that sixteen major league teams could produce just three other men capable of hitting as many as 40 home runs in a season?

I don't think so, and I'd like to suggest two other reasons that are related. The first is the strong prejudice that early baseball felt toward the home run. Back in 1845, Alexander Cartwright's original rules actually outlawed the home run—a ball hit over the fence was regarded as a foul. Hall of Famer Henry Chadwick, inventor of the box score, wrote in 1892 that "Long hits are showy, but they do not pay in the long run. Sharp grounders insuring the first-base certain, and sometimes the second-base easily, are worth all the hits made for home-runs." Chadwick felt that the number of strikeouts caused by players "swinging for the fences" far outweighed the value of the home run—a feeling that may have had some validity in his day when the number of errors in an average game was so high that putting the ball in play was of vital importance (in modern times the "sharp grounders" he called for would be swallowed up in Bill Mazeroski's and Ozzie Smith's gloves). That prejudice has never entirely disappeared from baseball. You saw it in Ty Cobb's relentless crticism of Ruth and how he had ruined "scientific" baseball. You'll see it pop up again in our next item in Branch Rickey's putdown of Ralph Kiner. In fact, on the day I write this, *Sports Illustrated* has published their "Overrated and Underrated" issue with Mark McGwire listed by Michael Bamberger in the former category because "In the batter's box he's one-dimensional. The harsh truth is that McGwire represents all that's wrong with modern baseball and modern life. . . . He strikes out every fourth time at bat." There you go, those strike-outs again. Makes you wonder what modern baseball writers think is so much more beneficial about hitting into double plays.

I don't have time to go into a detailed analysis here of McGwire's (and Barry Bonds's) achievements—tell enough of your friends how great this book is and I might get around to it in volume two—but in passing I'll say that McGwire did turn himself into a fine first baseman, that he was in fact much more adept at reaching base than many players with gaudier batting averages, and that the cell phone, *Entertainment Weekly* magazine, and Adam Sandler movies are far more indicative of what's wrong with the modern world than anything Mark McGwire ever did. And the harsher truth, whether Bamberger wishes to face it or not, is that in terms of winning baseball games it is relative slap-and-tickle hitters like Pete Rose and Tony Gwynn who are overrated. (Quick now: pick a batting order of Mark McGwires or Tony Gwynns or Pete Roses and bet your house or your children's college fund on which one is going to score more runs. *Now* tell me who's overrated.)

I think the other reason that the best players were slow to catch on to the home run is that well into the '20s, it appeared as if much of the old-timers' criticism was correct. In 1921 and 1922, the New York Giants of John McGraw, the ultimate exponent of hit-behind-the-runner-put-the-ball-in-play–type base-ball had beaten the Yankees in 9 out of 12 World Series games with Ruth hitting just 1 home run in 33 at-bats. I greatly suspect that not until 1923, when the Yankees won in 6 games with Ruth hitting 3 home runs, did many writers and fans truly see the home run as a great offensive weapon, much the way football fans and coaches and players didn't truly accept the forward pass until Notre Dame had beaten Army with it. And think about this: *before 1927, no player besides Ruth who had hit as many as 37 home runs had played on a team that had won a pennant.* In 1922, Hornsby became the first National Leaguer to break 40 when he hit 42, but the Cardinals finished third, 8 full games in back of the Giants. In 1925 he hit 39, but St. Louis finished fourth, 18 games behind Pittsburgh. In 1922 Ken Williams of the Browns hit 39, and St. Louis finished just 1 game behind the Yankees, but in 1923 Cy Williams of the Phillies hit 41, and his team finished dead last. It's likely that many veteran observers regarded the home run as a kind of desperation device to be used only when a team fell behind, much the way many football coaches felt (and still feel) about the pass. And, of course, only bad teams struggle to come from behind. I really believe that it isn't until the crushing one-two of Ruth and Gehrig in '27 and '28 that most baseball men gave into the home run and accepted it as the game's ultimate offensive weapon.

Because look what happens after that. In 1929, two players besides Ruth (Chuck Klein of the Phillies and the Giants' Mel Ott) hit more than 40 home runs, while two (Hornsby and the Cubs' Hack Wilson) hit 39, and four more in the two leagues hit more than 30. By 1930, fugedaboudit. Everyone is hitting big. Hack Wilson puts up Ruthian type numbers in the NL, including 56 home runs and a still-standing record of 191 RBI. By 1932, the year of Ruth's last World Series team, the A's Jimmy

Foxx has passed up Ruth (who is, after all, thirty-seven by now) and everyone else with a .749 slugging average and 58 home runs.

And so, the era of the lively ball that Babe Ruth ushered in had reached full flower. Right? Not quite.

There's a problem with that scenario, and it's basically this: the era of the lively ball started well before Ruth's influence. Let's take a glance at the American League hitting stats for the two years before Ruth became an outfielder as well as the three years after:

AL	BA	OBA	SLG A	HR	ERA
1917	.248	.318	.321	133	2.67
1918	.254	.324	.323	96	2.78
1919	.269	.334	.359	240	3.23
1920	.284	.348	.388	369	3.79
1921	.293	.357	.409	477	4.29
1922	.285	.349	.398	525	4.04

Hitting was on the rise—slightly—in 1918, and then, in 1919, it really started to take off, particularly in the area of home runs. The reasons *why* hitting was on the rise in this era have been recounted and argued in detail in numerous baseball histories, and it's likely that there is no one single reason for it (though I tend to favor Bill James's point that the major leagues started keeping large supplies of fresh, clean, new balls with life in them after Ray Chapman was killed by a dirty, hard-to-see ball in 1920. But that doesn't explain why home runs went up from 96 to 240 the season before that happened). Ruth became a full-time regular in 1919 and hit 29 home runs; take away his numbers and there's still a pretty big increase in for everyone else. You could, I suppose, make the argument that a lot of people were suddenly trying to imitate Babe Ruth—but then you'd have to explain why no one else in the league hit more than 10 home runs. In point of fact, individuals weren't hitting a lot more home runs; it was simply that almost everyone on the team was hitting a couple more. For instance, Cleveland and Washington, who finished second and third in the league in 1918, hit just 9 and 5 home runs respectively. In 1919 they hit 25 and 24, repetively. You'd also have to explain why the same kind of increases show up in the National League. In 1917 the NL hit .250; in 1918, .255; in 1919, .258; and in 1920, .270. NL hitters hit 139 home runs in 1918; in 1919 the figure went up to 207; and the next year to 261. Come on, now, are you going to tell me Babe Ruth was also responsible for these dramatic rises in the other league, too?

No, I'm sorry, the evidence in this case simply doesn't support the legends that have grown up around Ruth. Babe was a huge influence, and he did a lot to refocus baseball into a power game, and he was the single most spectacular example of that new power. But Babe Ruth did not create the "Lively Ball Era." Mickey Mantle, when asked by an idiot reporter whether he'd rather bat .400 or hit 60 home runs, gave an undeservedly sensible answer. "I'd rather hit .400," he said, "because the way I swing, if I hit .400 I'd get the 60 home runs." Allow for a slight exaggeration in numbers, and that's what happened between 1919 and the early '30s. Conditions were right for people to hit .400, or at least .375, and the way they were swinging, they got their 60 (or 58 or 56 or 42) home runs.

3. Babe Ruth the All-Around Player

In 1952, while trying to convince Pittsburgh Pirates owner John Galbraith to sell Ralph Kiner and then use the money to develop and buy new players, Branch Rickey composed the following free verse:

> *Babe Ruth could run. Our man cannot.*
> *Ruth could throw. Our man cannot.*
> *Ruth could steal a base. Our man cannot.*
> *Ruth was a good fielder. Our man is not.*
> *Ruth could hit with power to all fields. Our man cannot.*
> *Ruth never requested a diminutive field to fit him. Our*
>   *man does.*

Branch Rickey was, almost certainly, the greatest baseball mind ever. But even great minds have their blind sides. Why Rickey continually belittled and underrated Ralph Kiner, the only great player he ever had at Pittsburgh, is a mystery even Rickey's biographers have never explained, but that's not the point we're concerned with here. Ruth's reputation, as it has been handed down to us, is one of a great all-around player. Let's look at the evaluation of Ruth's all-around abilities from the man who invented the modern farm and scouting systems.

First, Babe Ruth could run. Yeah, a little, for a huge fat guy. Well, to be fair, they say Babe could haul it when he was young. All I can say is that we have more steals/caught stealing information for Babe Ruth than for most great early stars, including Ty Cobb and Honus Wagner, which is to say for fifteen of his twenty-one seasons, and if there is any case there to be made for Ruth's speed, I can't see it. From 1920 (when, after all, he was just twenty-five) to the end of his career in 1935, Ruth is known to have attempted 240 steals, of which he was successful just 123 times. This is such a miserable ratio—out of 240 base runners, Ruth was able to create perhaps 40 additional runs by moving to second where a single could bring him home, and as a trade-off he removed 117 other baserunners, killing an absurd number of scoring opportunities but also costing his team God-knows-how-many runs by using up outs on the bases that would have better gone to batters. In fact, Ruth was such a lousy base-stealer that one wonders today why he was even allowed to keep trying to steal. One possible answer is that everyone tried to steal bases back then, that it was such a common part of the game that even knowledgeable baseball people (and there is no more knowledgeable baseball person ever than Branch Rickey) simply did not stop to consider that a man who was thrown out as often as he stole was actually hurting his team.

Another reason might be that no one could keep a tight reign on Babe. Perhaps his most reckless and selfish moment on a baseball diamond was his unsuccessful attempt to steal second base in the ninth inning of Game 7 of the 1926 Series, depriving Bob Meusel and possibly Lou Gehrig of a chance to win the game and Series (One can only imagine Rickey's reaction if Kiner had tried such a stunt).

For the record, we have complete stolen base information on Ralph Kiner's stolen bases for just five years, 1951 through 1955. He was 9 of 11 in that period. I submit to Branch Rickey or anyone else that a team would have been better off with Ralph Kiner's stolen base record than Ruth's.

Second, Babe Ruth could throw. He is generally described as one of the greatest left-handed pitchers of his time; in point of fact he was one of the greatest pitchers, right or left, of the period. *Total Baseball* ranks him number one for 1916—not the number-one *pitcher*, the number-one *player*. In other words, his pitching made him perhaps the most valuable player in the league. In 1917, they rank him fifth-best player; in 1918, when he is still mostly pitching, they place him second, with Walter Johnson first.

But I think Rickey, as he was comparing Ruth with Kiner, meant "throw" in the sense of being able to make assists and hit the cutoff man from the outfield. Ruth seems to have been able to do this very well, with 203 assists to show for an 18-year career, though curiously, he never led the league. Like most outfielders with a strong arm, he had high assist totals early in his career—a high of 21 in 1920, and then 20 in 1923—and then fewer as his career went on and runners learned not to test him. He does not appear to be as good in his own time as, say, Roberto Clemente, who had 266 assists in eighteen seasons, leading his league four times and getting as many as 27 in 1961, was in his.

By the way, Kiner appears to have had about an average arm for a left fielder. Like Ruth, he never led the league in assists for his position. Overall, he had 80 assists in ten seasons, a slightly better average than Hall of Fame left fielder Lou Brock, who, according to the *Stats Inc. Major League Handbook*, had 142 in nineteen seasons, and several-time Gold Glove left fielder Barry Bonds, who had 129 for his first fourteen seasons.

Third, Babe Ruth could steal a base. Oops, that was already covered in the first item.

Fourth, Babe Ruth was a good fielder.

Hmmm, well, it was Branch Rickey who, after an extensive study of the subject, declared that there was "nothing you can do with fielding." So forgive me if I don't put absolute faith in range factor or fielding averages. Nonetheless, we have nothing else to work with, so, let's look at Babe versus his contemporaries. The Babe played 2,214 games as an outfielder in the American League and 26 in the National and compiled a range factor of 2.16 chances for 9 defensive innings with a fielding average of .968. How does that compare to other right fielders in his time? They put up a collective .966 fielding average with a range factor of 2.37. You can argue, if you wish, that this doesn't really prove anything, that maybe Yankee pitchers in Ruth's heyday struck out so many batters that there were simply fewer fly balls to go around, or that somehow for some unexplained reason the stat simply doesn't reflect Ruth's true defensive ability. And if you use these arguments I'm not going to argue too hard against you. But if you do that, you must still concede that there is no objective evidence that Ruth was anything more than an average outfielder—and the same is true of Ralph Kiner in left field, who had an average of .974 to the league's .978 and a range factor of 2.25 to the league's 2.40.

But, you might say, Kiner played only ten seasons, whereas Ruth's numbers reflect his declining years, when he had slowed down. Well, Ruth began playing the Yankee outfield full time in 1920 at age twenty-five, and from then till 1925, his first six seasons, he had a range factor lower than the league's in four of six seasons. So you figure it out how Ruth was supposed to be such a great fielder and Kiner was not. To me, more than half a century after the fact, they look about exactly the same.

Fifth, Ruth could hit with power to all fields.

I don't quite get this one. As long as one hits with power, what difference does it make what field or fields he hits to? For my own part, I never heard anyone say that Babe Ruth was good at hitting to "all fields"; in fact, I've never heard of a great power hitter who was known to hit to all fields. From period descriptions, Ruth seems to have been the quintessential pull hitter. (Kiner certainly was; opposing defenses always shifted sharply for him, and he never tried to take advantage of that by hitting to other fields, a stubbornness that, by his own admission, probably cost him a career batting average at or near .300. But, then, one wonders what difference it could have made to his team. Would hitting 20 points higher and hitting maybe half as many home runs have won more ballgames?)

I assume that Rickey meant that Ruth was a much more consistent hitter than Kiner, and that is certainly true. Ruth's lifetime average was .342 to Kiner's .279, which was a bit low even for a slugger in the late '40s and early '50s when batting averages had gone down. But the difference between the two is not so great as one might think at first glance. The National League batting average from 1946 to 1955, the ten short years of Kiner's career, was .2612. The American League's batting average from 1920 to 1929, Babe Ruth's peak years, was .2860. Now, unless you want to argue that hitters suddenly got worse in twenty years—and I'm sure that Branch Rickey was in as good a position to know that as anyone else and he never implied any such thing—then we have to assume that pitching or hitting conditions or something besides talent caused batting averages to drop so severely. Actually, we have a pretty good idea what it was: night ball, because even today we can see a huge gap between batting averages from day and night games. But we'll let that pass for now. The point is that it is not unreasonable to assume that Ralph Kiner, had he played in Ruth's time, would have had a career batting average of, say, .305, and since his on-base average (OBA) was an already sensational .398, we can certainly assume that would have gone higher, too, to about .430. Now, those are pretty sensational statistics, and I really have to wonder if Branch Rickey, observing Kiner hit .305 with all those walks and home runs, would have singled him out for criticism.

Or, stated another way, if Ruth had played in Kiner's time and beyond and had lost about 25 points off his average and wound up at about maybe .317 with a commensurate drop in other stats, would he then remain the yardstick against which all hitters are measured against? Uh-oh, better stop, we're getting into the area of heresy.

I'm getting off my path here, which is not really a comparison of Ruth and Kiner—and I'm not going to tell you that if it was that I'd contend that Kiner was Ruth's equal or even near equal—but an examination of Ruth's ability as an all-around player. Oh, okay, I'll do number six: No, to my knowledge, Ruth never asked for a more diminutive field to hit in, and since he first hit in the league's best hitter's park, Fenway, and then went to Yankee Stadium where the right-field porch was a mere 296 feet from home plate, he certainly shouldn't have. On the other hand, it makes perfect sense to me for a team like Pittsburgh to alter its dimensions a bit to suit its only offensive strength.

Okay, I'm finished with this, except to say that Branch Rickey was the smartest baseball man and one of the most compassionate baseball men who ever lived, but he was also a tightwad and cheapskate and enjoyed using management's power on players like Kiner when negotiating contracts, which may have had a lot to do with the animosity the two men had for each other ("With his parsimonious attitude to the baseball players," said Kiner years later, "Rickey did more than any other person to bring about the player's union."). And, frankly, I think there are a lot worse insults you can dish out for a player than to tell him he finishes second when being compared to Babe Ruth. But my real reason in quoting Rickey was to establish the fact that some pretty smart baseball guys have tried to make the case that Babe Ruth was some kind of great all-around player, and as near as I can see, there isn't a shred of objective evidence to support that conclusion. It seems to me that he was a mediocre fielder with a slightly overrated throwing arm who couldn't run very well (or at least didn't run very wisely) and who hurt his teams by his selfish and silly insistence on trying to steal bases.

4. Babe Ruth as the Most Dominant Team Player of the Century

Don't you hate silly arguments like this one? Remember, a year or so ago when people actually argued unanswerable questions like "Who's the most dominant team player of the millennium?" What does that mean, anyway, "dominant team player"? Does it mean "Who, as best as can be determined, is the best player in a team sport?" I don't think so, since then you'd pretty much wind up with the same players—Babe Ruth, Wilt Chamberlain, Jim Brown, et al.—who dominated all the other polls. I think the question was supposed to mean "Who, as best as can be determined, is the best team player on a dynastic team?" with "team" in this sense suggesting that his skills helped make his teammates better. In other words, Bill Russell or Michael Jordan over Wilt Chamberlain, Joe Montana instead of Jim Brown, because their teams won more championships. I'm not saying Russell was a better "team" player than Wilt, or at least I wouldn't say it without a chance to argue the question at length. I'm just saying that if you ask the question "Who is the most dominant player?" you'll mostly get Wilt for an answer, and if add the little word "team" as in "Who is the greatest team player?" you'll get Bill.

What's odd, though, is that Babe Ruth continued to dominate the baseball polls. Odd, I mean, because Babe Ruth wasn't any kind of "team" player and because—how to put this?—there are an awful lot of players whose record of *team* dominance surpasses Ruth's.

Does that surprise you? It sure surprised me when I began to research this chapter. I mean, if someone asked "How many championships did Babe Ruth win?" what would you answer? Seven? Six? I've been writing about baseball for more than twenty years, but that's what I'd have said. Babe Ruth was base-ball's most "dominant player," right? He played for baseball's most dominant team, right? He came along right at the time when power was starting to take over the game, and changed it forever, right? He was hitting 50–60 home runs at a time when everybody else was hitting 5 or 8, right? How could his teams have failed to win more than . . . four championships? Well, that's how many he won. (Fooled you, didn't I? He actually won six, including two with the Red Sox in 1916 and 1918. But of course we're talking about Babe Ruth the Yankee. The Red Sox were already winners before Babe arrived, having disposed of the Phillies, 4 games to 1, in 1915. What we're trying to find out is what Babe brought to the party on his own.)

In 1920—not 1921, as many historians have contended—Babe Ruth had his greatest season, hitting 54 home runs, and leading the AL in OBA (.532) and slugging average (SA) (.847) for the highest SLOB (see Chapter 15), .450, of his career (in fact, the highest of anyone's career). His Yankees finished third in the league behind Cleveland and Chicago. In 1921 Ruth had another fantastic season with 59 home runs, again leading the league in everything it is worth leading the league in, and the Yankees won the AL pennant and lost to their crosstown rival Giants, 3 games to 5, in the best-of-seven series. The next sea-son, Ruth was something like an ordinary great player (.315, 35 home runs) but the Yankees won the pennant, losing in the World Series to the Giants again, this time in a humiliating 0 to 4 sweep. In 1923 Babe rebounds a bit with 41 home runs and a career-high .393 average, and the Yankees win their first series ever, 4 games to 2 over the hated Giants. In 1924 he is almost as good, and the Yankees lose the pennant race to Walter Johnson and the Washington Senators. In 1925 Babe's career seems to disintegrate into a mess of problems, which we'll look at more closely in a couple of pages. On the field, the Yankees finish a horrendous seventh, next to last, in a league again won by the Senators and Walter Johnson.

Let's stop for a moment and review. By the end of 1925, Babe Ruth is thirty, past what most would consider his prime years, and where is he in baseball history? If he had been been killed in a plane crash at that point, or more likely, given his driving habits, in an automobile crash, he would still have made the Hall of Fame as a great pitcher and as a hitter who did more than anyone else to revolutionize the game. In the seven seasons he had had enough at-bats to qualify, Babe Ruth had led his league in OBA five times and—here's the key—SA seven times. In fact, seven straight times up to 1925, when he had his worst season. In five of those seven seasons, he had led the league in both, an absolutely awesome record of power and consistency. Forget for a moment the differences between the late teens and early '20s, when Ruth came to prominence, and the prime of Ty Cobb (which was roughly ten years earlier), or the even greater differences of the game in the prime years of Honus Wagner roughly five years before Cobb. If Cobb and Wagner had played at the same time as Ruth, they'd have had higher slugging averages; if Ruth had played in theirs, he'd have had a lower SA, with probably a higher batting average (BA) in Cobb's time and a lower BA in Wagner's. The numbers would have changed, but it wouldn't necessarily change one's chance of leading in a particular statistic, by which I mean that if Ruth led the American League in home runs in 1921 with 59 he probably would have led the league in 1911, too, even if his winning total was about 17 or so: well, maybe 20 or 25. After all, he was Babe Ruth. But in their own time, Cobb and Wagner did not dominate the two most important hitting stats, on base and slugging average, the way Ruth did in his. In twenty-four seasons from 1905 to 1928, Cobb led in OBA six times and in SA eight times and in both three times. Wagner, in twenty-one seasons from 1897 to 1917, led his league in OBA four times, in SA six times, and in both three times. But before age thirty, with just seven full seasons as a regular hitter under his belt, *Ruth had already led in both categories in the same season five times, and only a fourth-place finish (behind, respectively, Tris Speaker, George Sisler, and Ty Cobb) in OBA in 1922 kept him from leading in both categories for an incredible seven straight seasons.* So there is no doubt that Babe would have been remembered.

But would he have been remembered as dominant? As we said, he won two Series rings with Boston, but there he was pitching for a team that looked good enough to win anyway. As an everyday player with the Yankees, by age thirty, he had won just one championship ring.

Then, after a truly subpar 1925 season in which it looked as if he had peaked and was headed downhill, Ruth staged a second half of his career comeback. Over the next seven seasons he led the AL in OBA five times and in SA six times—that's six times in a row from 1926 through 1931. Four times he leads in both in the same season. The Yankees rebound to win the pennant again, but again they don't win the World Series, losing to the Cardinals, 4 games to 3 (This is the Series which ends with Babe inexplicably getting thrown out while trying to steal second base in the ninth.) Now, Ruth is thirty-one, and has just one championship as a regular player.

It is the 1927 and 1928 seasons that forever change our perception of Babe Ruth as a dominant team player. The Yankees storm through 1927, winning 110 games and clobbering the Pirates 4 games to 0 in the Series; in 1928 they win 101 and beat

the Cardinals 4 games to 0. That's a two-year record of dominance unchallenged until the Yankees of '98–'99 (As to who was
more dominant, it depends on how you look at it. The '27–'28
Yankees won 211 regular-season games, lost 99, and were 8–0 in
the World Series; the '98–'99 Yankees won 212 in the regular
season but lost 112 and were also 8–0 in the Series. But the
'98–'99 Yankees also had to play two rounds of playoffs each
year to get to the Series and were a combined 14–3 in those
games.) But something had changed from the Yankees of '27
and '28 and the pre–1925 Yankees. Or, rather, something had
been added. That something, of course, was Lou Gehrig.

I'm not suggesting that it took Lou Gehrig to make a super-
star out of Babe Ruth. I am suggesting that without Gehrig,
Ruth might have finished his Yankee career with just one New
York championship.

Who was more of a force on those 1927 and 1928 Yankee
teams? Let's look at both seasons using my favorite stat, SLOB
(slugging times on base), and, in the interest of bringing in
other points of view, *Total Baseball's* Batter Runs (created by
Baseball historian and statistician Pete Palmer and defined on
page 2492 of the seventh edition as "The Linear Weights
measure of runs contributed *beyond* those of a league average
defined as zero." There is a much more detailed explanation
in *Total Baseball*, but the formula is "Runs = (.47) 1b + (.78)
2b + (1.09) 3b + (1.40) HR + (.33)(BB+ HB) − (.25)(AB −H) −
(.50)OOB), and Bill James's Runs Created (which, as the text
on page 2498 of the seventh edition of *Total Baseball* says, has
"Many different formulas" but which, in its basic expression is
(Hits+ Walks) (Total Bases) over (At Bats + Walks) as well as
simple Runs Produced (runs batted in plus runs scored minus
home runs).

First, 1927:

	OBA	SLGA	SLOB	Ba. Runs	R Created	R Produced
Ruth	.486	.772	.3751	100.4	208	262
Gehrig	.474	.765	.3626	100.8	212	277

Now, let's do 1928:

	OBA	SLGA	SLOB	Ba. Runs	R Created	R Produced
Ruth	.463	.709	.3282	84.6	183	251
Gehrig	.467	.648	.3026	76.0	169	254

I'd say that overall all the numbers are so close that the differences between them fall into the "margin of error" category, though I think Ruth gets a slight edge. But it is not clear that Ruth was a more valuable player on those two championship teams than Gehrig. In any event, Ruth did not win his second and third World Series rings as a regular until he played alongside of a comparably great hitter. For the next three years, despite Ruth and Gehrig, the Yankees played second fiddle to the great and now largely forgotten Philadelphia A's teams of Jimmy Foxx, Al Simmons, Lefty Grove, and Mickey Cochran. In 1932, the Yanks, bolstered by a third great star, catcher Bill Dickey, pass up the A's to win the pennant and sweep the Cubs in the World Series. (This was the Series of the "called shot" home run, a topic I'm not going to touch with a ten-foot pole.) That gave Babe a thirteen-year stretch as a regular in which he played on seven pennant winners and four World Series winners. This is a terrific record of success, but it doesn't equal Mickey Mantle's thirteen-year achievement, from 1951 to '63, of playing for eleven pennant winners and seven World Series winners. It certainly doesn't equal Joe DiMaggio's thirteen-year stretch—

actually his entire career—of winning ten pennants and nine championships. (And while we're on the subject, Yogi Berra played in more than 100 games in fourteen seasons, during which the Yankees won eleven pennants and eight world series).

Bill James once made the very intelligent observation that any argument to the effect that Babe Ruth wasn't the greatest player in baseball history soon dovetails into something else. I suppose he's right, at least as the statistical argument is concerned. No one ever put up statistics like Ruth, and I very much doubt if anyone ever will again. But that answer doesn't satisfy me, not even a little. For one thing, it assumes exactly what we want to know: it starts out assuming that Ruth was the greatest. Let's try turning it around.

To do that I'm going to use a quote from a friend of mine, Allen St. John, a columnist for *The Village Voice*. "Ask someone," he wrote a few years ago, "who the greatest basketball player of all time is. They'll say Michael Jordan. Ask him who the greatest quarterback is. They'll say Joe Montana. Ask them to name the greatest heavyweight champion. It'll be Muhammad Ali. The greatest hockey player? Of course, Wayne Gretzky. Now, ask them the greatest baseball player of all time? And the answer will be Babe Ruth. Now, look over that list of names and ask yourself what's different about the last one." Exactly.

Every other sport gets to choose a current or modern player as its greatest, but a baseball fan always has to look to the past. No one who follows football would try to tell you that the Chicago Bears "Monsters of the Midway" from sixty years ago could stand with the recent NFL champions, and therefore no one would try to sell you Sid Luckman over Joe Montana. Yet, we are told that a baseball player of *seventy-five years ago is the standard by which all subsequent players should be measured*. A couple of years ago, at a lunch with some friends from *ESPN Magazine*, I proposed that Wilt Chamberlain and not Michael Jordan was the most dominant player in basketball history, "The Babe Ruth of Basketball." I was scoffed at; how could I say that when the conditions of the game have changed so greatly from the early '60s to now? And yet, when it came time to pick the greatest player in baseball history, four of five picked Babe Ruth without batting an eyelash (the other picked Willie Mays, the player people usually pick who don't pick Ruth).

Apparently the conditions of basketball had changed radically over the last thirty-five years but in baseball, over seventy years, not at all.

We could, of course, name hundreds of conditions that have changed in baseball over seventy to eighty years, but let's stick to the biggest ones. Babe Ruth didn't compete against black players. A black player, Hank Aaron, eventually broke Ruth's career home run record. Another black player, Willie Mays, probably would have done it first if he had not given two years of service to the Army. Another black player, Ken Griffey Jr., seems likely to pass up Ruth before he turns forty. But somehow, the fact that Ruth only competed against white players isn't supposed to matter to me. Does it matter that Ruth never batted against Pedro Martinez or Mariano Rivera? Does it matter that the big leagues of today are composed of the cream of white, black, Latin, and even Asian players, that stars of the modern game are drawn from a talent pool so huge and rich and refined by a process of competition so demanding that no one in Ruth's time and probably no one from the first half of the twentieth century can appreciate?

Am I dovetailing here away from a discussion of why Babe

Ruth is not the greatest player ever into a discussion of race and sociology? Not really, because I don't accept the premise. I simply refused to be pushed into it. The baseball I know, the game I grew up with, was and is dominated by Willie Mays, Mickey Mantle, Joe Morgan, Mike Schmidt, Barry Bonds, and Alex Rodriguez. I simply do not admit of anyone's right to assume that someone who played many years before them is automatically their superior without having justified their premises. I can accept that Babe Ruth was the best of the players in his own time, but I see that time as highly limited in comparison with my own, and I also see a highly unusual set of circumstances involving Ruth and his era that other great players in his time—and I'm not even talking about black players—simply didn't have the good fortune to stumble into.

Babe Ruth is an American creation myth. We've never been able to say for sure when baseball began, but we all recognize the game Ruth played as our own. Subsequently, we have built up myths around him, that he was some kind of great all-around player (he was not, unless you mean a great hitter and a great pitcher, though never at the same time), that he was the "savior" of the game, or that he was responsible for the "lively ball" era, or that he was great team player when in fact no player more self-centered and oblivious to the needs of his teammates ever lived, or that he called his own home run in the World Series (actually, I think he did do that). More than that, we have made him into a big, lovable clown and completely absolved him from any actions in his life that involve reason and accountability. The real Babe Ruth was a glutton, an adulterer, a heavy drinker, a carouser, a man who frequented brothels and partied with gangsters. He was, quite often, a selfish, childish, brutish and even bullying man—like Ty Cobb, he once attacked a fan in the stands, but who besides Ruth would have held his manager off the end of a train by his ankles?— who was constantly fined, suspended, and reprimanded in his own time. When movies are made about his life (such as the theatrical release a few years ago starring John Goodman and the TV movie starring Stephen Lange) they make it a high point of tragedy that he never got to manage, and to that any sane person can only shake their head and say "Thank God some team owners have the sense not to put men like that in positions of authority."

He was careless, crass, and no more averse to a fast buck than many a player today. Remember the boy in the hospital that Babe hit the home run for? He lent his name to a paper company to do a magazine ad telling the whole sob story.

Modern baseball writers who wouldn't tolerate Ruthian behavior in current players for a season regularly roll on press-box floors telling and retelling stories of his antics with showgirls and hookers.

The Babe gets a free ride from the modern historians and documentary makers, and his name is often evoked by people who in practice seem to abhor the very kind of big power–big strikeout, low emphasis on speed and defense game that Ruth was most associated with in his own time. Nobody ever gets tough with Babe Ruth.

What the hell, I love him, too, and I always will. That old Hartland statue with him standing there, a ghostly look on his face, a tiny finger calling his longshot, is one of my most precious possessions. If I ever get around to doing a follow-up to this book, I'll pick an all-time All Star team, and I can tell you now he'll be on it, in spite of everything I've said. The Babe is tough enough to take few knocks from me. Or anyone. Maybe even tough enough to put up with a modern reassessment and still stay a hero.

2

The Most Underrated
Team of the First Half of
the Twentieth Century

	W-L	ERA	R Per Game	FA	E	DP
1919 Chicago	96–44	2.24	4.21	.974	151	98
1919 Cincinnati	88–52	3.04	4.76	.969	176	116

There are anniversaries for the damndest things in sports, and I get letters on just about all of them. "Did you know," read an e-mail to me at *The Wall Street Journal* last August, "that coming up this September is the tenth anniversary of Shoeless Joe Jackson's banishment from baseball's Hall of Fame? And do you intend to do something about it?" Actually I did know that, or at least I thought I did. Jackson was banned from baseball by Commissioner Judge Kenesaw Mountain Landis's decision in 1920, but that had nothing to do with the Hall of Fame. That issue was settled in 1991 when the Hall of Fame officially ruled him "ineligible," or declared that he was ineligible because he was banned from baseball. The wording isn't clear; what *is* clear is that Landis did not specifically bar him from the Hall of Fame with his 1920 decision. There was no Hall of Fame to ban him from, and if there had been, Landis would probably have felt it was unnecessary to ban him from it, as no one in his right mind would argue a player for the Hall who had conspired to fix games.

Anyway, as any notion that I could "do something about it" is pretty silly—I suppose what the writer meant by doing something was that he wanted me to write not another plea for clemency but some kind of statistical analysis that would "prove" that Joe belongs in the Hall of Fame regardless of the charges that have been brought against him over the years in connection with the fixing of the 1919 World Series. That anyone thinks I, or anyone else, could do something like this is so absurd it doesn't bear further discussion.

What is my evaluation of Joe Jackson, the player? Someone, somewhere is supposed to have written something that proves Joe Jackson was not good enough to be in the Hall of Fame. I've never located the essay; if I do, I'll write the writer a letter telling him that he is an idiot. Jackson was not the great all-around star he is often made out to be in misty-eyed old-timers' accounts; all statistics for his time show him to be slightly below average as a fielder and base-stealer. For instance, despite his wonderful reputation as a left fielder, his range factor for thir-teen seasons was just 2.02 chances for 9 defensive innings, a lit-tle below the league average during that period, 2.12. In comparison, Ty Cobb, who wasn't regarded as a truly great out-fielder, was actually better, 2.35, than the league, 2.14, for his career. And consider that if Jackson's career had lasted several years more, that range factor would have dropped further as Jackson's speed declined. And as a baserunner, I just don't see it there, either. Like most of the fabled base-stealers in this period, Ty Cobb included, Jackson seems vastly overrated, at least from the available evidence. We have his stealing-caught stealing numbers for just four seasons, but the information is pretty eye opening: in 1914, '15, and '16, when he would be, presumably, at his peak, and in 1920, his last season, he stole a total of 71 bases and was thrown out 61 times. The only conclusion one can come to when reading numbers like this is that back then they simply did not realize the foolishness of letting runners try when their success rate was below 70 percent.

I can see no objective evidence to support the stories of Shoeless Joe's great speed, because he wasn't exceptional in the two areas of the game, in the field and on the bases, where speed matters. Ah, but as a hitter he played just ten full seasons and compiled a batting average of .356, third highest (after Ty Cobb and Rogers Hornsby) of all time. Despite the fact that he was a contemporary of Cobb, who led the league in just about everything every year, Jackson led the AL in hits once, doubles once, triples three times, total bases twice, SA once, and OBA once. In his last season, 1920, he hit .382, with a career high 121 RBI. It is reasonable to assume that, as hitting stats boomed in the '20s, Jackson's would have, too. He was just thirty-one at the time of the suspension and had 1,772 hits, and there would seem to have been no way that he could *not* have reached 3,000 hits had he played, say, till age thirty-eight. Mind you, for his time and place he was no Honus Wagner, Ty Cobb, Babe Ruth, Ted Williams, Mickey Mantle, Willie Mays, Hank Aaron, Joe Morgan, or Barry Bonds. But he was as good in his time as, maybe, Dave Winfield in his, with an edge given to Winfield for being a better power hitter in his day then Jackson was in his.

So, yes, the player rates Cooperstown. The man? Trying to hash through the jungle of who said what and who took how much and who thought who was dogging it in the field makes me weary. But in the end I have to say, reluctantly (reluctantly because I think he was basically what people sympathetic to him at the time thought he was: a big, not-so-bright, basically right-minded country boy who got mixed up with a bad crowd and let his frustration and resentment at low pay get the best of him), "Forget the arguments about his play, he agreed to do it, he took the money. He conspired to fix games. I'm sorry, he's out and that's it."

Well, you had to ask me. But while we're on the subject, I would like to make a statistical plea for justice as regards the real victims of the 1919 World Series. I don't mean Buck Weaver (whose case really should be reviewed—he didn't conspire and he took no money) or any of the other Black Sox players. My plea is for the winners of the 1919 World Series, the forgotten champions of twentieth-century major league baseball, the Cincinnati Reds.

For all the analysis of who took how much money and whose plays lost which game, the White Sox made exactly the same number of errors in the series as the Reds, 12, a not particularly high total in those days before big gloves.

I'm not suggesting that eight members of the White Sox weren't approached and paid by gamblers to lose. What I am saying is that simply because that was the case doesn't mean that the Sox had it in their power to turn it off and on when they chose. It's entirely possible that the Cincinnati Reds could and would have won the Series without help. In fact, that could well be what happened. Anyway, that's what all the numbers suggest. Before we talk about giving something to Joe Jackson or anybody else, let's start by taking the tarnished crowns off the heads of the 1919 Cincinnati Reds and replacing them with real gold.

Take a moment and study the small chart. Do the 1919 Cincinnati Reds really look that inferior to the 1919 Chicago

White Sox in most vital statistics? Do they really look like a team that gamblers would automatically make a significant underdog, a team that would give gamblers the idea to create a fix in the first place? Well, actually, now that I look a little closer, they do. I mean, the Reds scored .55 more runs per game, but that was more than made up for by the difference in runs allowed: the White Sox gave up .8 fewer earned runs per game. Fielding? Well, the Reds made 18 more double plays, but the White Sox made 25 fewer errors and had a better fielding average. Hmmm. Better pitching, better fielding, 8 more wins during the season . . . I guess I should concede and admit that I was wrong. The White Sox actually do look like the better team and probably deserve to have been the betting favorites.

Really? Well, time for a confession: I switched the two teams with their statistics. Yes, I understand, it's a cheap trick and I don't blame you for being angry, but hear me out. I want to make a point. Everyone who talks about the Black Sox Scandal assumes that the Cincinnati Reds were patsies, that gamblers were right in making them heavy underdogs. Now, I ask you: Look at those numbers and tell me what that assumption is based on? I have read Eliot Asinof's classic account of the scandal, *Eight Men Out*, and everything else I could find on the subject, including biographies of Joe Jackson and Bucky Weaver, and I still haven't got a clue.

Except for one thing: an assumption that any team that won the American League pennant was automatically superior. The American League had, after all, won eight of the previous nine World Series (after the National League had won four of the first six played starting in 1903) but three of the AL's champions after 1909–1910, '11, and '13, were Connie Mack's powerful Athletics with their famous "One Hundred Thousand Dollar Infield." The A's were simply the best in the period, beating three National League pennant winners by a total of 12 games to 4. But the A's beat the stuffing out of the AL, too, winning the pennants in their championship seasons by 14, 13½, and 6½ games. In other words, the American League wasn't superior to the National League: Mack's A's were just superior to everybody.

The World Series winners for the next four seasons were the White Sox in 1917—with virtually the same lineup as 1919, they won the pennant by 9 games and the World Series by beating the New York Giants 4 games to 2—and the Boston Red Sox (led by a terrific left-handed pitcher and pinch hitter named Babe Ruth). By 1919, the AL teams had won 16 of the previous 22 World Series games, and were 12–5 in the previous 17. The notion that this automatically signified a superior league may seem a bit naive to us nowadays; the Yankees won 16 of 19 World Series games from 1996 through last season and 12 of 13 from '98 through 2000, but few would make an argument for American League superiority based on that alone.

But remember that this was in the days before interleague play and fans, writers, and gamblers had nothing else to go by. If you go by regular season play, the 1919 Reds, who had a won-lost percentage of .686, were the second-best team of the decade, just 5 percentage points behind the 1912 Boston Red Sox. If you want my guess, I'd say that the likelihood is that the 1919 Cincinnati Reds were as good and maybe better than the 1919 White Sox.

3

Gary Cooper vs. John Wayne

"All I want out of life," Ted Williams is said to have said, "is for people to say, when I walk down the street, 'There goes the greatest hitter that ever lived.'" What, I wonder, did Joe DiMaggio want? It would seem that, at the end of his life, he settled for being introduced as "The Greatest Living Ballplayer." If so, both men got what they wanted, or at least what they got was close enough to satisfy them. I would guess that in a poll of baseball writers and researchers at least half would grant Williams his title as greatest hitter ever, and 60 percent or more would allow Joe his title of "The Greatest Living Ballplayer." (I'm not aware that sportswriters ever did take such a poll, but while working for Charlie Finley's A's in 1969, DiMaggio was honored at baseball's centennial celebration, as "The Greatest Living Player.")

I've never seen any statistics on it, but I'd be willing to bet that the influx of talent from the Far West in the 1930s, particularly from California, had almost as profound an impact on major league baseball as black stars did in the first half of the 1950s. Blacks comprised perhaps 5 percent of big leaguers by the mid '50s, and the white Western ballplayers who entered the big leagues in the 1930s must have, at the least, approached that percentage. Prior to the '30s, big league ball was not only the domain of white boys but Eastern (previously Southeastern) white boys. Lefty O'Doul, a star pitcher and hitter in the Pacific Coast League and a .349 lifetime hitter in eleven major league seasons, stands out in this era precisely because he was one of the few California-born stars. I don't think it's beyond the realm of possibility that there was enough talent in the Pacific Coast League alone to stock one or two additional big league teams, just as there was in the Negro Leagues at the time.

Both Ted Williams (San Diego area) and Joe DiMaggio (San Francisco Bay area) were Californians, and, along with Lou Gehrig, the two greatest everyday players in baseball from the '30s to the '50s. Joe DiMaggio, cool, aloof, controlled, and dignified, was often referred to as "the Cary Grant of baseball," though, given his shyness and taciturnity, Gary Cooper would have been a more appropriate comparison. Ted Williams, taller, rangier, more open and volatile, was more like John Wayne (though, unlike Wayne, Ted Williams was a real war hero, not just a celluloid one).

They were friendly competitors, the star players of the two oldest and most bitter rivals in American professional team sports. There were endless, unresolved debates as to who was the better hitter, who was the most "valuable." There were even ocassional talks, or at least rumors of talk, about a trade, though nothing that was ever confirmed by the front offices. What do four decades of hindsight tell us about their value? For one thing, there was never any doubt that DiMaggio was always regarded as the superior all-around player. There is no need to haul out baserunning and fielding statistics: DiMaggio was by far the more complete player. Williams worked himself into a capable baserunner, and, after switching from right to left field in 1940 to save his eyes from the sun—or so it was said, though others said he didn't have the arm for right—became a smart left-fielder and the first man to master the Green Monster of Fenway Park. But though there was little base-stealing in the late '30s and '40s, DiMaggio was always regarded as a tremendous baserunner with great speed and judgment. His manager Joe McCarthy called him "the best baserunner I ever saw" (and most of DiMaggio's contemporaries said pretty much the same thing). How many more runs was DiMaggio worth than Williams as a baserunner and fielder? I don't know of any scientific way of measuring this, nor do I know anyone who has seriously tried. Let's come back to it later. For now, let's look at their hitting.

Here are the career line numbers familiar to most baseball fans, capped by my favorite hitting stat, SLOB.

	G	AB	R	H	2B	3B	HR
DiMaggio, 1936–51	1736	6821	1390	2214	389	131	361
Williams, 1939–60	2292	7706	1798	2654	525	71	521

	RBI	BB	SO	BA	OBA	SLG	SLOB
DiMaggio, 1936–51	1537	790	369	.325	.398	.579	23.04
Williams, 1939–60	1839	2019	709	.344	.483	.634	30.62

DiMaggio's substantial edge in triples reflects both his speed and the huge gap in his natural power alley in Yankee Stadium, left-centerfield. The other big difference between them is in the walks and strikeouts column. Ted Williams was thought by many to have the sharpest hitting eye in baseball—Rogers Hornsby is the only player mentioned by many players in the same breath. Yet, DiMaggio had substantially fewer strikeouts, in fact, easily the lowest total of any great slugger in baseball history—lower, in fact, than most "contact" hitters (Phil Rizzuto, one of the toughest whiffs in his day, playing in 75 fewer games, struck out 102 more times). More on this later. But look at Williams's lead in walks! Williams played in 556 more games than DiMaggio, a little less than four full seasons, so he should have more walks. But DiMaggio could have played *twice* as many games as he did and not have approached Williams.

Of course, a combination of injury and military service—in Williams's case, two wars—cut a big chunk out of both men's prime years. Ted Williams lost all of 1943, '44, and '45 to World War II with the Marines; in 1950, he smashed his elbow into the wall at Comiskey Park at the All-Star Game and missed the remaining 65 games of the season; in 1952 and '53, he lost all but 43 games to the Korean War; and from 1954 through 1959, a series of injuries and operations left him constantly in and out of the lineup with such frequency that he never played more than 132 games in a season again. (In fact, after 1951, DiMaggio's last year, Williams had only one more season when he played as much as 136 games, and never again drove in a many as 90 in a season.) No other player in baseball history, not even Mickey Mantle, missed so many games in his prime years.

Ted Williams, like Mantle and DiMaggio, was simply injury-prone. We can't do anything about the injuries, but for a moment let's fantasize what Williams's career numbers might have looked like had he not served in two wars. Using Williams's numbers the previous two seasons, including 1950 when he played just 89 games, before each of his military stints, let's do an approximation of what his career numbers might look like if not for the wars, and where that would place him on the all-time lists (to make it as simple as possible):

	G	AB	H	R	RBI	HR	BA
Williams	2930 (10)	9500 (31)	3450 (6)	2380 (1)	2410 (1)	673 (3)	.350 (4)

Remember, these are just approximations, but I think the assumptions are reasonable. In each case I'm not assuming Williams would have been better if he'd had a chance to play those missed seasons, just about the same as the two previous seasons before he went in the service. So, giving him the minimum benefit of the doubt, he comes out tenth on the all-time list in games played but *first* in runs scored, *first* in runs batted in, third in home runs (with an outside shot to have surpassed Ruth), and fourth in batting average. Ted Williams probably *was* the greatest hitter who ever lived, and he certainly doesn't need my help to cop the all-time unofficial title. But I'd like to point out that if not for two wars there would be absolutely no doubt in the minds of the great majority of fans and writers that he was the greatest hitter who ever lived.

Joe DiMaggio, as you may have heard, was pretty good, too. The war and his physical problems limited his career to just thirteen seasons. There's no question the war took him in his prime; in 1939, '40, and '41, respectively, he hit .381 (his highest average), .352, and .357. There's no need for an elaborate chart on Joe's projected stats because even with the three restored war years he wouldn't have had enough at-bats to be among the all-time leaders in most categories. But I think it's all together reasonable to assume that if he'd played those three years he'd have added enough points to his lifetime average to approach .330, and that he'd have had about 430 to 450 home runs, and about 1,900 RBI—pretty spectacular numbers for a sixteen-year career.

Let's define "peak" performance as ten seasons, and compare Joe and Ted in their ten best seasons. For Joe, this is 1936 to '42, and 1947 to '49 (even though he played just 76 games that year); for Ted from 1939 to '42, '46 through '49, and 1957 and '58.

	G	AB	H	BB	SO	2B	3B	HR	R	RBI	BA
DiMaggio	1349	5378	1801	590	276	314	109	282	1123	1249	.335
Williams	1445	5052	1786	1316	468	365	59	329	1259	1210	.353

Looked at like this, they don't appear so far apart as many fans would imagine. Williams, injury-prone though he was, was still more durable than DiMaggio, and played nearly 100 more games in his peak seasons. Williams has more doubles and home runs, DiMaggio more triples, and, rather surprisingly, considering Williams's greater playing time, more RBI. Or perhaps not surprisingly when one considers that Red Sox opponents could pitch around Williams much easier than Yankees' opponents could pitch around DiMaggio. The real difference between them is that amazing walks total of Williams, more than twice as many as DiMaggio. It's what separates Williams as a hitter from DiMaggio; it's what separates Williams as a hitter from almost everybody.

No matter how you slice it, career-wise or for a peak ten-year period, there is no question that Ted Williams's hitting stats are superior to Joe DiMaggio's.

How much do those stats reflect their genuine abilities and how much do they reflect the parks they played in? Boston's Fenway Park was always recognized as a great hitter's park, though perhaps too much emphasis has been placed on the "Green Monster," the left-field wall that has made memorable sluggers out of people like Bucky Dent. There isn't a right-handed power hitter who hasn't had fantasies about a season at Fenway, and scarcely one who played in Fenway hasn't benefited from it. Yet in and of itself, the wall has never created great hitting stats. While the relatively short distance from home to the wall has tacked on many a homer or double that would have been a fly ball in most other parks, it has also cut down on a lot of singles—hard line drives that would drop in for base hits in other left fields get grabbed up by left fielders in Fenway who are at their normal depth. And singles to left often don't produce an RBI from a runner on second, since the cramped quarters often turn leftfielders with mediocre throwing arms into Roberto Clemente clones.

In truth, Fenway has been a great hitting park for *all* hitters, largely because the dark green backdrop allows hitters a better shot at picking up the ball as it leaves the pitcher's hand. In some ways, Fenway might have been a better park for left-handed hitters like Williams than for right-handed batters, since most visiting managers, when given a choice, have preferred to use righthanders to southpaws.

In recent years the construction of luxury boxes at Fenway has apparently affected air currents and diminished Fenway slightly as a power hitters' park, but in Williams's day, it was well-above the big league average for both average and power. Some historians have maintained that the construction of a right-field bullpen area in 1940 hurt Williams's power numbers, but if so, there are no stats to support the argument. Williams went from 31 home runs in his rookie season to 23 in 1941, but his overall slugging average dropped just 15 points from .609 to .594, and the next season he posted the highest slugging average of his career, a phenomenal .735. As we shall see, he did have a few more home runs on the road than in Fenway over eighteen seasons, but he hit far more doubles at home.

On the other hand, or field, there is absolutely no question that Yankee Stadium hurt Joe DiMaggio as a hitter. Yankee Stadium in DiMaggio's day had a huge left-center field area that peaked more than 460 feet from home plate, great for a center-fielder with DiMaggio's range, bad for a power hitter with DiMaggio's swing. The power area was, as it is today, the cozy right-field porch, which is almost but not quite the reverse of Fenway's left field.

How did their respective parks affect their hitting? Here, compiled by Retrograde, Inc., are their home-road stats. First, the home numbers:

WILLIAMS
HOME

G	AB	R	2B	3B	HR	RBI	BB	BA
1165	3887	973	319	35	248	965	1032	.361

ROAD

1127	3819	825	206	36	273	874	987	.328

DIMAGGIO
HOME

G	AB	R	2B	3B	HR	RBI	BB	BA
880	3360	648	186	73	148	720	398	.315

ROAD

856	3461	742	203	58	213	817	392	.333

This is quite an eye-opener. The first thing you notice is the substantial difference between Williams's home and road batting average—that's a whopping 33 points. Again, there is equally no doubt that Yankee Stadium hurt DiMaggio: he not only hit 18 points lower at home than in all other American League ballparks, he hit 65 more homers, scored 92 more runs, and had 97 more RBI away from home. It's normal for a hitter to have a batting average of, say, 5 to 10 points better at home, with proportionate increases in power, but Williams's batting average at Fenway is all out of proportion to the norm. The second thing you notice is how much Yankee Stadium cut down on Joe DiMaggio's power: had Yankee Stadium been just a neutral hitters' park for him, he'd have finished his career with a whopping 425 or so home runs in just thirteen seasons.

Just for fun, let's assume that Ted Williams and Joe DiMaggio had played their home games in ballparks that were absolutely neutral—or, phrased another way, parks that, in their effect on hitting and pitching, were like all the other parks in the league averaged out. In other words, let's take their road stats and double them and then pretend for a moment that these represent their career stats.

WILLIAMS

G	AB	R	2B	3B	HR	RBI	BB	BA
2254	7638	1650	512	72	546	1748	1974	.328

DIMAGGIO

G	AB	R	2B	3B	HR	RBI	BB	BA
1712	6922	1484	406	116	426	1634	484	.333

Williams, in our "neutral parks" scenario, has played 542 games more than DiMaggio, the better part of four seasons (in reality he played 556 more). Yet DiMaggio already leads him in triples, 116 to 72, a tribute to DiMaggio's greater speed and baserunning ability, and, at the pace established here, would surpass Williams in all the other categories if he had played a similar number of games. All categories except walks. (Of course, the scenario still assumes that DiMaggio would be batting in the Yankees' order and Williams in the Red Sox, which could affect RBI and run totals.)

Let's look at the home-road charts as well as our "neutral park" scenario a bit more carefully. First of all, it has to be admitted that seeing their hitting stats from a road perspective gives a solid boost to DiMaggio's stature. Williams was a better hitter, but not by so wide a margin as might be imagined. In fact, if they had played their careers for exactly as long as they did, and under the conditions imposed by our own "neutral park" scenario, then the average baseball fan might actually perceive DiMaggio to be the better hitter because of his slightly higher batting average and greater proportion of power hits (in this scenario, DiMaggio has 949 extra base hits to Williams's 1,130, a difference of just 181 in 542 fewer games). The perception would not be accurate, but it would be one that many, perhaps a majority of fans would hold.

And think of what might have happened if DiMaggio had been on the Red Sox and Williams on the Yankees. What difference might those circumstances have made and how might they have changed our perception even further? Judging from the boost all hitters get in Fenway and from the boost DiMaggio got hitting anywhere outside of Yankee Stadium, it's very likely that DiMaggio would have added 10 to 15 points to his thirteen-year batting average and finished around, say, .337 or .338. Likewise, he would have added at least 50 home runs—after all, he hit 65 more in other American League parks than he did in Yankee Stadium. But a total of 410 for thirteen seasons seems about fair without giving DiMaggio too much help.

Yankee Stadium wouldn't have done much to Ted's batting average one way or the other, and it might have helped his home run production a bit with that friendly right-field porch. But Yankee Stadium couldn't have helped Williams's home run total so much as being *out of Fenway* would have helped it. Strange as it seems, Fenway actually hurt Williams a bit as a home run hitter. If you refer back to the home-road chart, you'll see that Williams, over the course of twenty-one seasons, actually popped a few more homers on the road—25, to be exact—than he did in Boston.

If they had spent their prime years in each other's ballparks, it's very likely that our perception of Joe DiMaggio's and Ted Williams's hitting abilities would be different. What would *not* be different would be the reality. Williams was simply a better hitter, even when you allow for the artificial boost his stats got from playing his home games in Fenway Park. Williams didn't gain *that* much from playing in Fenway, and, anyway, how much can it be said that playing in Yankee Stadium *hurt* Joe DiMaggio? There is no question his overall numbers there were down, but how much of that was the fault of Yankee Stadium and how much was the fault of DiMaggio?

Great hitters are supposed to adjust to their surroundings. It must be said that Joe DiMaggio didn't adjust all that well to Yankee Stadium. If Yankee Stadium was simply a bad hitter's park that suppressed *all* hitters' averages, then the substantial difference between DiMaggio's home and road numbers would have to be allowed for in any comparison of DiMaggio's and Williams's relative value. After all, if runs were tough for everyone (or at least for every right-handed slugger) to come by in Yankee Stadium, then the runs DiMaggio produced would have to be accorded greater value. But Yankee Stadium wasn't really a "bad" hitter's park; it was, on the whole, a "neutral" hitter's park. It was bad for DiMaggio, at least relatively speaking. Many great hitters—and there is no questioning that DiMaggio was one of the greatest hitters of all time—almost invariably learn to make adjustments. Willie Mays, who modeled his stance on DiMaggio's and who, in his time, produced numbers similar to what DiMaggio produced in his, adjusted brilliantly to the strong wind in Candlestick Park that knocked potential home runs down and into outfielders' (and some would swear infielders') gloves. Candlestick Park was supposed to have "cost" Mays 100 or 140 or even 200 home runs to the wind blowing in from left field in Candlestick Park, depending on which Giant fan you talked to. But it turns out Mays did not lose 100 home runs or however many or even *any* to the winds at Candlestick (see page 79–80): it turns out that Mays adjusted his swing to hit the ball to right and right-center. Joe DiMaggio, who had what appears to be at least as much raw ability as Willie Mays, did not. DiMaggio should have hit a little better at home—most hitters do—but instead he hit worse. Why? Probably because he stubbornly insisted on swinging the same way and hitting the ball to the same part of the ballpark. Joe DiMaggio was too proud to change his style to suit Yankee Stadium, and his stubbornness hurt his numbers and, ultimately, his team.

Joe DiMaggio was a great hitter, one of the greatest ever, but no matter how you jumble the numbers, he was not the equal of Ted Williams. On the road, which is the best measure of a hitter's effectiveness, DiMaggio had a 5 point advantage in batting, .333 to .328, and Williams hit 60 more home runs, 273 to 213, while batting 426 fewer times, which gives Williams a slight edge in home run power, 1 for every 13.9 at bats to DiMaggio's for every 16.2. The real difference, though, as we said earlier, is in bases on balls: Williams, on the road, drew a breathtaking 987 walks in his career to DiMaggio's 392. In other words, Williams totaled 4,806 road plate appearances between at-bats and walks, and reached base 2,238 times, while DiMaggio was up 3,853 times on the road between at-bats and walks and reached base 1,546 times. That leaves 2,568 times that Williams *didn't* reach base—in other words, made an out, while DiMaggio failed to reach base 2,307 times—or, 2,307 outs. DiMaggio played in 271 *fewer* road games than Ted Williams and made 261 *fewer* outs. But Williams had 101 more hits and 595 more walks. In other words, he reached base 696 more times than DiMaggio.

I could go into an analysis of how many runs DiMaggio's superior baserunning was worth, but in the end the difference would be swallowed by the substantially greater number of times Ted Williams *reached* base while Joe DiMaggio was using up outs. I could, I suppose, do an analysis of how many more runs DiMaggio saved in the field than Ted Williams; even though they played different positions, it could be done. But I'm not going to do it, for the single reason that no amount of runs saved in the field—10 runs? 15? 25?—could account for how many more runs Ted Williams was worth as a hitter. (And is it worth mentioning that Ted Williams's range factor in left field was exactly 2.00, higher than Hall of Fame leftfielders Billy Williams, at 1.77, Lou Brock, at 1.81, and the man who followed Williams in left field for the Red Sox, Carl Yastremski, at 1.99?)

And so, if I had to choose between Ted Williams and Joe DiMaggio in their primes for ten seasons, I'd pick Ted Williams. I would? I would not. This book is largely about numbers and how to interpret them, and how to evaluate players on the basis of them. One of the important things to know is just how far stats can take you. Joe DiMaggio played for thirteen seasons, in which time his team won ten pennants and nine World Series. This is one of the most remarkable success records in sports, and DiMaggio was by far the biggest reason his team was able to accomplish what it did. Is there room for intangibles in a book such as this? Is there room for intangibles in the discussion of statistics? I don't know, but I do know that in every book I've ever read about DiMaggio I saw Yankees quoted as saying things like, "With Dage [the Dago, Joe's Yankee nickname] we always felt like we were gonna win." And with Dage they always did.

Maybe it was in all their heads, but were the results any less real for that? As Kevin Costner says in *Bull Durham*, if they *think* that's the reason they're winning, then that's the reason they *are* winning." I know what all the statistics I've flashed before your eyes told you about Williams's greater objective value, but even so, is it reasonable to argue, that if the Yankees had had Ted Williams instead of Joe DiMaggio they'd have won *ten* World Series? *The Yankees didn't win ten World Series with Babe Ruth.* In fact, the Babe Ruth Yankees won only *four* World Series. Yes, it's true that Ted Williams never had the opportunity to win as many pennants and World Series as Joe DiMaggio; his teams just weren't that good. But if you could go back in time and make that trade, would you? And *why* would you? Joe DiMaggio's Yankees won ten pennants in *thirteen* years; is there any reason to assume that Ted Williams or anyone else was so chock full of intangibles that he'd have helped those same Yankees to win *eleven* pennants in thirteen years?

Some men inspire awe, while others inspire confidence. Ted Williams, it seems to me, inspired more of the former than the latter, while DiMaggio inspired both but mostly confidence. He clearly made his teammates better players, or at least made them feel they were better players, which amounts to the same thing.

Think of John Wayne as the volatile trail boss in *Red River* who whips his men into line but whose own intensity causes him to spin out of control, after which the quiet, confident Montgomery Clift brings the herd in. Clift in that movie was like a younger, smaller version of the character Gary Cooper played so well, a character exemplified by his Sergeant York. Now, who do you want leading you in a tight pennant race, John Wayne or Gary Cooper?

4

What If
Jackie Robinson Had
Been White?

In 1997, when the fiftieth anniversary of Jackie Robinson's major league debut was being celebrated, an undercurrent of idiocy was sweeping through America's baseball writers. By no means did it affect everyone, but it got to enough to make an impression. It manifested itself in statements like "Jackie Robinson's accomplishments on a baseball field were not in themselves sufficient for enshrinement in Cooperstown," or in condescending praise such as "Jackie Robinson did so much for baseball that we can afford to look the other way a bit when it comes to his on-the-field credentials." Or even worse, "If Jackie Robinson had been white, he wouldn't be in the Hall of Fame today, but . . ." (I do these people a favor they don't deserve by omitting their names.)

"If Jackie Robinson had been white"? Is it possible that anyone without brain damage could make a statement more asinine? If Jackie Robinson had been white, he probably would have been one of the most obvious and popular choices for the Hall of Fame of the 1950s, or, if he had retired later, the 1960s.

Part of the problem, I suppose, in evaluating Jackie Robinson is that most analysts and historians don't know where to put him. I really don't think this is much of a problem, as Robinson played more than half of his big league games at second base. And since he didn't make his major league debut till age twenty-eight, I think there's a very good chance that had he broke in earlier, he'd have played nearly all his games at second base. Anyway, here are Robinson's career statistics compared with those of eleven other Hall of Fame second basemen. (I'm leaving out Bill Mazeroski, who wasn't much of a hitter, though I can tell you right now I'll take Robinson.) By the way, all fielding stats are for the player's time at second base.

	Year	Ba	H	HR	R	RBI	SB-C
Nap LaJoie	1896–1916	.339	3251	83	1503	1599	380–?
Eddie Collins	1906–30	.333	3311	47	1818	1299	743–?
Rogers Hornsby	1915–37	.358	2930	301	1579	1584	135–?
Frankie Frisch	1919–37	.316	2880	105	1532	1244	419–?
Charlie Gehringer	1924–42	.320	2839	184	1774	1423	181–81
Tony Lazzeri	1926–39	.292	1840	178	986	1194	148–?
Bobby Doerr	1937–51	.288	2042	223	1094	1247	54–64
Red Schoendienst	1945–63	.289	2440	84	1223	773	93–?
Jackie Robinson	1947–56	.311	1518	137	947	734	197–?
Nellie Fox	1947–65	.288	2663	35	1279	790	76–80
Joe Morgan	1963–84	.271	2517	264	1650	1133	686–162
Rod Carew	1967–85	.328	3053	92	1424	1015	353-187

	Fielding Avg	Chances/Game
Nap LaJoie	.963	5.73
Eddie Collins	.970	5.34
Rogers Hornsby	.965	5.36
Frankie Frisch	.974	5.84
Charlie Gehringer	.976	5.64
Tony Lazzeri	.967	5.34
Bobby Doerr	.980	5.74
Red Schoendienst	.983	5.38
Jackie Robinson	.983	5.56
Nellie Fox	.984	5.57
Joe Morgan	.981	5.03
Rod Carew	.973	4.88

Robinson has fewer hits, runs, and RBIs than any other second baseman on this list, which is the primary argument against him being in the Hall of Fame—"He has only 1,500 hits!" If you've read this book this far, you know how much this argument irritates me. Greatness, which is what the Hall of Fame is about, is not measured by the mere accumulation of certain statistics. All statistics must be mined for meaning, and meaning can only be found in relation to other statistics. I don't want to know who did *more*. I want to know who was *better*. Robinson played far fewer seasons—ten—than anyone else on this list, and spent far less time at second than others. Yet, he has more home runs than all but four of the others, and more stolen bases than all but five. That's a pretty good indication of his combination of power and speed.

It's difficult to know what conclusions to draw from the fielding stats; Robinson's range factor isn't higher compared to some of the others. But as we can see, the number of chances per game declines as the century goes on. The two highest in range factor are Frank Frisch, "the Fordham Flash," who was at his peak in the late '20s, and Nap Lajoie, who played his last game in 1916. After WWI, as more outs are made by strikeouts and fewer by batted balls, the chances per game start to decline; the two most recent second basemen on the list, Joe Morgan and Rod Carew, are, respectively, a shade of over 5 in range factor per game and a shade under. It's probable that Robinson's range was good-to-average for his time; His range factor at second base was 5.56, and the average for second basemen in his time was 5.59. Nellie Fox, considered the best American League second basemen of the era, is at 5.57, just .01 higher than Robinson's, (though 1.5 higher than AL second baseman in his time). Robinson's *fielding* average is excellent, only a point below Fox's and much better than those of the players who came before him—but fielding averages have gotten a bit higher as the century has gone on, reflecting, probably, the larger and better-made gloves of the fielders. One might conclude that Robinson was an average fielding second baseman—by Hall of Fame standards. And then perhaps just a bit better: in five seasons he led the league in double plays four times.

As a baserunner, most historians would agree that Robinson was at least on a par with Eddie Collins, Frankie Frisch, and Joe Morgan—surely the only candidates on this list who would be serious rivals for baserunning honors. Robinson led the league twice in steals over ten seasons. Of the dozen Hall of Famers on this list, only Collins, who led four times in twenty-two seasons, and Frisch, who led three times in nineteen seasons, ever led the league in steals. But there is a difference between Robinson's achievement and theirs: Jackie stole bases at a time when hardly anyone else was stealing. How good was he on the bases, really? Well, he was judged by nearly everyone who saw him in action to be the best baserunner of his time. And though some would say that was overstated because of his exposure on TV in a year when the televised World Series was still a novelty, there are many more who say that such exposure simply highlighted what everyone who played with and against him already knew. After all, the famous steal of home in the '53 series against the Yankees was hardly an aberration: Robinson stole home *sixteen times* in just ten major league seasons.

Indeed, what jumps out at a casual observer of Robinson's career is what he could do that other great second basemen of his time couldn't do. What do I mean by great? Well, Nellie Fox and Red Schoendienst are both Hall of Famers and are judged by nearly all historians to be, respectively, the best American and National League second basemen of the 1950s (that is, if one excludes Robinson). Lloyd Johnson, a former executive director of the Society for American Baseball Research, wrote a book— *Baseball's Dream Teams: The Best Players, Decade by Decade*— and he selected Fox number one and Schoendienst number two for the decade. Let's compare.

Nellie Fox and Red Schoendienst were practically the same player, and I've never been able to understand why anyone saw enough of a clear difference between them to rate Fox number one. Schoendienst played for eighteen seasons and hit .289 with 84 home runs, a .334 on-base average, and a .387 slugging percentage; Fox played for nineteen years, hit .288 and had 35 home runs with a .341 on-base average, and a .363 slugging percentage. Both were poor base-stealers; the caught-stealing information on Schoendienst is incomplete, but he was known to have stolen 33 and to have been thrown out 27 times, for a lousy 55 percent success rate. Fox was just 76 of 156 for just 49 percent. (It should be noted that both were considered smart baserunners who were better than their base-stealing stats would indicate.) In other words, neither was much of a hitter or a threat to steal, though by the standards of middle infielders in the '50s, they were pretty good.

Compared to the standards of 1950s middle infielders, Jackie Robinson hit like a first baseman. In fact, he *was* a first baseman in his first season while the Dodgers waited to see if he was a better player than Eddie Stanky (who batted .253 with 3 home runs in 146 games at second base). From his rookie season, 1947, through 1954, Robinson never hit fewer than 12 home runs in a season; from 1947 through 1954 he hit fewer than 31 doubles only once; and from 1948 through 1953, he drove in more than 80 runs in five of six seasons. Scarcely any middle infielders of Robinson's era could match that kind of power. In 1949, the Dodgers decided to bat Robinson cleanup for most of the season; he responded with 124 RBIs, the largest total of his career; in fact, the only time he ever drove in more than 100 in a season. Why didn't the Dodgers continue to bat him in the cleanup spot? Because they had plenty of power hitters—Carl Furillo, Duke Snider, Roy Campanella, Gil Hodges—but only one good hitter with the kind of speed to bat leadoff and bat control to bat second.

How good of a hitter was Jackie Robinson? How effective was his combination of power and speed? Figure it this way: Derek Jeter, going into the 2001 season, had a slugging percentage of .468, 6 points *lower* than Robinson's career mark. And Robinson's career on-base percentage was .410, 6 points *higher* than that of Rickey Henderson, generally considered by most baseball analysts to be the greatest leadoff hitter in baseball history.

I think, then, that it would be logical to conclude that Jackie Robinson, at his peak, was better than any other second basemen in the big leagues between World War II and Joe Morgan. (I'm going to eliminate Rod Carew from the discussion right now: despite his .328 career batting average, Robinson had a higher on-base average, more power, and more range in the field.) How does he stack up against Joe? Pretty much even, I'd say:

both were multidimensional players who could win games in the field, on the bases, at bat, and were MVPs for winning teams. Morgan had more home run power, but Robinson had the higher slugging percentage, .474 to .427. He had a better on-base average, too, .410 to .395. I would give Morgan a slight nod, not for any really clear reason but only because he performed at that level for much longer—he was a valuable player right up until 1985, his twenty-second season in the bigs—and because, as I mention in the chapter on Mike Schmidt, there was a general flattening out of statistics in the late '70s to mid-'80s, which was probably caused by the high level of talent and competition.

So, I've found one second baseman in the second half of the twentieth century that I might rank ahead of Jackie Robinson at his peak (and by the way, I do consider Ryne Sandberg a legitimate Hall of Fame candidate and would include him in this comparison, but I would not quite rank him as high as Joe Morgan or, at peak value, Jackie Robinson). Of Roberto Alomar, the best second baseman to emerge since Morgan, I must wait for another time. Anyway, Jackie Robinson is one of the two best at his position over a period of more than half a century. If that isn't your definition of a Hall of Famer, go play soccer.

Now, since you've paid so much money for this book, I'm going to do a little more than I promised: I'm going to compare Jackie Robinson to the great white Hall of Fame second baseman of the first half of the twentieth century. I'll eliminate Tony Lazzeri right off: he was a fine player, though a questionable Hall of Fame selection, and not quite in a class with Robinson or the others included from 1900 to WWII. I'm also dismissing Bobby Doerr, a good player and a Hall of Famer with terrific batting stats for a middle infielder (223 home runs and six 100+ RBI seasons in fourteen years), who nonetheless owed much to playing his entire career home games in Fenway Park (Neil Munro calculated that he hit 148 home runs at home and just 78 in all other parks) and having played for three of his peak seasons (1942, '43, and '44) in the war-depleted American League. Many think Doerr was not as good as Joe Gordon, the Yankees' second baseman from 1938 to 1948, who is *not* in the Hall of Fame. Gordon played eleven seasons to Robinson's ten; though Gordon hit 116 more home runs, Robinson's slugging percentage is 8 points better, and his on-base average average is 53 points higher.

This leaves Nap LaJoie, Rogers Hornsby, Eddie Collins, and Charlie Gehringer. There is simply no way around Hornsby's batting stats; even though he played at a time when hitting was booming, and in ballparks (for the Cardinals and Cubs) that favored hitters, his numbers are equaled in baseball history by only Babe Ruth and Ted Williams. He led the National League five times in runs, four times in hits, four times in doubles, twice in home runs, six times in batting average, *eight* times in on-base average, and *nine* times in slugging. I think I forgot to mention that he hit over .400 three times.

There is no way Robinson or any other second baseman in baseball history can match those numbers—Ty Cobb can't match them. But it's not inconceivable that Jackie Robinson, if he had played in Hornsby's era, would have put up even more impressive statistics than he did in the late 40s and early 50s. Let's look at how both Hornsby and Robinson hit in their four best seasons in relation to the rest of the National League:

HORNSBY	BA	League Avg	Diff
1922	.401	.292	.109
1923	.384	.286	.098
1924	.424	.283	.141
1925	.403	.292	.111

ROBINSON	BA	League Avg	Diff
1949	.342	.262	.080
1950	.328	.261	.063
1951	.338	.280	.058
1953	.329	.266	.063

Robinson is awesome—in all four of his best seasons he out-hit the league by at least 58 points. But Hornsby is beyond awesome—in his four best seasons he outhit the league by nearly twice as many points as Robinson outhit the league in *his* four best. But let's give Jackie a break. Let's put him back in the 1920s and assume he would have outhit '20s pitching by the same margin that he outhit pitching in his own time. Then those four best seasons would look like, say, .372, .349, .341, and .355. Then Jackie Robinson's career batting average would be at least .320 or .325 or maybe .330 or higher instead of .311—and then there would be no doubt in anyone's mind that he ranked with Hall of Famers like Rogers Hornsby and Eddie Collins and Frankie Frisch.

As it stands, hitting is the only area of the game that Hornsby surpassed Robinson in—if many who saw both in their prime are to be believed, it might be the only area he *approached* him in. Bert Randolph Sugar, the boxing writer and sports historian, has read me letters he received as a boy from Ty Cobb in which Hornsby's fielding is soundly berated, particularly his inability to field pop flies into short right. At least one other old time player recorded that and criticized him for always letting the shortstop take the throws to second—apparently Hornsby was afraid of being spiked, which certainly would have earned him Cobb's contempt right there. In fact, though his fielding stats are not at all bad, I can't find anybody in his own time who had anything good to say about Hornsby anywhere but at bat.

I honestly don't know who I'd pick if I had to choose between Jackie Robinson and Rogers Hornsby as my second baseman. It would probably depend on what era they played in. If it were, say, 1924, and both men were at their peak, I'd probably go with Hornsby. But if they were playing in the modern game—the one Jackie Robinson helped to create—I'd probably give the second base job to Robinson and ask Hornsby if he could play first.

This leaves me with four players—Nap LaJoie, Eddie Collins, Frank Frisch, and Charlie Gehringer. Anyone would make a superb choice for your all-time All Star team. They were all superb, multidimensional players who probably would be stars in any era. All four have statistics that, to the untutored eye, look better than Robinson's. But, starting with Gehringer, let's look a little closer.

Charlie Gehringer: You're not going to hear me bad-mouth Charlie Gehringer. He was a great player, an All Star from age thirty through thirty-five, and an MVP. As a player, he had a lot of things in common with Jackie Robinson. Like Jackie, he won an MVP award and a batting title. Like Jackie, he led the league's second basemen in fielding average (Robinson three times in five seasons at second base, Charlie seven times in sixteen seasons), and, like Jackie, he led the league in stolen bases (Gehringer once, Robinson twice). But though we don't have complete caught-stealing information on Robinson, we do on Gehringer, and it appears that Robinson was a much better base-stealer. Gehringer stole 189 bases but was thrown out 89 times, with just one truly outstanding season (1938, when he was 14 of 15).

Their on-base and slugging averages were almost identical: Gehringer was .404 and .480, Robinson .410 and .474—which, incidentally, leaves them with nearly identical SLOBs, .1943 for Jackie, .1939 for Gehringer. Who compiled his numbers in a tougher era for hitters? Let's compare their respective leagues from Robinson's debut in 1947 to his last good season in 1954—

eight seasons—to Gehringer's 1930 season to his best (when he hit .371) in 1937.

NL	BA	OBA	SLG A	ERA
1947	.266	.339	.391	4.07
1948	.261	.333	.383	3.96
1949	.263	.335	.390	4.05
1950	.262	.336	.402	4.15
1951	.260	.332	.390	3.96
1952	.253	.324	.374	3.74
1953	.267	.336	.412	4.29
1954	.266	.339	.408	4.08

AL	BA	OBA	SLG A	ERA
1930	.288	.351	.421	4.65
1931	.279	.345	.396	4.38
1932	.277	.346	.405	4.48
1933	.273	.343	.391	4.29
1934	.279	.351	.400	4.50
1935	.280	.352	.402	4.46
1936	.290	.363	.422	5.04
1937	.282	.355	.415	4.63

As you can see, hitters in Gehringer's time had a considerably better time of it than in Robinson's, the primary reason being night baseball, which lowered batting averages (and all other averages) substantially. In only one season, 1953, does the National League's ERA go as high as the lowest mark in the AL during Gehringer's prime.

As fielders they would seem to be close: Gehringer's range factor is higher, 5.69 to Robinson's 5.25, while Robinson's fielding percentage is higher, .983 to .976. Robinson's double-play totals are a little higher, too. Robinson was a better base-stealer, and, it appears, in relation to the times they played, a better all-around hitter.

That leaves Frisch, Collins, and LaJoie. Frisch was roughly a contemporary of Gehringer's, making his debut five years earlier (in 1919), and retiring five years earlier (1937). He benefited from most of the boom years in hitting as Gehringer (keyed largely though indirectly by the Ruthian revolution, NL averages and ERA went from .258 and 2.91 in Frisch's rookie season, to .290 and 3.78 in 1921, when Frisch became a full-time player). Frankie Frisch was a very good ballplayer, but except for stolen bases he does not appear to be Gehringer's equal in any way.

This leaves us with two, Eddie Collins and Nap LaJoie. There aren't too many flaws to be found in Eddie Collins's game. In a quarter century of baseball, first with the Philadelphia A's, as part of Connie Mack's "One Hundred Thousand Dollar Infield," then with the Chicago White Sox (he was the pillar of virtue on the 1919 Black Sox), and then, for a few games, with Mack's A's again, Collins was one of the great players in the game. He hit .333, led the league three times in runs scored, four times in stolen bases, and nine times in fielding average at second base. His strong suit was consistency: he had seasons of hitting over .340 in three consecutive decades, and had seventeen seasons with an on-base average over .400.

It's hard, almost impossible, to compare four or five of Collins's best seasons with Robinson's because Collins had so many seasons in so long a career that look very much like one another. Suffice it to say that during much of Collins's career, particularly after the hitting boom began in 1920, Collins played a game in which it was much easier to post high batting averages than in Robinson's years. Let's compare our look to just the years when he hit over .340:

Year	BA	League	Diff	Year	BA	League	Diff
1909	.347	.244	.103	1920	.372	.284	.088
1911	.367	.274	.093	1923	.360	.283	.077
1912	.348	.265	.083	1924	.349	.290	.059
1913	.345	.256	.089	1925	.346	.292	.054
1914	.344	.248	.096	1926	.344	.282	.062

Up to 1920, when hardly anyone is hitting home runs and batting averages are relatively low, Collins hits for some excellent averages. Then in 1920, when hitting takes off, Collins looks about the same. In 1920, AL batting averages are 10 points higher than in 1911 when Collins hit .367, yet Collins, who batted a career high .372, outhits the league by a smaller margin. In 1925, the league reaches the highest average it would attain in Collins's career, .292, and Collins hits for almost exactly the same average he hit for in 1909, when the league's average was 48 points *lower* than in 1925!

Of course, in 1925 Collins was thirty-eight years old, so you might expect him to be slowing down. Nonetheless, from 1920 on, when everyone else's average is going up, Collins's isn't. The margins he outhits the rest of the league by look about the same as the margin that Robinson outhit the league by. But Collins, by 1920, is even less effective than that might indicate. In the midst of a power explosion, Collins's hits become softer. Let's look at the same eleven years of .340+ and look at Collins's slugging average in relation to the league.

Year	SLG A	League	Diff	Year	SLG A	League	Diff
1909	.450	.309	.141	1920	.493	.388	.105
1911	.481	.359	.122	1923	.453	.389	.064
1912	.435	.348	.087	1924	.455	.397	.058
1913	.453	.336	.117	1925	.422	.408	.014
1914	.452	.324	.128	1926	.459	.392	.067

I'm not trying to build a case against Eddie Collins here. I'm trying to pin down the difference between what it might have taken a player to be a great player before 1920 and how that changed *after* 1920. Eddie Collins was about 5' 9" and listed at

175 pounds for most of his prime. He never had much power, but before 1919 that didn't matter much: he was fast, he had a terrific batting eye—he drew substantial amounts of walks in addition to his fine batting averages—and he could advance himself by stealing. Simply put, in the years when power wasn't part of the game, he was one of the game's most effective hitters. And when the game changed and power became more important, he *wasn't* one of the league's most effective hitters. He was just another good hitter. In the years 1909, 1911, 1912, 1913, and 1914, when no one is able to hit with much power and on-base average is more important, Collins's SLOB, slugging times on-base average, is high: He's second in 1909, fourth in 1911, fifth in 1912, fifth in 1913, second in 1914, and fifth in 1920. After that, in 1923, '24, '25 and '26, though his batting average remains constant and his slugging average relatively high, he isn't one of the *five* best in SLOB. In fact, not one of the ten best.

I guess what I'm saying is that Eddie Collins, with his lack of power, was a player ideally suited for the prepower era and no other. Well, that's not exactly true; a player with equal speed, fielding ability, and a great batting eye can be great in any era—say the words "Ichiro Suzuki"—but it's a lot harder in an era when power is at a premium. I won't say that Eddie Collins, if he had played in the '50s and '60s, would have been no more of a hitter than another 5'9", 175-pound player, Nellie Fox—who, let's remember, hit over .300 five times when not too many other players were doing it. Collins was much faster than Fox, and probably would have hit for a higher average. But his talents appear much closer to those of Fox than to those of Jackie Robinson, who was able to reach base with nearly the same frequency as Collins, and in a time when it was much more difficult to do so, and who hit with much greater power. What it comes down to is that Jackie Robinson's talents were much more suited to baseball in Collins's era than Collins's were suited to baseball in Jackie Robinson's time. If they both played in Robinson's time, I'd take Robinson, and if they both played in Collins's time, I'd take Robinson.

And that leaves Napoleon LaJoie. The case for LaJoie, in his own time, is greater than the one for Collins in his. His lifetime batting average for twenty-one major league seasons was .338—the seventh edition of *Total Baseball* lists just fifteen players in baseball history who are higher. He led the league once in runs scored, four times in hits, five times in doubles, once in home runs, three times in RBI, three times in batting—one at .426, the highest average of the last century—twice in on-base average, four times in slugging average, and six times in fielding average. He also stole 380 bases.

To deal with the last item first, LaJoie does not, by the standards of his own time, qualify as outstanding base stealer. Certainly nowhere near the class of Honus Wagner and Ty Cobb. Though he spent his entire career, from 1896 to 1916, in the era of the big steal, he never had as many as 30 in one season, and, in fact, he had 27 or more just twice. He never placed among the league leaders. This suggests to me that he did not have exceptional speed. He seems to have been an outstanding fielder, certainly so if judged by his fielding averages but also and perhaps more importantly by his field range: his 5.73 average is higher than most of the second basemen in his era, including Johnny Evers of Tinker-to-Evers-to-Chance fame, who, from 1902 to 1917, averaged 5.12; Miller Huggins, who, from 1904 to 1916, averaged 5.30; and Larry Doyle, who, from 1907 to 1920, averaged 4.79. In fact, by comparison with them LaJoie was outstanding.

As a hitter, though, there are mitigating circumstances to

some of those amazing averages. For instance, that .426 in 1901 is an outstanding aberration: he never came within 42 points of that mark either before the turn of the century or after. 1901 was far and away LaJoie's best season: he led the American League in runs (for the only time), hits (his highest total), doubles, home runs (his total of 14 was twice that of any other mark he put up in the twentieth century), and batting, on-base, and slugging (easily his highest averages in all—his .643 slugging average was the only time was over .600, in fact, the only time he was over .570). Without 1901, LaJoie's career wouldn't look quite so sensational, so it is worth noting that in 1901 the American League had just risen from the status of a minor league. It looks very much in retrospect as if LaJoie was the only truly great player in a mediocre league that season.

After 1901, his career came a little closer to the planet earth. After 1901, he never had more than 7 home runs in a season—in fact, in his sixteen seasons he hit 2, 1, or none ten times—and only once had over 100 RBI, in 1904, which was also the only time he topped 90. In an era which heavily favored stolen bases, he stole more than 25 bases only twice; and he never had more than 90 runs scored in a season.

Eddie Collins's lack of power would have hampered him in other decades, particularly recent ones, but it seems to me that Nap LaJoie not only lacked power but genuine speed. He seems to have had a great swing for base hits—he racked up 3,242, along with a .338 batting average, and had great hands at second base, but he couldn't hit home runs, he didn't draw walks, and he wasn't all that fast. It's hard to see how he could have been a great player in any period that didn't favor high-average singles hitters.

When I compare him with Jackie Robinson, one outstanding

fact jumps out at me: despite the huge 27-point bulge in career batting average over Robinson, .338 to .311, *Jackie Robinson's on-base average was better*. In fact, it is *much better*, a whopping 30 points better, .410 to .380. Jackie Robinson walked more times (740) in ten seasons than LaJoie did in twenty-one (516). And Robinson was a much more dangerous runner once he reached base. There is no clear edge to either in the field. So, tell me: if Jackie Robinson had more speed and power, and if he reached base with a far greater frequency, why do I want Napoleon LaJoie on my team at second base instead of Jackie Robinson?

If Jackie Robinson had had the career of an average good-to-great middle infielder, it would have gone something like this: maybe eight peak seasons and about seven more in slow decline. Robinson began to tail off sharply in 1955 due to injuries, age, and, of course the incredible toll that stress had taken on him. No one knew at the time that diabetes and heart trouble would leave him just sixteen more years of life.

In his last two seasons he played just 222 games, batting respectively, just .256 and .275. However, there were flashes of his younger self and his true greatness. For instance, he was 24 for 32 in stolen bases over the last two seasons, and still pulled in enough walks to post on-base averages of .378 and .382.

I've talked a lot here about this and that player's "prime," but the truth of it is that it really doesn't apply. This chapter is about Jackie Robinson and Jackie Robinson of all the players discussed here *never had a prime*. Jackie Robinson didn't make his major league debut until he was twenty-eight, an age when most players are in the middle of their prime; *he didn't move to second base till he was twenty-nine*, an age when most players are ready to slip a bit out of their prime. I had originally planned to run a chart here illustrating what Jackie Robinson's career numbers might have looked like had he come up the normal way under normal circumstances at, say, twenty-two, and struggled a year or so before his incredible natural talent and iron determination and competitive spirit began to kick in. There's no need to take up a lot of space, but the bottom line would have been something like: 2,220 games played, about 2,600 hits, maybe 210 home runs, in excess of 1,400 runs scored, and 1,200 RBIs, *at least* a .315 batting average and 300 stolen bases. As he would have started playing second base sooner when he was younger and faster, he would not only have better stats in the field, his range factor would have been higher, not probably as high as Bill Mazeroski, but pretty high—and probably higher than Nellie Fox and Red Schoendienst. And if he had career numbers like that, nobody would question that he was qualified for the Hall of Fame.

But Jackie Robinson didn't just lose those seasons because he was black: he lost them because of World War II. As with a score of other great and near-great players that we might consider here, Robinson lost his prime years to the military—though in Robinson's case, a couple of years might have been lost anyway because of baseball's reluctance to begin the Great Experiment. (If he had been white, Jackie Robinson might well have been in the majors *before* the war.) In any event, the point I'm trying to make is that in estimating a player's true greatness, there is a big, big difference between saying that "Jackie Robinson came up at age twenty-two played for ten seasons, hit .311, scored 947 runs, stole 197 bases and then, for whatever reason, never played baseball again" and saying "Circumstances kept Jackie Robinson out of the big leagues till he was twenty-eight, after which he played for ten seasons, hit .311, scored 947 runs, and stole 197 bases." What I mean is that it makes a big difference in your estimate of his "greatness" because in the first example you might conclude that Jackie Robinson was a great player for the first five years, and that he might have faded into a mediocre one afterward. But in the second scenario, I don't see how you could conclude anything but that Jackie Robinson was an obviously great ballplayer who would have been obviously greater had he had the advantage of playing baseball in his best years.

As the record now sits, what does it add up to? We see a player who was a superb second baseman and a more than capable first and third baseman, a terrific hitter for a middle infielder and a very good one for any position, a versatile offensive performer who hit for high average with excellent power and was by all counts a terror on the bases. What credentials does Jackie Robinson have for the Hall of Fame? Well, he was a Rookie of the Year, he won an MVP award, he won a batting title, he hit over .325 in four seasons, he led the league in total bases twice, he scored 99 or more runs seven straight seasons, he led the league's second basemen in double plays and fielding percentage three times each, he was an All Star for six straight years. And the teams he played for *won*—the Jackie Robinson Dodgers, as they have now come to be called, won six pennants in the ten years he played. Let's forget the question "What if Jackie Robinson was white?" Who cares? If you saw a player with such credentials, why would you keep him out of the Hall of Fame?

Whatever he *might* have done, the record Jackie Robinson left behind suggests that, along with Joe Morgan (and perhaps Ryne Sandberg, who could also hit, with power, steal, and cover ground), among all second basemen in baseball history, he had the talent and versatility to be a star in any era, at any position, at any spot in the batting order. If all the second basemen in the Hall of Fame from Nap LaJoie to Eddie Collins to Rogers Hornsby to Joe Morgan lined up to compete for the same job under the same circumstances, there is a very good chance that Robinson would get it. And if I could say that about any player, then I'd have to wave him around and into the Hall of Fame, no matter what his color or how many hits short of 3,000 he fell.

5

One-on-One, Once and for All: Mickey Mantle vs. Willie Mays

In Game 2 of the 1951 World Series, the New York Giants' twenty-year-old phenom, Willie Mays, lofted a fly ball toward right-center field. The New York Yankees' twenty-year-old phenom, Mickey Mantle, glided in front of centerfielder Joe DiMaggio to make the play. In doing so, he caught a spike in an improperly covered drain and badly wrecked his knee. (Just imagine if that happened today; what kind of lawsuit might result?). In hitting that fly ball, Mays had little impact on the Series, which the Giants eventually lost, but he had an enormous impact on baseball history. In essence, he settled for all time the debate as to who was the greatest player, Willie Mays or Mickey Mantle, years before it began.

When I was nine, my family, along with other commuters to Manhattan, the natives and the newcomers, the blacks and the whites, moved to a small town in New Jersey—Old Bridge—which was populated by locals whose families had lived there for generations, along with self-exiled New Yorkers. There was a wide cultural and social gap between the city kids and the small-town kids, but the common element was baseball. Everyone was a fan of some New York team, mostly the Yankees, maybe half as many fans of the Mets, and a few who, because of their parents, still swore allegiance to the Dodgers and Giants. The twin gods of this time and place were Willie Mays and Mickey Mantle. I have lived in a lot of places since then, but I have seen nothing close to the hold that these two athletes had on sports fans in that place and time.

Mays and Mantle were the constant, year-round objects of affection, admiration, and debate. Ours was a Willie Mays household. My father bought books about Mays and taught me how to read a box score so we could check the *Newark Evening News* or *New York Times* to see how Willie had done the day before. On Sunday morning, there was no clear distinction between religion and the sports pages and items about Willie Mays. Mantle was never ignored; we checked his box score, too, just to keep pace. We respected Mantle, but we worshiped Mays. I still remember the catch in my father's throat as he'd read accounts to me of Willie Mays playing stickball with kids in the streets of Harlem, and the scorn in his tone when he related stories from the papers about Mantle kicking his helmet or smashing a water cooler. Willie Mays was my father's ideal of what a professional athlete should be: enthusiastic, charismatic (even though the word wasn't in vogue back then) and *grateful* for the chance to play baseball and be an American hero. My father never articulated it this way, but I'm sure that Willie Mays embodied all his hopes for an integrated, tolerant America. This, of course, was shortly before the Newark riots erupted and the '60s officially began.

Our family baseball outings were built around the San Francisco Giants' trips to New York. I'll never forget the goose-bumps I got on hearing Mays announced at Yankee Stadium during a 1961 exhibition game. It was billed as his return to New York after four years (though he had played in the All Star Game in Yankee Stadium the year before), and the full-throated roar of the packed house as Mays came to bat left me with the feeling that the real loss most New York–area baseball fans felt in 1958 was not the departure of the Dodgers or even the departure of the Dodgers and Giants, but the loss of Willie Mays. (Mantle, batting left-handed, hit a home run into the right-field porch, the first I had ever seen in person. But Mays later won the game with a two-run single.) A year and a half later, we went to the fifth game of the 1962 World Series where I vividly remember someone shouting to Mickey, "Hey, Mantle, we came here ta see who whuz da best, you or Mays. Now we're wonderin' who's da woist." After Mantle popped out, the same fan shouted, "Hey, Mantle: you win."

Most of us, no matter who we rooted for, had to have a Mantle thing to match every Mays thing we collected, or vice versa. If you were staggeringly fortunate to get a Topps Mays card, you tried hard to trade something for a Mantle card, and usually felt your collection was then complete. My mother bought me a Willie Mays Hartland statue for $4.98—swear to God—at Whelan's Drug Store on Route 9. Instead of enjoying it, I kept running down to Whelan's every day after school just to make sure no one bought the Mantle statue before I accumulated enough lawn-cutting money to buy it. My mother soon gave in and got me that one, too. Today, both stand proudly in a glass case on the third floor of my house. (Mantle doesn't always stand so proudly; that knee that he twisted in the 1951 Series still gives him trouble, and he wobbles a bit when you open the case.) I wouldn't dream of selling either (for the $300 to

$400 they go for) for anything less important than my daughter's college fund.

No more fit subjects for a Plutarch-style "parallel lives" ever existed in sports. There will never be two ballplayers like them at the same time again. There may never be another like *either* of them; that there were two players so great and so similar at the same time is phenomenal. Mantle and Mays were both 5'11" and, at their peak, about 190 (though some guides list Mantle at about 200). They both made their major league debuts in New York in 1951 at the age of twenty (Mays was a little more than five months older). There's a wonderful photograph of the two taken before the Series, holding bats, Mickey, with a bulge in his cheek, laughing at something Willie has apparently said to the photographer. Two splendid young men, just approaching their physical peak, two magnificent careers ahead of them. It's the way you want to remember them.

Both were Southern boys, Mick from Oklahoma, Willie from Alabama, bred by their dads—Mickey's father was nicknamed "Mutt," Willie's was "Kitty Cat"—to play ball. The dads' nicknames described the sons: Mantle ran like a dog, Mays scampered like a cat. Both had plenty of incentive to escape their dads' lives, Mantle's from the mines of Commerce, Mays's from the steel mills of Fairfield, a suburb of Birmingham.

Both were blessed with an astonishing combination of power and speed; both were born centerfielders. They were the most complete players of their times, perhaps of all time, and the answer to the question, "Who was the greatest, Mantle or Mays?" just might be the answer to the question, "Who is the greatest player who ever lived?"

So, who was better, Mickey Mantle or Willie Mays? I'm not proud to admit that in my formative years I spent more time thinking about this question than I did pondering the meaning of existence—and I spent a *lot* of time pondering the meaning of existence. When one is no longer a child one puts away childish things, at least until one can find time as an adult to be a little childish all over again, and, so, in 1985, while reviewing *The Bill James Historical Baseball Abstract* for *The Village Voice*, I came across the first objective attempt to compare Mantle and Mays and found myself caught up in the question all over again. James's brief but brilliant study concluded that Mays was clearly the greater player in terms of career value, but we all knew this; Mays played longer and without serious injuries. What I wanted to know was who was *better*, not who was good *longer*. James was unequivocal on the subject: "Mickey Mantle was, at his peak in 1956–57 and again in 1961–62, clearly a greater player than Willie Mays—and it is not a difficult decision." I can tell you that when I read those words, I was as shaken as the day when I was eighteen and sitting in a park and read Camus's *The Myth of Sisyphus* and Dostoevsky's *Notes from Underground* and realized that all of my cozy perceptions of a rational universe would never float again. James's opinion was simply too informed to be disregarded, no matter how hard I might try. But perhaps someday, I thought, I could make my own analysis and discover something James and other researchers had missed. Maybe I could still win the debate for Willie Mays, once and for all.

On one point at least Bill was certainly misinformed. "It was only after the fact," he wrote, "when the final statistics were in the book, that people began to say Mays was the greater player." I can think of very few subjects on which I would say Bill James is completely and totally wrong, but this is one (maybe the only one). In point of fact, in their own time, Mays was almost always regarded as the better player. I have a scrapbook of magazine articles and newspaper columns on the issue, and almost all of them choose Mays over Mantle. In 1960, the Associated Press chose its all-decade team and Mays, though he had missed two seasons in 1952 and '53 to the Army, edged out Mantle to join Ted Williams and Stan Musial in the outfield.

Even better examples of Mays's superior reputation can be found in a special 1962 issue from *Sport* magazine devoted entirely to Mickey Mantle and Willie Mays. In the issue, edited by Al Silverman, and with contributions by Arnold Hano and Dick Schaap (who wrote, respectively, the Mays and Mantle biographies for the *Sport* magazine paperback library), numerous players, managers, and coaches were asked who they thought was the better player. Here are some of the responses:

"There may be one or two better hitters, but for all-around ability, I've got to stick with Mays."

—WALTER ALSTON

"Willie's the best—easily."   —ALVIN DARK

"He shows me everything there is to see in a ballplayer. There may be others close to him, but Willie's the greatest."   —JIMMY DYKES

"He beats you every way imaginable. If there's anything like a complete ballplayer, Willie is it." —DEL CRANDALL

There's no doubt about it, Mays is the best ballplayer in the big leagues today."   —HARVEY KUENN

"Mays may be more than the best ballplayer in the majors today. He may be the best who has ever played baseball."   —JOHNNY TEMPLE

And so on. Alvin Dark, of course, was Mays's manager. Mantle was picked as the best by Casey Stengel, his manager,

Whitey Ford and Phil Rizzuto, both former teammates, and Hank Greenberg and Al Lopez. Lopez's judgment was qualified: "When he's right [sic], he can do everything." Greenberg's was not: "On sheer ability, it has to be him." Though on second thought, maybe it was, as Greenberg might have been implying that Mantle had greater "potential" but Mays gave a greater *performance*.

Anyway, of all the people interviewed, including players, managers, and coaches who had been in both leagues and had seen both players, Mays was the clear favorite. And it's important to remember that the poll was taken right after the 1961 season when the Yankees had just crushed Cincinnati in the World Series and Mantle had spent a season locked with teammate Roger Maris for the all-time single season home run record, finishing just four votes behind Maris in the MVP balloting. Mays's Giants finished fifth, well out of pennant contention, while Mays was a distant sixth in the MVP vote won by Frank Robinson. So, in a poll taken the year after one of his two or three greatest seasons, when his team was easily the most dominant, Mays was still widely regarded as the greater player.

That was in 1962. Even though Mantle would win the MVP award at the end of the 1962 season, everything that happened from there till the end of their careers could have done nothing but reinforce the persisting opinion. Mantle faded, mostly from the effects of his injuries and his osteomyelitis-ravaged legs but also, as we now know, from the ravages of drink and dissipation. Mays went on to win the 1965 MVP award, to surpass Mel Ott as the National League's all-time home run leader, and became the first player since Ruth to reach 600 home runs.

So Bill James is wrong: the idea that Willie Mays was the better baseball player was not something that came along after the statistics were added up and the returns were in. At their peak, the baseball establishment was pretty much decided on the issue, and despite the occasional voice to the effect that Mantle's potential was cut short from injury, there really wasn't much controversy. Those who were supposed to know were in agreement that while Mantle was a close second, Mays was not only the greatest player of *his* time, he was the era's candidate for greatest of *all* time.

And he remains so today. In the All Century voting, Mays placed third to Mantle's thirty-second, and in the *Sporting News'* Top One Hundred, he left Mantle in the dust, placing second to Mantle's seventeenth. So James's and his colleagues' expert analysis to the contrary, it can be reasonably argued that Mantle is not, and never was, regarded as a greater player than Mays.

Why did the experts in their own time regard Mays as superior? The case was summed up neatly in *Sport's* Mantle–Mays issue: "Mays remains the choice today. For the same reasons he has been picked so often through the years: He can do more things better. It is possible, some people say, that no player in history has ever been able to do so many things so well." According to the story, the Dodgers' chief Alex Campanis—yes, *that* Al Campanis—set a point value rating system for all the things a player could do on a baseball field: hitting for average, hitting for power, speed on the bases (stealing and going for the extra base), strength and accuracy of arm, and fielding. (How refreshing, by the way, to see the terms "hitting" and "fielding" used instead of "offense" and "defense.") The only one judged to have a perfect score in every category was Mays.

How were they rated in their own time? What was their relative value? Here, Mantle appears to have a surprise advantage over Mays. From 1952, his second season and the first in which he played in over 100 games, to 1964, his last great year, Mantle had an astonishing run. He won three Most Valuable Player awards—1956, 1957, and 1962—and deserved at least one more. Roger Maris beat out Mantle in two close votes in 1960 and 1961, the year both were racing toward Babe Ruth's record of 60 home runs in a season and Maris won. Let's compare those two seasons:

1960	G	BA	HR	RBI	R	BB	SO	OBA	SLGA	SB-CS	SLOB
Maris	136	.283	39	112*	98	70	65	.374	.581	2-2	21.74
Mantle	153	.275	40*	94	119*	94	111*	.402	.558	14-3	22.43

1961	G	BA	HR	RBI	R	BB	SO	OBA	SLGA	SB-CS	SLOB
Maris	161	.269	61*	142*	132*	94	67	.376	.620	0-0	23.31
Mantle	153	.317	54	128	132*	128	126*	.452	.687*	12-1	31.05

°Denotes lead league

In 1960, it's close. Maris, batting in front of Mantle, drove in more runs. Considering that Maris missed 18 games, his numbers, particularly in a down year for hitters, are pretty impressive. He delivered almost the same number of total runs (210) in 136 games as Mantle (213) did in a rare, for him, near-complete season. Mantle struck out much more often, but that was probably unimportant. Maris outhit him by 8 points, but in the really important hitting stats, on base and slugging, Mantle led by 28 points in the former while Maris led by 23 in the latter. Both were superb fielders, though Mantle, of course, was in center. Mantle was obviously much the superior baserunner with 14 steals in 17 attempts, while Maris was 2 of 4. Anyway, missed games or no, Mantle was the better hitter and baserunner and probably the better fielder and should have been the MVP, but Maris was a new force on the scene and it's easy to see why many could have favored him over Mantle.

But in 1961, it's not close; it's not even close to close. Maris played in 8 more games, and, of course, had 7 more home runs to break baseball's most famous record. But Mantle outhit Maris by a whopping 48 points *and* walked 34 more times, and, despite the 7 fewer homers had a slugging average 67 points higher *and* stole 12 of 13 bases to Maris's none *and* scored 132 runs, same as Maris, without having a Mickey Mantle to bat behind him. His SLOB was a whopping 7.74 greater than Maris's. There is absolutely no question that Mantle should have won the American League MVP award in 1961, and if he had, it would have given him a record *four* MVP awards.

Still, Mantle won three, while Mays won only two—though it's a measure of how good Mays was for how long that he won his awards farther apart (1954 and 1965) than any player in baseball history. Mays, too, had his shafts. In fact, in 1962, the year after Mantle and Maris chased Ruth, Mays was involved in perhaps the biggest shaft in MVP voting history. In 1962, Maury Wills beat out Mays by six votes, 208 to 202. Here are their numbers for that season:

1962	G	BA	HR	RBI	R	BB	SO	OBA	SLGA	SLOB
Wills	165	.299	6	48	130	51	57	.349	.393	13.01
Mays	162	.304	49	141	130	78	85	.385	.615	23.67

In 1962, Willie Mays was responsible for at least 50 more runs than Maury Wills and possibly 60, and no nonsense about "intangibles" (what intangible could Maury Wills have had over Willie Mays anyway?) could make up for that difference. There is no logic, no reading of statistics, no interpretation of the value of Wills's then-record of 104 stolen bases that could possibly justify calling Wills more valuable than Mays. Whatever Wills's value to the Dodgers, they'd have won more games if they had replaced

Wills with someone off the bench and put Mays in their outfield. In 1962, Mays was the victim of the media hype surrounding Maury Wills's pursuit of Ty Cobb's stolen base record, just as Mantle lost out in '61 because Maris was the one who passed Ruth.

The only problem with giving Mays the MVP award for 1962 is that Frank Robinson, the MVP of the previous season, who led the league in both on-base and slugging average and tallied a SLOB of 26.45, had the better year at bat. Mays was better in the field and on the bases, and his team did win the pennant. You might consider that these things offset Robinson's superior batting, but it's not clear that Mays should have been the MVP over Robinson, whereas there is no reasonable argument that Maris should have won over Mantle in 1961. Probably better arguments could be made for Mays in 1955 (when a year after winning the MVP award, he finished a puzzling fourth to Roy Campanella, Duke Snider, and Ernie Banks, despite putting up better statistics than all of them) or 1960 (when he finished a ridiculous third to Pittsburgh shortstop Dick Groat and Don Hoak, two players whose best seasons couldn't crack Mays's top eighteen seasons).

But, then, Mantle finished an inexplicable fifth in 1955 behind Yogi Berra, Al Kaline, Al Smith, and Ted Williams despite leading the league in home runs, triples, on-base average, and slugging average, and stealing 8 of 9 bases—in other words, having the best season, on paper, of anyone in the league. It could be argued that Berra was valuable to the Yankees' pennant drive that year, but why did the others finish ahead of Mantle? In 1958, Mantle also finished fifth, this time behind Jackie Jensen, Bob Turley, Rocky Colavito, and Bob Cerv, despite leading the league in runs, home runs, and walks, stealing 18 of 21 bases, and finishing second to Williams in on-base average and third to Colavito and Cerv in slugging average. Mantle was a superior all-around hitter, baserunner, and player to all of them, and his team won the pennant. Second-place finisher Bob Turley did go 19–6 and win the Cy Young, but he wouldn't have been able to do so without Mantle's support. The only explanation that fits here is that after Mantle easily won two straight MVP awards, the voters decided to spread the honors around.

No matter what should have been, Mantle dominated American League MVP voting from 1955 through 1964, his last great season, in a way that Mays never did in the National League. Mantle was first or second six times, while Mays finished first or second four times in his entire career. Bill James makes a major point of this in proclaiming Mantle the superior player; Mantle, he argues, had the greater respect of his contemporaries. I don't buy the argument. Mantle and Mays weren't competing with *each other*. Mays had far tougher competition in the National League than Mantle had in the American League. In the '50s, Mantle's major competition was a great catcher, Yogi Berra, and an aging slugger, Ted Williams; in the '50s, Mays's major competition was a great catcher, Roy Campanella, an aging slugger, Stan Musial, another great centerfielder, Duke Snider, the greatest slugging shortstop in baseball history, up to that point, Ernie Banks, the greatest slugging third baseman up to that point, Eddie Mathews, and from the late '50s into the '60s, the two greatest slugging rightfielders in the game (Roger Maris not being one of them), Frank Robinson, and the most prolific home run hitter of all time, Henry Aaron. Simply put, the American League of Mantle's time didn't have superstars like the ones Mays competed against in the National League. And Mantle had another advantage over Mays in MVP voting: his team won much more often, and it simply can't be denied that, except for spectacular exceptions such as Ernie Banks, voters pay more attention in MVP voting to players from winning teams.

So, whatever stock one places in the evidence of MVP vot-

ers, we really don't know who ranked the highest among contemporary observers, because they didn't go head-to-head
against each other.

So what, then, does the record book tell us? A statistical comparison of Mickey Mantle and Willie Mays is a baseball analyst's
dream. Their prime years occurred at exactly the same time,
with park conditions and rules virtually the same for both
leagues. The National League had more superstars in this
period, almost all of them black, but as black players overall con-
stituted about 8 percent of major league players by the end of
the '50s, it really can't be said that, on the whole, Mays competed against better players than Mantle. In terms of what Mantle and Mays faced day to day, the competition and conditions
are strikingly even. Here are the career lines from *Total Baseball*, the game's official encyclopedia:

	G	AB	R	H	2B	3B	HR	RBI	BB
Mantle, 1951–68	2401	8102	1677	2415	344	72	536	1509	1733
Mays, 1951–73	2942	10851	2062	3283	523	140	660	1903	1464

	SO	BA	OBA	SLG A	SB-CS	Field Avg
Mantle, 1951–68	1710	.298	.423	.557	153–38	.982
Mays, 1951–73	1526	.302	.387	.557	338–103	.981

I've looked at those numbers so many times over the years
that I'd stopped *seeing* them. I'd always assumed, for instance,
that Mantle was clearly a superior power hitter, but the record
doesn't make that clear. Mantle had a greater home run percentage, that is, Mantle averaged a home run every 15.1 times at
bat, while Mays averaged 1 for every 16.4. But Mays hit doubles

and triples with more frequency. Mantle's career stolen base percentage is actually better than Mays's (who led the NL in stolen bases for four straight years from 1956 through 1959 and was regarded by many as the best baserunner of his time). And Mantle's walk total is particularly impressive: he had 269 more walks despite playing in 541 fewer games.

Let's pause and look at those numbers again. They had identical slugging averages; it's on base-average that separates them. We'll come back to that soon. It has always been argued that Mantle's career numbers would look much more impressive if not for serious injury, and of course they would, but how about cutting Mays some slack? It has always puzzled me that Mays was never given hypothetical credit for the 270 or so games he missed while in the service. Let's fantasize for a moment. As a twenty-year-old rookie in 1951, Mays hit 20 home runs in 121 games, scored 59, and drove in 68. As a twenty-three-year-old in 1954, he hit 41 home runs, scored 119, and drove in 110. He played only 34 games before going in the service in 1952, with 4 home runs, 17 runs scored, and 23 RBIs. For the sake of argument, let's split the difference between Mays's 1951 and 1954 seasons and give him 31 home runs, 79 runs, and 79 RBIs for both 1952 and 1953. And for further argument, we'll add these two years and subtract what he *did* do in 1952 before entering the Army (we don't want to credit him with too much). Here's what Mays's career numbers on the all-time chart look like in 1999:

HR: 660—3rd
R: 2062—5th
RBI: 1903—8th

Now, let's add our hypothetical numbers and see what the record book might have looked like:

HR: 718—2nd
R: 2223—4th
RBI: 2058—3rd

There are already a great many people who consider Mays the greatest all-around player of all time, but think what it would have done for his career reputation if he could have been the first to break Ruth's career home run record, placed fourth on the all-time runs scored list, and third in RBIs. In fact, in one hypothetical projection, Mays finishes just 2 runs scored behind Pete Rose, so, considering that we have given him just minimum numbers on this, and since we're fantasizing, we may as well place Mays third on the all-time home runs and RBIs list behind Babe Ruth and Hank Aaron—and fourth in runs behind Rose and Rickey Henderson—and remember that this is a guy who led his league *four times* in stolen bases and who many call the best defensive outfielder they've ever seen.

Is there anything that would mitigate the career numbers for either Mantle or Mays? Were they particularly helped or hurt, for instance, by their home ballparks? A home-road breakdown shows that Mantle hit .305 with 266 home runs and 743 RBIs at home, with a .291 average, 270 home runs, and 766 RBIs on the road—that's a near-perfect balance. The same, in fact, is true for Mays, who hit .302 with 335 home runs and 932 RBI at the Polo Grounds and Candlestick Park, and .301, with 325 home runs and 971 RBIs on the road. Mantle was a switch-hitter and thus was not hurt by Yankee Stadium's deep left-center field power alley. Oddly enough, though, Mays, contrary to popular belief, lost nothing from the Polo Grounds's similar left-center configuration or from that famous but apparently mythical wind that was supposed to have cost him, in the familiar litany of his fans, "at least a hundred home runs." In fact,

Mays actually hit *ten* more homers at home than in all other NL ballparks.

But, again, all of this comes under the heading of career value. We already know Mays lasted longer and performed at a quality pace for longer. Who was the *best* at their respective peak? Well, what do you regard as "peak"? Is fifteen years okay? Let's try their fifteen peak seasons, 1951 to 1965 for Mantle; 1951 and 1954 through 1967 for Mays:

	G	AB	R	RBI	HR	BA
Mantle, 1951–65	2015	6894	1517	1298	454	.306
Mays, 1951, 54–67	2264	8505	1662	1552	560	.310

	BB-SO	SB-CS	PCT	OBA	SLGA	SLOB
Mantle, 1951–65	1463–1424	145–34	81.0	.427	.567	24.21
Mays, 1951, 54–67	1054–1049	283–86	69.6	.386	.586	22.62

This brings them closer together in career numbers, but Mays still has an edge because Mantle missed so many games. In 1963, for instance, the year after winning his third MVP award, Mantle missed 89 games due to injury. But note that Mantle's *quality* numbers are terrific; he leads Mays in the most important number, on-base average, by a wide margin, and even has a higher stolen base percentage, *81 percent* to *70 percent*. And though Mays has batted more than 1,600 times more than Mantle, Mickey is only 106 home runs behind. Mays's only edge is in strikeouts, but we have no real evidence that strikeouts hurt Mantle's ability to produce runs.

Let's try it another way: let's define "peak" as the twelve best seasons. Let's eliminate the rookie seasons for both, and Mantle's 1963 season even though he hit .314 for the year. Coincidentally, this brings us through Mays's two MVP seasons, 1954 and 1965. Here's how they look in their twelve best seasons:

	G	AB	R	RBI	HR	BA
Mantle, 1952–62, 64	1722	6020	1372	1198	426	.321
Mays, 1954–65	1850	7003	1421	1311	481	.317

	BB-SO	SB-CS	OBA	SLGA	SLOB
Mantle, 1952–62, 64	1308–1242	131–25	.433	.589	25.50
Mays, 1954–65	876–816	264–81	.393	.556	21.85

At first, this looks like another clear advantage for Mays; more home runs, more runs, more RBI, more hits, more stolen bases. But it doesn't take long to see that Mantle is the superior hitter, and by a decisive margin. In their dozen best seasons, Mays played 128 more games—about 80 percent of an additional season more than Mantle—but the differences in their *total* production aren't that great. Let's use one more table:

	AB	BB	PA	H + BB
Mantle, 1952–62, 64	6020	1308	7327	1871 + 1308 = 3179
Mays, 1954–65	7003	876	7879	2224 + 876 = 3100

PA—plate appearance

Please, look at that again so I can't be accused of stacking the argument in Mantle's favor. Though Mays was in 128 more games than Mantle in their twelve best seasons and had nearly 1,000 more at bats and 557 more plate appearances, *Mantle has reached base 79 more times.* And in their fifteen best seasons, Mays batted more than 1,600 times *but reached base just 121 more times.* Not only that, but measured over a fifteen-season or twelve-season span, Mantle's SLOB was superior to Mays's.

And over a twelve-year span, Mantle had a superior on-base *and* slugging average.

I don't know how else to interpret these numbers except to conclude that Mantle was a superior hitter, at least if you interpret the term "superior hitter" as the hitter who does the most to produce runs. What does SLOB say? When you multiply slugging times on-base average, Mantle jumps into a clear and resounding lead, 25.50 to 21.85, or 3.65 more runs per 100 at bats.

Are there any factors that could possibly mitigate Mantle's superiority as a hitter? If there are, I haven't been able to find any. In fact, the deeper I dig, the more superior Mantle appears. Stolen bases, for instance. It was generally accepted when I was a kid that Mantle was the fastest runner in baseball—every biography and profile mentioned that he had been clocked running down to first base faster than any player in history—but that Mays was smarter and a superior baserunner. (In the 1962 *Sport* magazine special issue, Mantle was given by the panel of experts the nod for "speed" while Mays got the edge in "baserunning.") Many regarded him as the best baserunner in the game, and, indeed, there were times in the spotlight when he certainly seemed to be. In the 1960 All Star game at Yankee Stadium, for instance, Mays looped a single off Whitey Ford to right-center. When Mantle loped in casually to scoop it up, Mays made a sudden break for second and made it easily in a play that must have been enormously satisfying, coming as it did on Mantle's home turf. And in 1963, he stole 2 bases and scored 2 runs in the National League's victory.

Any Willie Mays fan could think of a dozen other such moments. Mays was regarded as a dazzlingly "instinctive" baserunner (black athletes were "instinctive" back then, white athletes were "hardworking"). And Mays was beautiful to watch, rounding bases with a wide sweep that took him right out from under his cap but gave him a straight angle at second. Mantle could probably have beaten Mays to first by a step, but I don't think any runner in baseball could have beat Mays from home to second. Mays led the National League in stolen bases for four straight seasons, from 1956 through 1959; in fact, from 1956 through 1958, he led *both* leagues in stolen bases, creating a tremendous impression on sportswriters all over the country. This was an era when hardly anyone stole bases; Mays's total of 40 in 1956 was the highest NL mark of the decade and the highest in the major leagues till Luis Aparicio stole 56 in 1959. Nothing was more indicative of Mays's amazing versatility than his ability to lead the league in home runs one season and stolen bases the next. Think of it this way: from 1956 through '59, while Mays was leading the National League in stolen bases for four straight seasons, Luis Aparicio was leading the American League in stolen bases for four straight years. For those four seasons, Mays had 136 steals, Aparicio had 134. And that was Aparicio's job, to steal bases. Over those four seasons, Aparicio hit 14 home runs; Mays hit 134, the same number as Aparicio's stolen bases.

It's difficult for me to accept even as I write this that Mickey Mantle was a better baserunner—or at least a better base *stealer*—than Willie Mays. I simply never looked at the numbers. Mantle's stolen base percentage is not only higher than Mays's, it's higher than such other stolen base champions as Jackie Robinson (78 percent), Luis Aparicio (79 percent), Lou Brock (75 percent), and much higher than (though we don't have his stolen base records for every season) Ty Cobb (65 percent). If I had to pick the most impressive display of power and speed in baseball history, I'd say this: from 1952 to 1964, including 1963 when he played in just 65 games, Mickey Mantle hit

443 home runs and stole 133 bases in 159 attempts, a success rate of 83.6 percent.

It can be objected, too, that Mays, after all, stole many more bases than Mantle; and that, as one baseball researcher wrote to me in a response to a column about Mantle in *The Wall Street Journal*, that because the Yankees were so dominant, Mantle could pick and choose the spots in which he wanted to steal. After careful consideration, I have to reject both arguments. As has been demonstrated time and again, stolen bases by themselves generate very few runs. Give Mays credit for his 185 additional stolen bases and then subtract the additional 65 outs he made trying to steal—not to mention the additional 65 baserunners he removed in the process, and I doubt if the extra runs Mays produced through stolen bases amounted to 3 or 4 per season.

But that's not even the point. I see no rational reason why, if circumstances had called for it, Mickey Mantle couldn't have stolen more bases than Willie Mays. If you have a higher percentage of steals in, say, 190 attempts, I don't see any reason why you would have a lower rate of success in, say, 440 attempts. Mantle's Yankees won much more often than Mays's Giants so there was far less *need* for stolen bases. The argument that Mantle could afford to be more selective than Mays could easily work in reverse: on a team that hit as well as the Yankees, Mantle most likely would attempt to steal only in the toughest situations. Why bother to steal a base in a laugher?

There's another area concerning speed that Mantle shows up well in: GIDP, or grounded into double plays. Researcher Neil Munro did some eye-opening work for Bill James on the subject of great hitters and their GIDP totals; let's collect them in a chart to compare Mantle with other Hall of Famers:

	Years	Games	GIDP
Mickey Mantle	1951–68	2401	113
Willie Mays	1951–73	2992	251
Johnny Bench	1967–83	2158	207
Jackie Robinson	1947–56	1382	113
Eddie Mathews	1952–68	2391	123
Mike Schmidt	1972–89	2107	122
Luis Aparicio	1956–73	2599	184
Ted Williams	1939–60	2292	197
Stan Musial	1941–63	3026	243
Lou Brock	1961–79	2616	114
Joe DiMaggio	1936–51	1736	130
Duke Snider	1947–64	2143	166
Roberto Clemente	1955–72	2433	275
Hank Aaron	1954–76	3298	328
Pete Rose	1963–86	3371	235
Reggie Jackson	1967–87	2705	180

That's quite a variety of players including great all-around hitters to sluggers to base-stealers, and it spans more than six decades. Of all the players on that list, Jackie Robinson alone failed to hit into more GIDP than Mantle—*and Mantle played in 1,019 more games!* Ted Williams, considered by many to be the greatest hitter who ever lived, played in 119 fewer games than Mantle but hit into 84 more double plays. Luis Aparicio, who is in the Hall of Fame precisely because of his speed, hit into more double plays. Mantle drew a lot of criticism from writers who worshiped Joe DiMaggio because Mickey struck out far more often. But in 1,000 fewer games, DiMaggio hit into 17 more double plays—and we don't even have the GIDP information for the first three years of DiMaggio's career. We have to ask ourselves if the occasional advanced runner or rare errors that occur from "putting the ball in play" that Mays (or DiMaggio) were responsible for are worth all those extra outs and baserunners erased by that many double plays. And after careful consideration, I'll take Mantle's combination of high strikeout, high walk, low GIDPs.

And so, neither at bat nor on the bases can I make an objective case for Willie over Mickey. Perhaps Mays's best chance is in the outfield. There were a couple of writers who thought Mantle covered as much ground as Mays, but none that I know of who thought that in their prime Mantle was better or had as good an arm as Mays—though everyone acknowledges that Mantle had an excellent throwing arm. But what exactly was the difference between them in terms of *value*? For what it's worth, Mantle's career fielding average was a point higher than Mays, but most baseball experts don't put much stock in fielding average. Throwing assists is also difficult to figure, if only because outfielders with truly great arms don't get challenged very often. In 1967, his sixth full season, Roberto Clemente gunned down 27 runners from right field; he never had more than 19 in the rest of his career. Al Kaline, in his fifth full season, 1958, had 23; he never had more than 14 again. Joe DiMaggio had 20 or more in his first three seasons, then never topped 16 again. It's a similar story with Mays. In 1955, his second season back from the Army, he had a career-high 23 assists; for the rest of his career he topped 14 only once. Either these great players' arms got weaker as they matured, or the runners wised up. The problem is that there's no way to measure the runs that are prevented by an outfielder's "reputation."

Mantle, too, may have developed an early reputation with his arm. In 1955, he had a career-high 20 assists; he never had more than 11 for the rest of his career. For their careers, Mays averaged 10.6 assists per 154 games, while Mantle averaged 9.0. The difference between them might amount to a run per season.

What, then, of range in the outfield? For his career, Mays averaged 2.56 fly balls per game, while Mantle averaged 2.26. That means, roughly, that Mays got to about one fly every 3-odd games that Mantle didn't get to. Both played in spacious center-field areas with plenty of room to move. Could the difference between them be accounted for by the Yankees' pitching staff allowing fewer fly balls? The Yankees pitchers almost always struck out more batters than the Giants; and Casey Stengel, you may recall, always had a fondness for selecting pitchers who, in his famous phrase, could "throw ground balls." Maybe the other Yankee outfielders had more range than the other Giant out-fielders so they intruded upon Mantle's territory more and took away a fly ball or so every 3 or 4 games. I don't really think so. I don't think there's any reason to believe the difference represents anything other than Willie Mays being just a little better at pulling down fly balls than Mickey Mantle.

Can the difference be calculated precisely? Well, the difference between 2.56 fly balls per game and 2.26 would be about 35 over 150 games. I asked several baseball observers to consider what they thought, on average, those 35 flies would be worth in terms of runs prevented scattered at random over 150 games. Rob Neyer, who has cowritten several "By the Num-bers" columns with me at *The Journal*, who used to work with Bill James, and who currently writes a baseball column for ESPN's on-line magazine, estimated "7 or 8 runs." Alan Schwarz, an editor with *Baseball America* and a sometime cowriter in my *Journal* column, calculated "9 or 10." Allen St. John, baseball writer for *The Village Voice* and likewise my occasional *Journal* colleague, estimated "7 to 10." Bill James in his Mantle–Mays comparison thought the difference between Mantle and Mays in the outfield to be worth 5 or 6 runs a year.

I think it might be worth a little more than that. If, say, every third fly a centerfielder doesn't get to become an extra-base hit, I think you can calculate 10 runs right there. But this might tip the scale too much in Mays's favor. After a serious tear of a thigh muscle while running out a ground ball in May of 1962, Mantle was never quite the same in center; he went from 2.38 flies per game in 1962 to under 2.00 for the rest of his career. If we take Mantle and Mays at their peak years, Mantle from 1952 to 1961 (Mantle played right field in 1951) and Mays from 1954 to 1963 (he averaged 2.57 flies per game that season and never got that high again), their numbers would look like this:

	G	PO	PO per Game
Mantle, 1952–61	1427	3436	2.41
May, 1954–63	1526	4077	2.67

That makes it a little closer, .26 flies per game, advantage Mays. In terms of what those flies would mean translated into runs, it probably means less of a difference between Mays and Mantle than most outfielders, because Mays played so shallow a centerfield that most of the flies Mays got to that Mantle didn't were singles. Still, I want to be careful about giving Mays too many runs here—I want to say 20 runs since each additional ball that drops for a hit not only has a good chance of scoring a baserunner but of putting a runner on base who will score—but then I'd have to deal with the fact that Richie Ashburn, playing centerfield in the same era, averaged 2.98 flies per game. Could he possibly have been worth 40 runs *more* than Willie Mays over 150 games? It doesn't seem possible. To give Mays the edge in the field and still preserve common sense, I'll say that at his best Mays saved at most 8 to 10 runs per season more than Mantle at his best.

That's not going to make up the difference between Mantle

and Mays as hitters. The only conclusion I can come up with is
that all the objective evidence points to Mickey Mantle, in his
prime, being a better ballplayer than Willie Mays in his prime. I
may not have convinced anyone else, but at least, after all these
years, there's no doubt in my own mind. Thank God my father
isn't alive to read this.

Am I leaving something out? Should I consider all the qualities
that are supposedly lumped together under the heading of "intangibles"? Willie Mays's attitude was said to be wonderful, and Mantle's, we know, was childish and temperamental, at least until
Roger Maris's arrival in 1960 took some of the focus off of him.
But if you take Mantle's prime seasons, starting in his rookie year
of 1951 and going through '64, the Yankees won pennants in '51,
'52, '53, '55, '56, '57, '58, '60, '61, 62, '63, and '64. And one of the
years they didn't win, 1954, they had their best regular season
record under Casey Stengel, winning 103 games. They won the
World Series in '51, '52, '53, '56, '58, '61 and '62—Mantle had
more championship rings at a comparable age than Michael Jordan. Mays's Giants won pennants in '51, '54, and '62, and went to
the playoffs in '71. (Willie also put in a stint for the Mets in their
pennant drive in '73). Yes, I know, Mantle's Yankees were a better
team than Mays's Giants; they *should* have won more. But when
you win twelve pennants in fourteen years, how can you really say
a guy's attitude is hurting his team? If Mantle played with pain and
led his team, and his team won, then it's hard to make a case that
he was bad for team morale. It seems ridiculous to criticize him for
not being more mature before age thirty—should the Yanks have
won eleven pennants in twelve years if not for Mantle's "attitude"?

By the time he died in 1995, most of Mantle's early attitude
problems had been forgotten or at least forgiven by the press and
public. He seemed to be on the verge of being accepted as an
elder statesman, and his comments about his personal life, partic-

ularly his own apologies for being such a bad father, touched a genuine nerve with fans. Joe DiMaggio was pretty much acknowledged by the baseball establishment as "the greatest living ballplayer," but Mantle was without doubt the most beloved. In contrast, Mays has become more moody and withdrawn, given to public displays of temper and jealously, particularly as regards Mantle's superior clout on the autograph circuit. And, oddly enough, all of this had no effect on the public's perception of their careers; in fact, at the end of the century polls, Mays's stature had increased and Mantle's had slipped. To many, they are no longer locked together for all time in the pantheon. Why? I suspect because Mantle left no easily identifiable records or marks behind. Mays hit 4 home runs in a game; he hit 660 home runs, and was just 54 behind Babe Ruth on the all-time list before Hank Aaron passed him by. Aaron has 755; DiMaggio has 56. Ted Williams was the last hitter to top .400. These are easily identifiable marks. A generation of younger fans has to search a list to find Mantle's true greatness. Some might look at the .298 career batting average, the RBI totals—just *four seasons* over 100! (How many players not in the Hall of Fame can boast more 100 RBI seasons? Twenty? Thirty?)—the relatively low (compared to the '70s, '80s, and '90s) stolen base totals, and consider them outside of the context of his time and place and wonder what the fuss was all about.

The RBI, for instance. Leaving aside the seasons when injuries kept him from accumulating enough at-bats for a 100 RBI season—1962, for instance, when he batted just 377 times, drove in an incredible 89 runs, and won the MVP award—it does seem remarkable that Mantle had just four seasons over 100. One reason is that for most of his career he batted third, and generally behind some really terrible leadoff hitters. Bobby Richardson, for instance; in 1961, for no reason anyone has ever been able to figure out, manager Ralph Houk had Richardson lead off for 162 games, and he responded with an on-base average of .295. With Mantle batting two spaces behind him, and Roger Maris batting after that, Richardson had just 80 runs scored all season. Mantle finished with 128 runs batted in. If he'd had a leadoff hitter in front of him with just a mediocre on-base average of .360, he could easily have driven in 140 to 150 runs.

And Willie, too, suffered from a relative lack of good leadoff hitters; it seems odd that so many fans' and writers' candidate for the greatest player of all time never once, in twenty-two seasons, led his league in runs batted in. With both Mantle and Mays, you sometimes have to look a little below the surface to see the greatness. Mays had ten 100+ RBI seasons and never led the league, but he *scored* more than 100 *twelve* times, and led the NL twice. Mantle was awesome in this department. Though he drove in more than 100 just four times, he *scored* more than 100 *nine* times and led the league *six* times.

I think it's fair to say that they were the two most complete players ever to dominate the game at the same time; I might argue, if I hadn't already taken up so much space here, that they were the most complete players of *all* time, the greatest combination of power and speed ever to play the game.

The thing is, I wouldn't have to make the argument for Mays, because he is already perceived that way, but with Mantle, in the eyes of many, it's still very much a case of what *might* have been. Here are some epitaphs about Mantle I saved from newspapers: "could have been one of the truly greats," "never quite lived up to his enormous potential," "squandered so much of his enormous talent." Well, he *did* squander a lot of his talent, largely because of a fatalistic attitude about life instilled in him by his father at an early age. But let's give a lot of blame to those injuries; essentially, that fly ball Mays hit to him in the '51 Series was an obstacle he never quite surmounted.

But what about what Mantle *did* do? We spent so much of Mantle's career judging him from Casey Stengel's perception as the moody, self-destructive phenom who never mastered his demons, and we spent much of the rest of Mantle's life listening to a near-crippled alcoholic lament over and over about what he *might* have been able to accomplish. For an entire generation of fans and sportswriters who saw their own boyhood fantasies reflected in Mantle's career and their worst nightmares fulfilled by his after-baseball life, Mantle's decline became the dominant part of the story.

It's time to dispel this myth. Mickey Mantle played more games in a Yankee uniform than any player in the history of baseball's greatest team, more than Ruth, Gehrig, DiMaggio, or Berra. He played more games than Ted Williams. *Potential?* He was one of the most complete players ever to step on a big league field, a hitter with a terrific batting eye—as evidenced by one of the top twelve on-base average in this century, a better OBA than that of Stan Musial, Joe DiMaggio, Wade Boggs, or Tony Gwynn—spectacular power, blinding speed, and superb defensive ability. He could do things none of his contemporaries could do, not Duke Snider, not Hank Aaron, not Ted Williams, and, yes, not even Willie Mays. He could switch-hit for high average and power, and he could bunt from either side of the plate, and no great power hitter in the game's history was better at stealing a key base or tougher to catch in a double play. He was an All Star centerfielder for eleven straight seasons, he won three MVP awards and should have won two and perhaps three others, and he had more championship rings by age thirty than Michael Jordan had in his whole career. That his life is a cautionary tale on the dangers of success and excess can not be argued, but as a player he has a right to be remembered not for what he might have been but for what he was.

6

61*—Or, Should Roger Maris Be in the Hall of Fame?

Billy Crystal's HBO film *61**, on the Mickey Mantle–Roger Maris chase of Babe Ruth's home run record in 1961, revived interest in a part of baseball history as no film had since John Sayle's recounting of the Black Sox Scandal, *Eight Men Out*. It also revived in many fans the candidacy of Roger Maris for the Hall of Fame.

While *61** is surprisingly fact-based for a baseball movie, it nonetheless propagates a couple of myths about the 1961 season that need to be laid to rest. Among them are:

- The notion that the great home run race of 1961 was caused largely by the "watered-down pitching" brought on by expansion from eight to ten teams. This is always a great fallback when hitting records are being challenged; what is never explained is why expansion wouldn't "thin" hitting as well as pitching. In point of fact, the AL's batting average in 1961 was .256, exactly the same as it had been the year before expansion, and the league's ERA of 4.03 was only a slight increase over the 3.88 in 1960. Interestingly enough, the league's worst team ERA wasn't posted by one of the new teams, the Los Angeles Angels or Washington Senators, who were ninth and sixth, respectively, both well behind Kansas City, the team that posted the worst ERA in the two previous seasons.

- the idea that Yankee Stadium's "friendly" (that is, short) right-field porch (played by Tiger Stadium's friendly right-field porch in the film) substantially helped Maris set the record—or, for that matter, that it helped Babe Ruth or Mickey Mantle. In their best home run seasons, all hit more home runs *on the road* than they did at Yankee Stadium (Maris hit 31 on the road, 30 at home in '61; Mantle was 30 and 24; Ruth was 32 and 28).

But the biggest myth of all is the myth of the asterisk. With the possible exception of Abner Doubleday's invention of baseball, the game's most enduring myth has been the Roger Maris's asterisk. Now, thanks to Billy Crystal's otherwise admirable film, the asterisk has sole possession of the top spot.

The asterisk is supposed to be beside Maris's name in the record books, indicating that he broke the most famous of all baseball records, Babe Ruth's 60 home runs in one season, over a 162-game span instead of the 154 that Ruth played in. In point of fact, no such asterisk was ever put beside Maris's name in any record book; it never existed.

That anyone ever thought there was an asterisk is at least as much the fault of sportswriter Dick Young as of Commissioner Ford Frick. Frick worshiped Ruth and was at his bedside the day before he died (and made much of that in interviews and after-dinner speeches). Maris had the bad luck to have his greatest season in 1961 at a time when Frick was commissioner of baseball. As early as July 17, when Maris and several other sluggers were ahead of Ruth's 1927 pace, Ford, apparently distressed that the new 162-game season would give someone an unfair crack at Ruth's record, called a press conference and issued this ruling:

"Any player who may hit more than 60 home runs during his club's first 154 games would be recognized as having established a new record. However, if the player does not hit more than 60 until after his club has played 154 games, there would have to be some distinctive mark in the record books to show that Babe Ruth's record was set under a 154-game schedule."

Did I say "ruling"? Actually, Frick was offering his opinion; he had no power whatsover to make a ruling on this subject. Crystal's film (with veteran character actor Donald Moffit as Frick) gets the press conference right but fails to tell us that Frick was simply grandstanding, probably because Crystal and his screenwriters never quite understood what happened. They were, and are, in good company. Judging from my experience on radio shows, not one fan in a thousand understands what happened. What the film doesn't say, and what escaped most of the baseball writers present at Frick's press conference, was that major league baseball has no "official" record book and didn't have until *Total Baseball* got the job a few years ago. So, in essence, Frick was trying to pressure publishers over whom he had absolutely no authority whatsoever that they had to print something in their books on his order.

It's possible that little or nothing would have come out of the incident if not for the crusty and acerbic sports columnist Dick Young, then writing for the *New York Daily News*. According to a later Maris biographer, Maury Allen, Young said out loud, "Maybe you should use an asterisk on the new record. Everybody does that when there's a difference of opinion." Of course, there was no "difference of opinion"; the issue didn't exist until Ford created it, and it wouldn't have lasted unless Young had kept it alive. When the 1962 record books appeared, there was no asterisks anywhere. *The Sporting News* did begin to list records set in 154 seasons and 162 seasons separately, but the editors swore it was their idea and had nothing to do with the commissioner's ruling—er, opinion. Some simply listed Ruth's record and Maris's record on separate pages. It could be said that this was in itself a form of anti-Maris discrimination, and in any event it long ago disappeared from any record books. Today there is no more question that Roger Maris held the record for home runs in one season than there is that Hank Aaron holds the record for career home runs.

And yet, the myth persists that Roger Maris's record is somehow qualified, and it has even survived the denial of Ford Frick himself in his autobiography, *Games, Asterisks, and People* (Crown, 1973). "No asterisk," he wrote, "has appeared in the official record in connection for that accomplishment." But, he couldn't resist reminding us, "His record was set in a 162-game season. The Ruth record of 60 home runs was set in 1927 in a 154-game season." For all the mentions that's still made of that fact, few fans or writers realize that Maris hit his 60th home run in his 684th plate appearance, while it took Ruth 689.

There is a bizarre postscript to the Maris asterisk story. In 1991, Commissioner Fay Vincent issued a statement that indicated that he supported "the single record thesis," which is that Maris hit more home runs in a season than anyone else. The committee on statistical accuracy then voted to remove the asterisk from Maris's record. Thus, a commissioner of baseball voiced his support for removing an asterisk which a previous commissioner had denied ever existed.

If baseball's record books had actually put an asterisk beside

Maris's name in 1962, it would have soon been removed and the whole incident would have been forgotten. The fact that the asterisk never really existed has made it impossible to kill the myth. (Of course, one can argue that the fact that Maris died thinking that it existed made it just as real as if it had been on the record books.)

Still, *61** gets a number of things right, the most important of which is that Roger Maris was not, as many of his critics claimed at the time, a "one-year wonder." In fact, in 1960 Maris led the league in slugging and finished only 1 home run behind Mantle, 39 to 40, leading the league with 112 RBI. He edged out Mantle for the AL MVP award. In 1962 he was pretty good, too, hitting 33 home runs, driving in 100 runs and generally supplying much the glue the team needed with Mantle out for much of the season. So his value was probably much greater that year than the simple statistics indicate (the oft-injured Mantle drove in 89 runs that season in just 377 at-bats, the fewest of any MVP winner excepting pitchers). In the Mantle–Mays chapter I argue, quite soundly, I think, that Mantle should have won the MVP awards both seasons that Maris won. But that's not a knock on Maris: Mantle was one of the greatest players of all time, especially during his '61 season. For those three seasons Roger Maris was a terrific ballplayer, and for several others he was very good to good.

There are a number of other myths about Roger Maris that need to be done away with, such as the notion that his only contribution to his team was the ability to hit home runs. Maris was regarded as a fine outfielder with an excellent arm; all Yankee fans old enough remember his peg to Bobby Richardson in the ninth inning of Game 7 of the 1962 World Series. Following Willie Mays's opposite-field double, Maris threw a one-hop strike from the right-field corner of Candlestick Park that held Matty Alou on third base and saved the Yankees' lead. (An odd thing about Maris's fielding stats, though: in 1960, '61, and '62, when he was younger and faster, his range in right field was considerably below the league average; in '61 it was absurdly below, 1.77 chances per game to the league's 2.10. In 1967 and '68, when he was older and slower, he was well above the league average in range, 2.26 to 2.02 and 2.14 to 2.02. The only logical explanation is that the Yankees must have loaded with "ground ball" pitchers in the early '60s just as in the Casey Stengel years.) He was considered an excellent baserunner, too.

But Roger Maris does not, on the basis of his career numbers, deserve a plaque in the Hall of Fame, and Billy Crystal's movie shows you precisely why: He burnt out from the pressure of the '61 race and despite playing substantial roles on five other pennant winning teams (three with the Yankees, two in St. Louis), Maris played just two more full seasons after 1961. I could make a comparison with ten to twenty players at least as deserving as Maris; I'd like to see Ron Santo and Ken Boyer and maybe Joe Torre (as a player) get in, and I think Minnie Minoso and Tony Oliva, to pick two outfielders off the top of my head, should get in well before Maris. And yet, it's that damned asterisk, which the movie has now cemented in everyone's minds, that helps convince people that he belongs there. I could put up charts to show you, but what would be the use? If you are advocating Roger Maris for the Hall of Fame, it isn't a logical argument you're making but an emotional one.

You want to say to me, as you've said on numerous radio shows or in your e-mails, that he deserves to be in because of his "fundamental decency"—and from everything I've ever heard or read he was certainly that—or that he showed great character in keeping himself together under pressure while pursuing and finally breaking the most famous record in American sports. I'll give him that, too. But how many men would we admit to Cooperstown if good character under pressure was the criterion? I'd certainly start with Orestes "Minnie" Minoso, the first black Hispanic player in major league baseball (with Cleveland, 1948). I think Minoso had more to endure than Maris or practically anyone besides Jackie Robinson, and I would argue that he was a better player as well (see Chapter 12, "The New Latin Dynasty").

Or you want to hit me with the Great Unwritten Sandy Koufax Rule, namely, that unquestioned greatness over a short period ought to be sufficient to get a player into the Hall of Fame. I have no problem with that rule in theory; in practice, unfortunately, the only person I've ever been able to apply it to is Sandy Koufax. Sandy Koufax was great for six years; for six years, or at least five, he was *the* pitcher in baseball, or at least so great that the overwhelming weight of available evidence says so. Was Roger Maris that great for five years? Was he ever really the greatest for one year? Can you really say with certainty that he was one of the ten best players in the game for even five years? For three? Maybe for three; *maybe*. And if you can't immediately answer yes to that question, how can you seriously say he should be in the Hall of Fame?

Roger Maris is one of my first vivid childhood sports heroes, and I'm forever grateful to Billy Crystal for bringing him back, along with Mickey Mantle, to help me explain to my ten-year-old daughter why the summer of '61 meant so much to me. But the Hall of Fame is about greatness, unadulterated, unalloyed, undeniable greatness—or at least I think it should be and if you don't, then don't talk to me about it. And for whatever reasons that were locked up in his mind and heart, Roger Maris shied away from true greatness. Think of it this way, folks: Roger Maris would have been the first one to tell you that he didn't quite deserve to be in the Hall of Fame. You know that he would. A less than honest response to the question of "Does Roger Maris belong in the Hall of Fame?" dishonors his memory.

Clearing the Bases

It's gospel, isn't it, that Roger Maris didn't blossom as a power hitter till he came to New York? Well, here are Maris's home-road stats for his entire career.

Year	Team	HR	Home/Away
1957	Cleveland	14	8/6
1958	Cleveland–KC	28	10/18
1959	KC	16	6/10
1960	NYY	39	13/26
1961	NYY	61	30/31
1962	NYY	33	19/14
1963	NYY	23	11/12
1964	NYY	26	10/16
1965	NYY	8	4/4
1966	NYY	13	7/6
1967	StL	9	4/5
1968	StL	5	0/5
Total		275	122/153

Roger Maris played in four different home parks, and hit more home runs on the road than he did in each of them. That's amazing. No only didn't Yankee Stadium help him—he hit 13 more home runs in *other* AL parks than he did there—but none of the others did, either. Just imagine: If Roger Maris had hit as well at home as he did on the road—or perhaps if he'd had a couple of better home parks to hit in—he would have had 306 home runs in just twelve major league seasons and then his fans would have a solid argument for his Hall of Fame candidacy. If he'd have hit about 10 percent better at home like most players do, he'd have finished with over 330 homers—and then he'd probably be in the Hall of Fame.

7

Juan Marichal and Bob Gibson: A Reassessment

MARICHAL

When Juan pitched
he kicked holes
through the blue
San Francisco sky
and reaching above
China Bay, he
plucked flame-tipped
stars from the
Milky Way.

Through celestial storms
and Pacific gales,
I couldn't believe
he never lost
his cap when
he kicked so high
and Mercury glistened
on the bottom
of his left shoe.

—ED MARKOWSKI

The preceding poem is from the *FAN*, a baseball quarterly. It is accompanied by a silhouette of Juan Marichal in highest kick. If you ever saw Marichal pitch, no illustration is necessary; was there ever a pitcher so easily identifiable by outline?

I don't know that Juan Marichal was my favorite pitcher— I'd probably give that honor to Tom Seaver, if pressed. But Marichal was easily my favorite to *watch*. He had style to burn, and the most distinctive windup of any pitcher I ever saw.

To my mind, no one has ever completely explained the disappearance of the windup from the big leagues. Japanese pitchers still use them, and judging from Orlando Hernandez, so do the Cubans, but hardly any American pitchers do. Are you old enough to remember the windup of the great pitchers of the '60s? Think Warren Spahn and you recall that beautiful left-handed kick and fluid come-down with his glove covering the grip on the ball until the exact moment of release to the batter. Sandy Koufax was even more fluid, a lower leg kick, more of a sweep, really, culminating with a snap! of the wrist and elbow—you wondered how his arm could sustain it (as it turned out, it couldn't). Don Drysdale's long, gangly arms curling over his head and a side-arm (later in his career, three-quarters) sweep that must have made right-handed batters think the ball was coming in from around third base. Jim Bouton, nearly great before the shoulder blew, launching himself off the mound with such force that when his left leg came down, the momentum often left him several feet off the dirt of the pitcher's mound (and his cap several feet to the left).

Why did they stop throwing like that? In the '80s, it seemed, they started throwing more with their *arms* and less with their bodies. How many pitchers today even use a windup? Was it the emergence of the running game that caused pitchers to abandon the high kick? Did too many backs (like Juan Marichal's, actually) get thrown out of whack? Whatever the reason, the big windups are gone, and I think we shall never see their like again.

Juan Marichal had the most fun windup of all. Joe Garigiola once described Marichal as looking like "a double-jointed drum majorette stooping to pick up a dime during a parade." That's good, but it doesn't get at the whole picture. As my father once observed, Marichal seemed to wind up in sections. First, he'd rock, with both arms swung high up behind him, then they'd swing up over his head as his torso began to twist to the right and his left leg started to whip up from underneath. Then the leg soared high—"Nobody," he once bragged to an interviewer, "kicks higher than me" (and no one did, not even Warren Spahn)—while his right arm reached back so far the ball nearly touched the ground, all the while in perfect line with the leg. Actually, that famous high-kick windup was only one of several; he used it for the fastball, curve, slider, and, occasionally, a screwball, but he could throw the first three and a change-up from three-quarters, as well as a dandy curve from an almost comically exaggerated side-arm windup.

No pitcher was more fun to watch, but how good was he at his best? As an anonymous *Time* magazine writer wrote in a June 10, 1966 cover story, "Better than Koufax or not, Juan Marichal without question 1) has the best right arm in baseball, and 2) is the most complete pitcher in the game today, or any other day." That was pretty much how he was regarded back then, but in recent years his reputation has faded. In the All Century team, he was passed up for Bob Gibson and—insult of insults—Nolan Ryan.

Actually, the erosion of Marichal's reputation began earlier than that, as evidenced by the Hall of Fame votings, beginning in 1981, the year both Marichal and Bob Gibson were eligible for the Hall of Fame. First, let's look at their respective records. Gibson and Marichal were almost exact contemporaries, Gibson breaking in a year earlier in 1959, both retiring in 1975. Here's the career line:

	G	GS	W-L	PCT.	ERA	IP	H	SO
Gibson	528	482	251–174	.591	2.91	3884	3279	3117
Marichal	471	457	242–142	.631	2.89	3507	3153	2303

	BB	CG	SHO	OAV	OBP
Gibson	1336	255	56	.228	.299
Marichal	709	244	52	.237	.278

These stats, by the way, are from *Total Baseball*; OAV is opponent batting average, OBP is on-base percentage against. So, if Bob Gibson was a better pitcher than Juan Marichal, I can't see it from their career numbers. Gibson started 25 more games, won 9 more, and lost 32 more; Marichal's won-lost percentage is 40 points higher. Complete games, shutouts, hits-to-innings pitched, and earned-run average are all about even. Hitters hit Marichal for 9 more points, but reached base substantially less often via the walk. If anything, the overall numbers, particularly won-lost percentage, seem to indicate a small but definite edge for Marichal.

And yet, when the Hall of Fame balloting started, Marichal was left in the dust. In 1981, Gibson passed all HOF contenders, walking home with 337 votes, 36 more than were needed. Marichal placed only sixth; two other pitchers, Don Drysdale and Hoyt Wilhelm, neither of whom were in Marichal's class for overall value, finished ahead of him. Gil Hodges, who still hasn't been elected to the Hall of Fame, also finished ahead of him.

That wasn't the end of it—the next season Hank Aaron and Frank Robinson waltzed in while Marichal finished six votes short (at least this time he outpolled Wilhelm and Drysdale, 306 to 236 and 233; what happened over a twelve-month period to make him better than they is a mystery). The next year he made it, 313 votes of a required 281. But it was qualified: Brooks Robinson outpointed him by *thirty-one votes*. *Thirty-one.* Brooks Robinson, at his peak, was not the equal of Juan Marichal in value. If Brooks Robinson were a pitcher, he'd have been about the equal of Gaylord Perry, not Juan Marichal.

Juan Marichal was one of the greatest pitchers in baseball history. At his peak, from 1961 to 1971, he stands comparison with the best. Over an eight-year span, from 1962 to 1969, he was possibly one of the five or six best in the lively ball era. If he hadn't been stopped cold by back injuries in what could well have been his peak years, he might well have put in a valid bid as the best of all time. The line drive from the bat of Gil McDougald that effectively ended the career of Herb Score has often been called a baseball tragedy. But so was Juan Marichal's severe reaction to a penicillin infection in 1970 that led to severe arthritis. Juan was thirty-two at the time, and the illness cost him his fastball. He slipped to 12–10 in 1970, the worst record of his major league career. Working with guts and guile he came back the next season to win 18, but that was his last hurrah. He struggled through three more seasons and 2 games into a fourth, compiling an overall 22–33 record for 72 starts. With his smarts and wide pitching arsenal, he was precisely the model of a pitcher who could have been a big-gamer into his forties. He was 191–88 before the illness, 52–54 after. One doesn't have to disregard his illness altogether to see what might have been. Allow 1970 and '71, and then cut him a little slack. If, from 1972 on, he could have pitched till forty, going just 15–10 for five more seasons, he'd have finished an awesome 296–154. A seventh 20+ win season would certainly not have been out of question; he would then have had over 300 wins along with one of the best won-lost percentages in the Hall of Fame.

But never mind what he might have been. Juan Marichal won 243 games; he won 18 or more eight times, more than 20 six times, and 25 or more three times. He was the best pitcher in baseball over a twelve-year span from 1960 through 1971, Bob Gibson and Don Drysdale not excepted, and what the Hall of Fame voters did to him is a disgrace. He was every bit as deserving as Bob Gibson, Hank Aaron, and Frank Robinson, and more deserving than Brooks Robinson. He should have strolled into Cooperstown on the first ballot.

Clearing the Bases

Let's take him at his peak and compare him with Bob Gibson (asterisks denotes led league).

MARICHAL

Year	W-L	GS	IP	CG	ERA
1961	13–10	27	185	9	3.89
1962	18–11	36	262	18	3.36
1963	*25–8	40	*321	18	2.41
1964	21–8	33	269	*22	2.48
1965	22–13	37	295	24	2.13
1966	25–6	36	307	25	2.23
1967	14–10	21	202	18	2.76
1968	*26–9	38	*326	*30	2.43
1969	21–11	37	299	27	*2.10
1970	12–10	33	242	14	4.12
1971	18–11	37	279	18	2.94

GIBSON

Year	W-L	GS	IP	CG	ERA
1961	13–12	27	211	10	3.24
1962	15–13	30	233	15	2.85
1963	18–9	33	254	14	3.39
1964	19–12	36	287	17	3.01
1965	20–12	36	299	20	3.07
1966	21–12	35	280	20	2.44
1967	13–7	24	175	10	2.98
1968	22–9	34	304	*28	*1.12
1969	20–13	35	314	23	2.18
1970	23–7	34	294	20	3.12
1971	16–13	31	245	23	3.04

Gibson, to be fair, had one more great season in 1972, going 19–11 with an ERA of 2.46. Gibson needed that edge to catch Marichal. At the end of 1971, including 1959 and 1960 for Gibson (in which he was a combined 6–11) and 1960 for Marichal (when he was 6–2), Marichal was 221–109 for a percentage of .670; Gibson was 206–130, for a percentage of .613.

In how many of the seasons was Marichal a better pitcher than Gibson? Let's review.

- In nine of the eleven seasons, Marichal had a better won-lost percentage.
- In seven of the eleven seasons, Marichal had a lower ERA.
- In seven of the eleven seasons, Marichal completed more games.
- In seven of the eleven seasons, Marichal won more games and had a lower ERA.

The more one looks at this, the more puzzling history's judgment becomes. Puzzling, that is, unless one considers the three World Series that Gibson pitched in, Series in which the Cardinals won twice (in 1964 and '67) and lost one close one (1968) and in which Gibson was a combined 7–2 with 2 shutouts and 2 games in which he allowed just 1 run. In the 1964 and 1967 World Series, Gibson was the most dominant player, and he came within a wisp of being so again in 1968.

I'm not attempting to take anything away from Bob Gibson's World Series victories; they weren't aberrations but a clear reflection of how good his performance was in those years, perhaps raised just a notch for the occasion. That's what great pitchers do in big games. The injustice is not that

Gibson's reputation is raised by those extra games, it's that Marichal's is *lowered* for the ones he didn't get to pitch. Marichal got to the postseason just twice, once in the 1962 World Series, in which he started Game 4 and was lifted after 4 innings after getting hit on the hand by a Whitey Ford pitch during a bunt attempt; he gave up just 2 hits and no runs—and the 1971 playoffs against Pittsburgh in which he went 8 innings while allowing 4 hits and 2 runs. So, his career postseason record stands at 2 starts, 0–1 record, 12 innings pitched, 6 hits, 2 ER, 1.50 ERA, 10 strikeouts, 2 walks. I don't know how you can do much better than that in 12 innings, and he never got another chance.

It's odd that Marichal's only two postseason appearances would come after seasons when he was very good but not great. In 1962, he won 18 games and began his brilliant ten-year run; 1971 he won 18 games, his last winning season. In between, per-haps no pitcher of the modern era was plagued with stranger luck. Here are the Cy Young award winners during Juan Marichal's four best seasons. (One award was given for both leagues until 1967).

1963	Marichal	25–8	Sandy Koufax	25–5
1964	Marichal	21–8	Dean Chance	20–9
1966	Marichal	25–6	Sandy Koufax	27–9
1968	Marichal	26–9	Bob Gibson	22–9
Total		97–31	Total	94–32

I don't know how you could have worse luck than that— in your four best seasons, you lose to a flash-in-the-pan (Chance), and to Sandy Koufax twice, and then to Bob Gibson the year he decides to post one of the lowest ERA's in major league history. (Not to take anything away from Gibson's achievement that year, but it was somewhat on the flukish side. Great as he was, in only one other season did he post an ERA less .than twice the mark of 1.12.) And despite that, *Marichal's overall won-lost record for those four years was better than the combined records of the pitchers who won the Cy Young awards.* And how's this for even stranger luck: Juan Marichal was the winningest pitcher in the major leagues from 1960 through '69, 191–88, with the best won-lost percentage of .685 (Bob Gibson was 164–105 for .610). Yet, *Juan Marichal never got a single first-place vote for the Cy Young award.* Not one.

There's a lingering prejudice about Marichal to the effect he wasn't as good as the numbers suggest, or, as the host of a Chicago radio sports show once phrased it to me, "How could a guy with Willie Mays, Willie McCovey, and Gaylord Perry on his team, all those Hall of Famers, not win some pennants?" (I could as easily turn that argument around and ask why the other three Hall of Famers couldn't win more pennants, but let that pass.) What people forget is that, top to bottom, the Dodgers and Cardinals, winners of every National League pennant from 1963 through 1968, were better teams than the Giants, even with Marichal, Mays, McCovey, and (for some of the time) Perry. The Giants, of course, did win in 1962, edging out the Dodgers, but Marichal (18–11) wasn't the ace that year. Jack Stanford (24–7) was. Here are the records of Marichal, Koufax, and Gibson for '63 through '68, with the team's won-lost records when those three didn't get the decision:

	Koufax	Dodgers	Rest of Staff	Plus/Minus
1963	25–5	99–63	74–58	+16
1964	19–5	80–82	61–77	−16
1965	26–8	97–65	71–57	+14
1966	27–9	95–67	68–58	+10
1967	—			
1968	—			

	Gibson	Cardinals	Rest of Staff	Plus/Minus
1963	18–9	93–69	75–60	+15
1964	19–12	93–69	74–57	+17
1965	20–12	80–81	60–69	−9
1966	21–12	83–79	62–67	−5
1967	13–7	101–60	88–53	+35
1968	22–9	97–65	75–56	+19

	Marichal	Giants	Rest of Staff	Plus/Minus
1963	25–8	88–74	73–66	+7
1964	21–8	90–72	69–64	+5
1965	22–13	95–67	73–54	+19
1966	25–6	93–68	68–62	+6
1967	14–10	91–71	77–61	+16
1968	26–9	88–74	62–65	−3

From 1963 through 1966, Koufax's last year, Sandy was
97–27 for a team that was otherwise 274–250. Over the same
period, Marichal was 93–35 for a team that was otherwise
283–246. This is very nearly equal, with an edge to Koufax. But
it's slightly misleading: In 1965, the year of the Marichal–John
Roseboro incident (more on this later), Marichal had his least
impressive of these four seasons, 22–13, while the Giants, over-

all, had their best record (95–67). If you take the other three seasons in which they went head-to-head, 1963, '64, and '66, Koufax was 71–19 for teams that were otherwise 203–193, while Marichal was 71–22 for teams that were otherwise 206–192. This is practically a dead heat, close enough to fall into the margin-of-error category.

And what of the relative support given to Marichal and Bob Gibson? In 1964, '67, and '68, the Cardinals won the National League pennant, and Gibson's record was 54–28 while the Cardinals were otherwise 239–166. In those years, the Giants, when Marichal didn't get the decision, were 218–190; when he did get the decision, they were 61–23. Even in the years when the Cardinals had the better team and won the pennant, Marichal out-pitched Gibson.

Okay, let's not pretend we don't know the real reason Juan Marichal has been insulted by baseball. On August 22, 1965, in the heat of a pennant race, Marichal, as he so often did, faced off against Sandy Koufax in one of the biggest games of the year. (Perhaps this is the place to dispel another "couldn't win the big game" myth about Marichal: he won 24 of 25 decisions over the Dodgers at Candlestick Park.) The Dodgers got off to a 3–1 lead, despite two knockdown pitches from Marichal against Maury Wills and Ron Fairly. In the third, with Marichal batting, Dodger catcher John Roseboro called for a retaliation pitch from Koufax. Sandy wasn't big on retaliation, preferring to intimidate by domination, but he obliged first by brushing back Willie Mays, then with an inside fastball that moved Juan off the plate. No problem, part of the game. But Roseboro dropped the ball, and picked it up—looking to some as if he was trying to get an angle closer to Marichal when he tossed it back to the mound. At any rate, it was a close throw—Marichal always claimed it nicked his ear. "Why did you do that?" he screamed at Roseboro. "Why did you do that?"

What has often been overlooked in rehashes of the incident is that it was Roseboro who charged Marichal. Marichal clubbed the Dodgers' catcher three times with the bat, causing a deep scalp wound. By the time order was restored, a shaken Koufax surrendered a 3-run home run to Willie Mays in a 4–3 Giants win, but the Giants' season was effectively over. Fined $1,750 by National League President Warren Giles—that doesn't sound like a lot now, but remember that Koufax was at the time the highest-paid pitcher in baseball at $130,000—Marichal was also suspended for nine days, including a crucial road game in Los Angeles. Many thought the punishment wasn't enough, but it was enough to finish the Giants, who lost to Los Angeles by 2 games. Marichal was 19–9 before the incident, 3–4 after.

There was in fact a subtext to the incident. Roseboro was deeply disturbed by the rioting in the Watts section of Los Angeles, while Marichal, a fervent patriot, was tormented over the bloody civil war in his native Dominican Republic (two weeks before the Roseboro incident, he had taken out a full-page ad in a Santo Domingo paper urging his countrymen to vote. And his cousin, also named Juan Marichal, was the running mate of presidential candidate Joaquin Balaguer). Juan Marichal, "The Dominican Dandy," the smiling warrior, the man described by his wife Alma as "never angry, even when he gets up in mornings," the practical joker who liked to pass around perfume bottles loaded with stink bombs, the man who Maury Wills (one of the Dodgers Juan brushed back in the August 22 game) called "a nice guy, a great individual," was so strung out he probably should not have been pitching at that point—and certainly not in a pressure-packed Giants–Dodgers match.

There is no excuse for what Juan Marichal did to John Roseboro, but Roseboro forgave him and even campaigned for his election to the Hall of Fame, a gesture for which Juan thanked him in his induction speech. Baseball should do likewise. Doing the All Century vote once again would be a nice starter.

8

My Player of the Century

In March 1999, following Joe DiMaggio's death, I was surprised by a rumor that Reggie Jackson was now demanding (as DiMaggio had) that he be announced at all public appearances as "The Greatest Living Ballplayer." I wrote a column for *The Wall Street Journal* on the subject of "The Greatest Living Player." (By the way, I never confirmed the rumor about Reggie.) Essentially what I did was take a quick poll of friends, colleagues, writers, and the researchers I use in *The Wall Street Journal* "By the Numbers" column and asked for nominations for the player they regarded as, well, the Greatest Living Player. Outside of being great and being living, I gave no criteria.

My colleagues chose to exclude pitchers from the mix; whether because they didn't think pitchers as valuable as regulars or because they thought it simpler to confine the discussion to everyday players, I didn't ask.

Anyway, the lists everyone came up with were practically

identical to each other and also pretty much identical to mine. The players included were Ted Williams, Stan Musial, Yogi Berra, Willie Mays, Hank Aaron, Johnny Bench, Joe Morgan, Mike Schmidt, Ken Griffey, Jr., and Barry Bonds. Reggie Jackson, Frank Robinson, and Rickey Henderson just failed to make the cut; Pete Rose wasn't close. Tim Raines, I thought, should have been, but that's a subject for another chapter.

Now, such categories as "Greatest Living Ballplayer" have no real meaning and obviously exist just for fun—for debate fodder. But the impact of the silly story was enormous, a spate of e-mail, letters, and calls on radio talk shows on who deserved to be on the list who was not (mostly Tony Gwynn, whom I love as a human being and enjoy as a player but who definitely does *not* deserve to be in such a group), and who was on the list but shouldn't have been (mostly Mike Schmidt, as in, "I remember a time when a guy who hit .270 couldn't make the team"). And who might have made the list if I had only waited another year or two (mostly Alex Rodriguez, though Pudge Rodriguez drew some votes). Some objected to the chart, which listed the number of times each candidate led his league in home runs, batting, runs batted in, runs scored, on-base average, slugging average, and stolen bases, saying that it didn't "weigh" the categories in order of importance (true, but not relevant since this wasn't an attempt at a scientific measurement), some because it didn't measure fielding (true), and some because it was unfair to players who played tough defensive positions as Morgan, Bench, and Berra had to do (also true).

But most of all I was surprised by the *interest* the column stirred up. I got cards and letters and email till summer, and several expressed some variation of this thought: in picking the greatest living player, you may well be picking the greatest player of all time.

I hadn't thought about that when doing the piece, but of course I was and I am prepared to agree with it. I've never understood why other sports get to call a current player the greatest but baseball always has to settle for someone whose prime was sixty or seventy or eighty years ago. I began to develop the idea that a closer examination of the proper players might indeed yield the greatest player of all time, an idea that had always seemed too daunting to me to actually attempt. But why couldn't the greatest player of all time be a modern player? And if he was, why not take a stab at it?

So, after thinking it over and deciding it was a bad idea, I've gone ahead and done it anyway. I've gathered together all the players mentioned in the original column and added Mickey Mantle to the pool (I still can't get it into my head that he's dead), shifted the question from Greatest Living Player to Greatest Player of the Integrated Era, and this time, after careful examination, I've done what I didn't do the first time: I've come up with a winner.

First off, I must also do here what I did not do in the *Journal* story, namely, offer an explanation for starting this debate with players from the second half of the twentieth century. As I've indicated elsewhere in this book, I've never understood why there is an automatic assumption among so many baseball fans that the best players and teams came before 1950. 1950, or even a decade or so later, is where football and basketball fans *begin* to date their games' histories from. No football fan really thinks the Chicago Bears' "Monsters of the Midway" are a match for the Lombardi Packers or Walsh 49ers or any other modern NFL teams; no basketball fan would dare compare the George Mikan Minneapolis Lakers to the Shaquille O'Neal LA Lakers. But you'll find millions of quite knowledgeable baseball fans willing to pick, without hesitation, the 1927 Yankees as the greatest baseball team of all time and Babe Ruth as the greatest player.

This is not a subject I want to argue at length at this time or, really, any other. What I want to do is move my argument forward by making what I regard as some very simple assumptions. First, that the overwhelming weight of evidence is that the other major sports have evolved toward excellence in the last half century and that there is no reason to believe that baseball has done otherwise. Second, that if the first proposition is true then it is also very likely that the players in that sport have evolved for the better, too. In another chapter I deal with the impact that black and Latin players have had on the game. Is it such a leap to suppose that if Ty Cobb and Babe Ruth and Cy Young had had to compete against the ancestors of Willie Mays and Hank Aaron and Bob Gibson, that they wouldn't have dominated as they did in a time when major leaguers were drawn from a relatively small portion of white men from, mostly, the eastern and southern and a few midwestern states?

Okay, so if you don't fully agree with the direction in which I'm heading, at least grant that I *could* be right and, for the sake of argument, let me follow this proposition through to its logical conclusion: that the only fair comparison of candidates for the title of Greatest Player must be drawn from those who played from 1951 to the end of the century. So, then, who are the usual suspects? I would wager that most baseball fans would agree with the list in my chart.

Fewer, probably, will agree with my decision to cut Ted Williams and Stan Musial from my list. I'm certainly not denying that they were great players, or at least that they had great moments after 1950. But clearly their best seasons were in preintegrated ball, and no one would argue that by the mid- and late '50s that either was making a substantial contribution in the field or on the bases, and that with the exception of Ted Williams's incredible 1957 season, neither was hitting as he had in the '40s.

So let's proceed. I think we can all agree that one way of perceiving greatness is to look at the number of categories a player leads his league in. I'm not saying all categories are equal. RBIs, runs, Most Valuable Player awards? Aren't the first two too dependent on who hits in front and in back of you, and the latter too much on the attitudes and prejudices in both? Yes and yes, but I'm not putting absolute faith in any categories, I'm simply using them all as indicators. I'm assuming that great players cannot be great without leaving a trail in at least some of these categories. And, yes, we must cut Berra, Bench, and Morgan some slack here for playing tough defensive positions; it's hard to lead the league in runs scored when your job is to squat behind a plate 140-odd times a year, or in home runs when the prerequisite for your position is to be nimble enough to make a double-play pivot to first.

But there is someone on that list who played a defensive position that, judging by the sparseness of its representation in the Hall of Fame, might be even tougher than Berra's, Bench's, and Morgan's. Third base has fewer representatives in Cooperstown than any other position, and yet Mike Schmidt was able to play it and win eight home run titles while playing it.

Eight home run titles. Did you realize that Mike Schmidt led the league eight times in home runs? I didn't, and his career spanned the time when I was writing about baseball for a living. If you'd ask me, I'd have guessed five or six. Mike Schmidt played only 13 games in his first season, 1972, and 42 in his last, 1989, so that means in sixteen full seasons, he led the league in home runs in half the seasons he was a regular. Let's put that in perspective. Competing against roughly 180 nonpitching players a year, in sixteen seasons Mike Schmidt won eight home run titles. Babe Ruth, of course, has the most impressive home run title credentials of any player in history, and he won twelve titles in seventeen full seasons. (I am counting Ruth's 1918 season in which he batted only 317 times and won the home run title with 11.) But Ruth only had to compete against roughly 120 players a year. Ruth's achievement is fantastic, but Schmidt's is pretty damn good. If Ruth's achievement over seventeen seasons is the most impressive power hitting feat in baseball history, where does Schmidt rank? Third, I think, behind Ruth and then Ralph Kiner's feat of seven home run titles in a row from 1946 through 1952.

Let's put that into an even clearer perspective: Mickey Mantle and Willie Mays had a combined thirty-five seasons of over 100 games played, and Mike Schmidt had sixteen. Mike Schmidt won twice as many home run titles as Mickey Mantle and Willie Mays *combined*. Let's turn that perspective focus one notch sharper: Hank Aaron and Mickey Mantle played a combined *thirty-eight seasons* of more than 100 games played, and they won as many home run titles *combined* as Mike Schmidt did in sixteen. That's as many home run titles in thirty-eight seasons, playing for much of their careers in *eight-team leagues* as Mike Schmidt had in *sixteen seasons* playing in *twelve-team leagues*, competing against one-third more players (Schmidt also had to compete against more players to win his titles than Ralph Kiner, who played in an eight-team league).

Does that mean Mike Schmidt was a greater slugger than Mantle, Mays, Aaron, Kiner, or anyone else on that list? Not necessarily, but it sure doesn't mean that he wasn't.

Hitting is the most important single criterion for any great player, and I think we can state without fear of contradiction that Mike Schmidt ranks among the great hitters in at least one important aspect: power. But what about consistency? There's absolutely no doubt in my mind that the greatest single stumbling block in the minds of many fans in accepting Schmidt's greatness is his lifetime batting average of .267, which has got to be one of the lowest of any nonpitcher in the Hall of Fame. I'm not even going to look; I promise you it's one of the lowest. But what of that? Why should this archaic, lingering prejudice toward a devalued statistic block our acceptance of a great player? On-base average is a much more important statistic, and Schmidt led his league *three times* in on-base percentage, which is as many times as Mickey Mantle led his. Once again, let's put that in perspective: in sixteen full seasons competing in a twelve-team league, Mike Schmidt led his in on-base average as many times as Willie Mays and Hank Aaron, two players who outhit him by more than 30 points each over their careers, did in a combined thirty-eight seasons. In the twentieth century, both Barry Bonds and Joe Morgan led their leagues more often in on-base percentage, both four times each, but Schmidt led the league in slugging average *five times* to Bonds's three and Morgan's *one*.

Since all of the candidates on our list are excellent all-around players, let's examine some other key areas. Baserunning? It should certainly be conceded that Schmidt was less of a base-stealing threat than any other candidate with the obvious exception of our catchers, Berra and Bench. But for a period of nine seasons, from 1974 through 1982, when he stole 155 of his 174 bases, Schmidt was pretty good for a slugger, or, really, for just about anyone, with a success rate of 72 percent (155 of 215). Everyone who saw him play acknowledges that he was fast, smart, and tough on the bases until his knees gave him too much trouble in the last couple of seasons. Anyway, the difference between Joe Morgan, the most prolific base-stealer among our candidates, and Mike Schmidt would amount to a few odd runs per season in Morgan's favor.

Let's look at another statistic that measures speed and baserunning ability: GIDP, or Grounded into Double Plays.

GIDP wasn't a stat considered to be of any great importance till about sixty-five or so years ago. We don't know how many double plays, for instance, that Ty Cobb hit into. Of Babe Ruth, we know that he hit into 2 in his final season, 1935. But let's compare Mike Schmidt to the other players included in the "Greatest Living Player" comparison, and a couple more besides:

	Games	AB	GIDP
Joe DiMaggio	1736	6821	130
Ted Williams	2292	7706	147
Stan Musial	3026	10972	243
Yogi Berra	2129	7555	146
Mickey Mantle	2401	8102	113
Willie Mays	2992	10881	251
Eddie Mathews	2391	8537	123
Hank Aaron	3298	12364	328
Frank Robinson	2808	10006	269
Johnny Bench	2158	7658	201
Reggie Jackson	2705	9528	180
Joe Morgan	2649	9277	105
Pete Rose	3371	13411	235
Mike Schmidt	2404	8352	156

I think I've included just about every former player from the 1930s up to Mike Schmidt that might be substantially supported as the best player from then till now. Of the other thirteen only five hit into fewer double plays than Mike Schmidt. Of those five, Joe DiMaggio hit into 26 fewer but played in 688 fewer games. Yogi Berra, a very tough DP, especially for a catcher, hit into 10 fewer but played in 275 fewer games.

So, we can say with some certainty that of the fourteen best players between the retirement of Babe Ruth and the end of Mike Schmidt's career, only three, Mickey Mantle, Joe Morgan, and Eddie Mathews, were harder to catch in a double play (and before we move on to other subjects, let me say that Eddie Mathews's GIDP total of 123 is, for a relatively slow-moving power hitter, one of the most remarkable statistics I came across while researching this book).

Fielding? Mike Schmidt was a superb third baseman, the winner of ten Gold Gloves. Most place him among the top four or five fielding third basemen of his time, and many include him with the all-time best at his position. Mike Hoban, author of *Baseball's Complete Players,* ranks him fifth by his HEQ (Hoban Efficiency Quotient) among third basemen over the span of 1956 through 1996. There is no fielding statistic in which he does not compare well with the best ever at his position. Of all the players in our comparison, I would guess that Willie Mays is the only one that many fans and writers would chose as the best ever at his position. (I don't know that he was, but I'm sure many people would say that he was; see earlier chapter, "One-on-One, Once and for All: Mickey Mantle vs. Willie Mays" for a detailed discussion.) I don't know of anyone who ever called Mike Schmidt the best fielding third baseman of all time, but I don't think it's a stretch to say that outside of Mays, Schmidt was on a defensive par with every other player on our list. Let's use the *STATS Inc.'s All-Time Major League Handbook* (second edition) to compare Schmidt to some of the best at his position (the number in parenthesis next to the total indicate times leading the league).

	G (at 3B)	PO	Assists	DP
Jimmy Collins	1683	2372 (5)	3702 (4)	225 (3)
Home Run Baker	1548	2154 (7)	3155 (3)	259 (3)
Pie Traynor	1863	2289 (7)	3521 (3)	303 (4)
George Kell	1692	1825 (2)	3303 (4)	306 (2)
Eddie Mathews	2181	2049 (2)	4332 (3)	369 (1)
Ron Santo	2130	1955 (7)	4581 (7)	396 (6)
Brooks Robinson	2870	2697	6205 (8)	618 (3)
Clete Boyer	1439	1470 (1)	3218 (3)	315 (1)
Mike Schmidt	2212	1591	5045 (7)	450 (6)
George Brett	1692	1372 (1)	3674 (2)	307 (1)

	Range Factor	Leag. R. Factor	FA	Leag. FA
Collins	3.64 (1)	3.48	.929	.907
Baker	3.44 (3)	3.35	.943	.937
Traynor	3.15 (5)	2.99	.947 (1)	.947
Kell	3.21 (3)	3.21	.969 (7)	.954
Mathews	3.02	3.01	.956	.950
Santo	3.14 (6)	2.92	.954 (1)	.948
Robinson	3.20 (3)	3.09	.971 (11)	.953
Boyer	3.42 (3)	3.03	.965 (2)	.951
Schmidt	3.14 (2)	2.87	.955 (1)	.949
Brett	3.13 (2)	2.98	.951	.953

These are ten terrific third basemen on this list, and their careers span a century—more than that, actually, since Jimmy Collins started in 1895. Of the ten, eight are in the Hall of Fame—Clete Boyer wasn't quite a good enough run producer, and the exclusion of Ron Santo is a scandal. There isn't a man on this list who could be called substantially better in the field than Mike Schmidt.

Of course, judgments made about players from different

eras must always be imprecise, but with fielding this is especially true. Fielding statistics have been changing all through the century, and on the whole, chances per game for third baseman have been slipping by the decades as more and more outs were made by strikeouts. Probably no modern third baseman will match the range factor of Jimmy Collins at 3.64, and Collins played from 1895 to 1908. It ought to be said, though, that Clete Boyer's career range factor of 3.42 is probably the single most impressive defensive stat posted by a third baseman in this century, because *nobody* else in his league was getting to ground balls like Boyer in his day. Collins's range factor was 16 points better than the other third basemen in his league; *Clete Boyer was 32 points better than the third basemen in his.*

But look whose range, in relation to the rest of the third basemen in his league, is second best: *Mike Schmidt's range factor* (though he only led the league in this category twice) *is a full 27 points higher than the NL average for third basemen over the same period.*

That's perhaps the strongest argument for Schmidt's excellence in the field: how much better he was than most third basemen of his time. As we said, fielding statistics are always difficult to make sense of, and the problem is even greater when comparing fielding statistics from players in different eras. Jimmy Collins, for instance, is often regarded by historians as the best third basemen of his time. Yet, his fielding average of .929 is eye-openingly low by modern standards. He also participated in fewer double plays than any third basemen on this list. We must cut Mr. Collins some slack for the time he played in; fielding equipment was so poor relative to today that errors were much more a part of the game. Still, Collins's fielding average was 22 points better than the fielding average of other third basemen in his time, and that's what he deserves to be judged by.

All of which suggests a couple of common sense rules when rating fielders. First, they should be judged by the standards of fielders in their own time, and, second, they should be judged by the most important statistics. Most experts are pretty much in agreement that the most important statistics for infielders are range factor—how much ground a man can cover—and double plays. And by those standards Mike Schmidt was a very, very good third baseman. Brooks Robinson is generally regarded as the finest fielding third baseman of the last four decades, if not of all time (though I might call for a reevaluation of Clete Boyer's credentials for that title). Schmidt compares favorably with Robinson in every key area. His range factor is slightly lower, but his assists per game (2.28) is slightly better than Robinson's (2.16), and his double plays per game (2.16 to 2.28) is only slightly lower. Robinson's range factor is just .11 better than AL third basemen of his time; Schmidt is .27 higher than NL third basemen of his. In eighteen seasons (really sixteen full seasons), Schmidt led the league in assists 7 times and double plays 6 times; in twenty-three seasons (really seventeen full seasons), Robinson led the league in assists 8 times and double plays 3 times.

Those are the stats that offer the best perspective on a third baseman's ability. In fact, putouts not only don't add anything to the picture; one might argue that they detract from it. I include putouts here because *Total Baseball* does, but most putouts are relatively easy chances and don't tell you much of anything about how Schmidt or Brooks Robinson played their positions (catching pop-ups is the one thing I think I could do as well as Mike Schmidt or Brooks Robinson). Most analysts and historians of the game would argue that the criteria for judging the fielding ability of a third baseman are assists and double plays, and on that basis, I can't see a reason on paper for arguing that

Brooks Robinson was much better than Mike Schmidt—or for that matter, that either was better than Ron Santo, but that's another chapter in another book.

Will I insist, then, that Mike Schmidt is better or even as good a fielder as the man regarded by most as the best in baseball history at third base? No. Robinson's reputation is too formidable to be assaulted without more information than I've had time to gather. All I can say for sure is that Mike Schmidt must have been very, very close to Robinson in ability or there would be some statistical evidence to the contrary.

What else is there to consider? Intangibles? Schmidt was popular and well respected, and a winner. In sixteen full seasons, his team was in the playoffs six times, including two World Series.

Respect of his contemporaries? Schmidt won three Most Valuable Player awards in sixteen full seasons, the same as Mickey Mantle and Yogi Berra and the same as Barry Bonds through fourteen seasons in the last century. He won as many MVP awards as Willie Mays and Hank Aaron *combined*.

So, what exactly am I trying to prove here, that Mike Schmidt is the greatest baseball player in history? To be honest, I'm not sure where I'm trying to take this. Perhaps it's no more than this: in putting together a newspaper column, I saw some things about Mike Schmidt that I didn't see before—things I hadn't heard anyone else say, and wanted to see how far I could push the point that Mike Schmidt wasn't fully appreciated by the fans of his day. There is no question in my mind that Mike Schmidt was the greatest player at the least represented position in the Hall of Fame, and I think there is a general consensus among hard-core baseball researchers that he is one of the ten or twelve or at least fifteen best players ever; he would certainly be on almost every knowledgeable fan's all-time All Star team at

third base. Bill James ranked him the number-one third baseman of all time for both peak and career value, and that was four
years before his career was over, and the groundbreaking *The
Hidden Game of Baseball* (Pete Palmer) ranked him the fif-
teenth best everyday player of all time.

And yet, even at that, I can't help but shake the feeling that
Mike Schmidt remains underrated. More than that: that he's
very underrated. Certainly during his own career, appreciation
among his local fans and press was slow in coming. I followed
quite a bit of his career through my father's family in South Jersey and probably read the Philadelphia sports pages as much as
if I'd lived there. I used to regularly clip all sorts of negative
comments about Schmidt from the Philly press, which was, on
the whole, as nasty toward a truly great player as any I've ever
seen (I admit I did not see what Boston writers regularly bombarded Ted Williams with, but Mike Schmidt was a heck of a lot
easier to get along with than Ted Williams). Here's a fragment I
saved from about 1977 from a columnist whose name I no
longer remember: "A Texas computer couldn't calculate the
number of runs the Phillies lost because of Mike Schmidt's
walking on hittable pitches." What a criticism! He's *walking* too
much! Leaving aside the obvious response—if they were "hittable pitches," why did the umpires call them balls?—I'd have to
say the comment is fairly typical of the dumb things written
about Schmidt in the Philadelphia-area press, at least before his
back-to-back MVP awards in the '80 and '81 seasons. "He'll
never be a .300 hitter," "He strikes out too much," "He doesn't
have the skills of a classic third baseman," were all bandied
about in one form or another (the last was particularly silly,
since, except for his incredible power, ability to accumulate
walks, and speed on the bases, he *did* have the skills of a classic
third baseman, which is to say he hit about .270 and could field).

You heard those criticisms of Schmidt pretty much every-
where in Philadelphia and South Jersey back in the late '70s, in
the papers, the radio call-in shows, and, especially at the ballpark, Veterans Stadium, where, as someone (Bob Uecker, I
think) once said that "Phillies fans would boo cancer patients."
It really wasn't until after Schmidt's great 1980 season, when he
lifted the Phillies to their only World Series victory of the twentieth century, that attitudes toward him began to change and
that Phillies fans began to regard him as one of the greatest and
possibly *the* greatest player in the game. Even then, I felt,
Schmidt's stock was higher around the country, where it was
common to hear him referred to as the best player in the game,
than in the Philadelphia area. I very much doubt that even after
he won his third Most Valuable Player award that the sports
media and most Phillies fans regarded him as the greatest third
baseman ever. Even at the end of the decade in which he won
three MVP awards, led the Phillies to their only World Series
championship, won five home run titles, led the league in walks
and *slugging* four times each, and hit more home runs than any
player in either league, local fans didn't quite seem to understand that they were watching one of the all-time greats.

Might it have been different if Schmidt had been a much
heralded product of the farm system? Maybe. Mike Schmidt got
a late start for a baseball superstar. He was discovered by the
legendary scout Tony Lucadella, immortalized by Mark Wine-
gardner's wonderful book *The Prophet of the Sandlots*. Lucadella
was an unaffiliated scout with ties to the Phillies. Lucadella, who
sent forty-seven players to the big leagues, including Ferguson
Jenkins and Mike Marshall, was probably the last great inde-
pendent scout the game will ever see. With scouting so sophisticated, it's doubtful any superstar will slip under the radar as
Schmidt did. He almost slipped right back again. His first two

seasons were wretched. Breaking into the big leagues at the advanced age of twenty-three, he batted .206 in thirteen games played in 1972 and just .196 in 367 at-bats with 136 strikeouts in 1973. It wasn't till 1974, at age twenty-five, that he batted more than 500 times in a season, and he blossomed, leading the league in home runs and slugging, and stealing 23 bases. From then through 1981, he had a string of great seasons broken only by 1978 when he hit .251 with a mere 21 home runs and 78 runs batted in. It was the only season from 1974 through 1984 that he didn't lead the league in *something*, and he had the bad luck to have such a season after signing a multiyear contract, thus giving fuel to cynical Phillies fans who felt that players "dogged" it after signing multiyear deals. In truth, he was pressing, trying too hard to live up to his billing.

That was the only time he was to bat over 400 times in a season and failed to place among the top players in both leagues. In the end, 1989, he retired honorably when he couldn't play up to his own standards. He had just fourteen seasons with more than 400 at-bats, the shortest career of any player in our comparison and one of the shortest of any great player in baseball history.

Anyway, in 1995 he was an easy first ballot Hall of Famer, getting 28.7 percent more votes than he needed for the Hall of Fame. Of all the players in our comparison, only Hank Aaron, at 30.1 percent got a higher percentage of the votes needed. (Mantle got an inexplicably low 17.5 percent while Mays had to settle for 26.2 percent.)

So, do I really think Mike Schmidt was the greatest baseball player of all time, or am I just trying to convince myself—to pump up a case that, once I began to explore it, caught me by surprise? Once again, I'm not entirely sure. But now that I've made the argument, there's a lot about it that I like. Of course I can't feel comfortable dismissing Ted Williams and Stan Musial the way I did, and in my heart the great players of my youth, Mickey Mantle and Willie Mays, can never be supplanted. But I can tell you this: the record gives no immediate evidence that Mantle or Mays were that much better, if at all, than Mike Schmidt. Mike Schmidt played in the most competitive era in baseball history. The evolution of baseball in the late '70s and '80s was generally toward a flattening of statistics, a trend disguised by such aberrations as George Brett's .390 batting average and Rickey Henderson's 130 stolen bases in 1982. The strike zone was a little smaller when Schmidt played, and didn't get wider till 1987, by which time Schmidt was at the tail end of a career. Expansion in the '90s perhaps gave veteran hitters an edge, which resulted in some sensational hitting stats (Mark McGwire's and Sammy Sosa's home runs, Manny Ramirez's RBI totals, etc.) that probably could not have happened twelve to twenty years earlier. He had more players to compete against than Williams, Musial, Mantle, Mays, and Aaron had to in most of their careers. Relief pitching evolved into an art during Schmidt's career. Mike Schmidt dominated batting statistics for a fourteen-year period like no player since Ted Williams in his prime, and he did it during a span when competition was keener than ever before.

And what about Babe Ruth? Am I really going to tell you that Mike Schmidt was better than Babe Ruth? Obviously there is no statistical argument I can make; Babe Ruth dominated batting stats like no player before him and like no player ever will again. But, for a moment picture them on the same field together, as they would be in an all-time position-by-position All Star team. Assume they'd both be playing in an era of relief pitching and night ball, at a time when black and Latin talent are thrown into the mix. Then look at that overweight guy in right field, and look at that sculptured athlete at third base, and ask yourself if, in the same time and under the same conditions they might be equals. (Yes, yes, I know, if Ruth played in today's game there would be better weight training and nutrition available, though whether someone of Babe Ruth's temperament would take advantage of them is problematic at best.)

Ask yourself if evolution works in reverse.

LED LEAGUE IN . . .

	Total Seasons	HR	BA	RBI	R	OBA	SLG	SB	MVPS
Yogi Berra	19	0	0	0	0	0	0	0	3
Willie Mays	22	4	1	0	2	2	5	4	2
Hank Aaron	23	4	2	4	3	0	4	0	1
Joe Morgan	22	0	0	0	1	4	1	0	2
Mike Schmidt	18	8	0	4	1	3	5	0	3
Barry Bonds	14	1	0	1	1	4	3	0	3
K. Griffey Jr.	11	3	0	1	1	0	1	0	1
Mickey Mantle	18	4	1	1	6	3	4	0	3
Johnny Bench	17	2	0	3	0	0	0	0	2

9

The Most Overrated and Underrated Players Over the Last Thirty Years— Pete Rose vs. Tim Raines

Three Charts on Tim and Pete

Raines vs. Rose, Career

	G	AB	H	BB	HR	BA	R	RBI	OBA	SLG	SB
ROSE	3562	14053	4256	1566	160	.303	2165	1314	.377	.409	198-149
RAIN.	2353	8694	2561	1290	168	.295	1548	964	.388	.427	815-124

Pete Rose (who played from 1963 to 1986) and Tim Raines (1979 to this season) are both switch-hitters with similar talents, namely the ability to reach base consistently and hit with unusual power for men who bat early in the batting order. But while Rose played in many more games and been to bat many more times, the numbers don't show that he was better than Raines, who has reached base at a greater frequency, hit with greater power, and shown immeasurably more speed on the bases.

Raines vs. Rose, Relatively

Hitting was a bit more difficult in Rose's time than Raines's. Here's a short comparison of National League averages in those periods:

NL	BA	OB Pct	SLGA
1963–83	.2537	.3169	.3716
1981–95	.2580	.3244	.3882

If we want to assume that Raines, had he played twenty years earlier, would have had stats lower by exactly the same number of points as the overall league, Raines and Rose would look like this, careerwise:

	BA	OB Pct	SLGA
Rose	.303	.377	.409
Raines	.290	.379	.409

Rose, of course, would get points for his durability; Raines should get credit for his vastly greater speed, which produced more than 600 stolen bases and fewer throw-outs on steal attempts. Who would you take?

Raines vs. Rose, Peak Performance

I chose the best fifteen seasons from both men for an idea of peak performance. How did I decide which were the best? I didn't; in the interests of being objective, I went by *Total Baseball's* Total Player Rating and took the fifteen best-rated years for each. Here's what those years produced:

	G	HR	RBI	R	H	BB	SB-Caught	GIDP*
Rose	2256	129	861	1469	2837	1040	117–96	173
Raines	2052	149	825	1366	2294	1134	770–136	57

*GIDP-grounded into double plays

So, in their fifteen best seasons, Rose reached base by walks and hits a total of 3,877 times to Raines's 3,428—445 more, total, or about 34 more times per season—and produced 2,330 total runs (RBI plus runs scored) to Raines's 2,191—139, or, about 9.3 more runs per season. That Rose had to play in 204 more games to do that convinces me that Raines was, perhaps, more skilled than Rose in the art of producing runs. The *question* is: does Rose's durability automatically make him more valuable? After all, he did accumulate more total runs.

Actually, the question is a great deal more complex than that. First of all, although he played alongside some fine hitters such as Gary Carter and Andre Dawson, Raines had nothing like the career-long quality in teammates that was afforded to Pete Rose. Rose played nearly all of his best years on the Reds with Hall of Fame teammates such as Johnny Bench, Joe Morgan, Tony Perez, and Dave Concepcion, and on the Phillies he batted in front of Mike Schmidt and Gregg Luzinski. Given Raines's greater home run total and far superior speed, I think if he batted in front of the same hitters Rose had, he would have produced not only more runs but significantly more runs per season—and, remember, that's in 200 fewer games. Second, think of how many fewer outs Raines would have used up to produce those runs, and how many more runs those outs would have produced spread around the lineup.

If it sounds like I'm saying that in his fifteen best years, Tim Raines helped create more runs than Pete Rose did in his fifteen best despite playing in over 200 more games, that's what I'm saying. In that fifteen-year stretch, Raines stole 643 more bases than Rose while being thrown out just 40 more times. In his prime, Rose was a bad base stealer; with a miserable total of just 117 in 213 tries, you wonder why he ever attempted to steal. Surely, to use up 96 outs and remove 96 baserunners to advance 117 runners to second base was counterproductive in a big way; Rose certainly cost his team runs with his base-stealing attempts. Raines, on the other hand, was one of the great percentage base stealers in baseball history, and in his fifteen prime years, he stole 770 bases in 906 tries, or an average of about 51 steals in 60 tries per season. I submit that the combination of the runs Rose cost his team by trying to steal and that Raines created with all his steals, closes the gap on that 9.3 runs per season edge for Rose, and tilts it into Raines's side of the ledger. And if I'm wrong, if the difference in stolen bases doesn't quite give Raines the edge, look at the enormous difference in double plays. In this fifteen-year comparison, Raines averaged less than 4 per season (he had just 72 for his entire career) while Rose averaged better than 11. That's at least 7 more outs and 7 more runners removed from the bases by Rose per season.

And you know what I haven't even touched on here? The extra, uncounted bundle of runs Raines got for his teams by going from first to third or second to home when Rose had to settle for one base.

At their peaks, Tim Raines was a more valuable and more productive player than Pete Rose, and this includes the greater number of games Rose played where Raines was lost to injury. I strongly suspect this claim would hold up for a twenty- or twenty-two-year study, but what I've seen of their peak years is enough for me to proclaim Tim Raines a greater player than Pete Rose.

As I write this chapter, Tim Raines—or "Rock," as he was

identified on some of his baseball cards, the nickname deriving from his football player's build—is making a courageous comeback with his old team, the Montreal Expos, after having lost a year of his career to the disease Lupus (to say nothing of a bout with cocaine addiction, for which he voluntarily sought treatment a few years ago). If he does well, he could eventually become one of the few players in modern baseball history to be voted into the Hall of Fame without setting a single record, or even reaching an awesome total in any statistical category.

How good has Tim Raines been over the last twenty-two years? Well, despite his lack of recognition from the mainstream sports press, Tim Raines has long been recognized by baseball analysts as one of the six to ten best active players in baseball from the early '80s until now. He made seven successive All Star teams playing for the Montreal Expos, which is not unlike winning a Pulitzer Prize while writing for a newspaper in North Dakota. In the '80s, he was often referred to as "the National League's Rickey Henderson," which is not inappropriate as he stole 70 or more bases every year from 1981 to 1986. Like Rickey, he remained, after his prime, a valuable player that a veteran team could rely on. After years of toiling on second-division teams, no one begrudged him the World Series rings he picked up with the '96 and '98 Yankees.

Perhaps the best way of measuring Tim Raines's greatness is to compare him with a much better known but not necessarily better player. Over the last six years at *The Wall Street Journal*, I have probably gotten more questions about Pete Rose—where I rank Pete Rose as a player, what I think of him as a person, do I think he bet on baseball, and whether or not I support his bid for the Hall of Fame—than about anyone else. I've never had time to properly deal with them, but I'll try now. To take them in order, I think Pete Rose is a great player. I say that grudgingly. I do not think he is nearly in a class with the truly great players of his time—Mike Schmidt, Joe Morgan, Johnny Bench, Rickey Henderson, and possibly Reggie Jackson and two or three others. As a person, he is, in my opinion, an arrogant, shallow, self-centered jerk who hung around years after he had any value on the field simply to eclipse Cobb's record. You're a fan, you want to pay money to watch that kind of circus junk, then you pay your money. I stopped caring about the so-called record two years before Rose surpassed it.

As for his betting on baseball, I'll confine my comments to observing that the Dowd report presented by Major League Baseball presents not a shred of evidence that Rose bet on baseball. As for the Hall of Fame, of course Rose belongs in it. If he doesn't, then end the hypocrisy of charging people money to see his balls and bats.

But I don't see anything wrong with Pete Rose having to wait a while to get in. Pete Rose was really no better than his teammate on the Big Red Machine, Tony Perez, and he had to wait a while. I'm really not sure that Rose was better than Gary Carter, who is still not in, and there are players at least as great as Pete Rose who will probably have to wait longer. For instance, if Rose was eligible for inclusion at the same time as Tim Raines, I'm certain that Rose would have been voted in first, and equally certain that Raines is more deserving.

Hall of Fame voters in recent years have become too influenced by "totals" such as 500 home runs, or 300 wins, or 3,000 hits. The one that bugs me the most is "200 hits." I'm so tired of hearing people say "Look how many times Pete Rose got 200 hits in his career" when telling me that I have underrated him. Tell me, average reader, off the top of your head: Who do you think is the greatest hitter in baseball history? Did you say Ted Williams? Did some of you say Babe Ruth? Well, Babe Ruth had exactly three seasons with more than 200 hits, and Ted Williams had zero. Now, I ask you: How important can any hitting category be in which Ted Williams has a zero? Has anyone ever stopped to think that one of the reasons Pete Rose got so many of those hits is because pitchers didn't fear him more? Or stated another way, Williams and Ruth didn't have more hits because they were feared. Pitchers walked them too much.

Most veteran writers decry the use of statistics by the younger generation in arguing the case for and against certain players. Peter Gammons of ESPN is especially maddening in this area, constantly telling us "You can't trust the statistics where this guy is concerned." Why can't you trust the statistics for this or that particular player? Because Peter Gammons, by God, likes that guy—or doesn't like him, as the case may be? The point is that you can cite all the evidence you want about a certain player only to hear Gammons not refute it but disregard it; he has seen the player or players in question and the final word is that this player or that is better or worse because he says it's so. Never mind that you have seen the same players. The very fact that you would be foolish enough to make a statistical case for a player you could have argued irrationally for automatically makes your observations suspect.

"Stat Nerds" they snort contemptuously at me, and probably at you, too, if you're smart enough to have picked up this book— but the truth is that they depend as much on numbers as anyone else when it comes to making decisions. What else, after all, are you going to rely on? What, in the final analysis, are statistics but a record of what a player does when you're not watching him? And we don't have time to watch 99 percent of the players 99 percent of the time. No one does. But you can be locked into a mindset where you give too many free passes for certain impressive-looking but insufficiently considered statistics. Thus, quantity wins out over quality, longevity over value. In Pete Rose's case, surpassing Ty Cobb's total of 4,190 hits overwhelms discussion of Rose's other qualities and deficiencies as a ball player. Primarily because, off the record, or at least the hype that surrounded Rose's pursuit of it, HOF voters would, I'm sure, vote Pete Rose in before Tim Raines if given the choice, despite the fact that Raines's speed and power and consistency were greater than Rose's. Why? In Raines's case, there is no 4,000-plus hits or even 3,000-plus hits to point to; Raines walked too much to accumulate hit totals like that. Nonetheless, Tim Raines reached based more often than Pete Rose, used up fewer outs in doing it, and, for most of his peak years, had more power than Rose in his (though he played in nearly 2,000 fewer games, he hit 8 more home runs) and speed (again, 2,000-odd fewer games and more than four times as many stolen bases).

Simply put, all the indications are that under the same conditions and in the same situations, Tim Raines would have produced at least as many and probably more runs than Pete Rose. That's not going to make him as hot an item on the autograph circuit as Pete Rose, but it ought to be good enough to get Tim Raines a plaque at Cooperstown—if he decides to retire someday.

10

The Dynasty That Never Was: The 1986 Mets

I see the boys of summer *in their ruin.*

—DYLAN THOMAS (emphasis mine)

I love old-timers' games, but if the New York Mets have an anniversary for their 1986 championship team, I think I'll pass. With most championship teams, you can pass the time away celebrating what happened, and I suppose Mets fans will remember the amazing playoff series against Houston and Mookie Wilson's ground ball to Bill Buckner as long as they live. And they should; I don't want to take anything away from that team. The '86 Mets won 108 games, most in the major leagues that season (in fact, the most by the amazing margin of 12 over the NL's Western champions, the Houston Astros.) They were the only major league team that year to win more than 100 games; the only team, in fact, to win more than 96.

The 1986 Mets were one of the best teams since the second World War, and they might have been even better than that. In the recent *Baseball Dynasties—The Greatest Teams of All Time*, Rob Neyer and Eddie Epstein make a case for the '86 Mets as one of the great teams of the century. In his 1987 Baseball Abstract, Bill James called them "a great ballclub, a beautiful demonstration of what talent can do when assembled with planning and guided by intelligence."

And yet, 1986 was the beginning and end of the dynasty. The Mets almost lost to the Red Sox, a team whose pitching might have been as good as theirs but whose hitting and bench most certainly weren't (and if Bill Buckner had been able to pick up a batting practice grounder, the Mets wouldn't have won the Series), so really, their postseason play was substandard. But no matter how tight the situation, they won, they always pulled it out. They looked like a team full of gamers, a group that aimed to be around for a long while. And yet, the core of the '86 Mets, a lineup filled with players who looked like Hall of Fame candidates—and I'm going to make a case that no team in baseball history had so many players who, at their peaks, seemed to be heading for the Hall of Fame—never won another World Series, and never even went to another. Their defeat by the Los Angeles Dodgers in the 1988 Championship Series is perhaps the most bitter memory in team history.

Try looking at the '86 Mets as the 1955 Brooklyn Dodgers in reverse. The Dodgers of that era featured several Hall of Famers (Jackie Robinson, Duke Snider, Roy Campanella, Pee Wee Reese) and several near-misses (Certainly Don Newcombe would have been a likely candidate if not for two prime years lost to the army, or several seasons lost later to a losing battle with alcoholism, and Gil Hodges has his defenders and always will) but could never quite win the big one (that is, they couldn't beat the Yankees). When they finally did in 1955, the victory had an autumnal flavor to it, and not just because it was October. In little more than a year, the team was broken up and in two the franchise would be forever relocated. The Mets (the expansion result of the Dodgers' move to California) also had numerous Hall of Fame candidates or players that looked as if they would be, and a fine, proven manager in Davey Johnson to guide them. Unlike the Jackie Robinson Dodgers, though, the '86 Mets won it all relatively early in what should have been the prime years of their best players. Then they began, season by season, to fall apart, until, by 1991, the dream was gone. They didn't lose most of their best players to free agency, either. They lost them to . . . life.

Were the '86 Mets perhaps a flash in the pan, a collection of cocky, talented prospects whose potential we overrated? Not a chance in this world. Begin with Darryl Strawberry, who began impressing scouts and sportswriters as "the Black Ted Williams" or at least the next Mantle or Mays while he was still in high school. So, if Darryl Strawberry wasn't quite Willie or Mickey or even the Duke, he was certainly, after about 800 or so games, in their class.

How good was Darryl Strawberry at his peak? How good might he have been? We'll never know the answer to the second question, but the first is perhaps best answered by comparing him to New York's three great power-hitting outfielders of the 1950s. The chart below picks up Strawberry's career after the 1988 season when the Mets somehow managed to lose the National League pennant to the relatively punchless Los Angeles Dodgers. Everything seemed to unravel for the Mets and Strawberry after that—the Mets finished second in the East in both '89 and '90, races they always seemed to be on the verge of putting away—despite Strawberry's 66 home runs over the two years. Neither Darryl Strawberry nor the Mets was quite good enough in '89 and '90, and many Mets fans began to feel that once upon a time would never come again. Still, it is undeniable that, after the 1988 season, in a comparable number of games in their careers, Darryl Strawberry was on par to put up the kind of power-speed numbers that were posted by Willie, Mickey, and the Duke in their prime years.

	G	AB	HR	RBI	BB	SB
Darryl Strawberry	823	2885	188	548	449	165
Willie Mays	762	2899	183	519	351	161
Mickey Mantle	806	2924	173	575	524	43
Duke Snider	798	3062	151	538	325	44

And, really, would he even have had to have been that good to have made the Hall of Fame? In 1991, fed up with not fulfilling everyone's expectations in the East, Darryl went home to Los Angeles with a $23.5 million contract. Though its largely forgotten now, Strawberry earned a lot of goodwill by coming back from injuries to hit 28 home runs and drive in 99 runs in 1991 and lead the Dodgers to a late-season run that threatened the Atlanta Braves' remarkable run from last place in 1990 to the World Series. Perhaps it was the back injuries that did him in, but over two more frustrating seasons, he was able to play just 75 games. Strawberry started the '94 season at Betty Ford, and ended it under indictment for tax evasion. What is remarkable about Darryl Strawberry's life from then till now was how much worse it was actually able to get. But that's a discussion for a biography; for our purposes the point is that if he had been able to maintain not the level of his greatest seasons with the Mets but simply the level of his 1991 season with the Dodgers (28 home runs and 100 RBI) for, say, just three more years—and he was just twenty-nine when he left the Mets—he would probably now have, together with his comeback as a role-player on the Yankees' pennant-winning teams of the '90s, sufficient credentials for the Hall of Fame.

And Darryl Strawberry wasn't the best of the '86 bunch. In 1986, everyone was arguing not about whether Darryl was as good as Ted or Willie but over who was better, the Boston Red Sox' sensational twenty-two-year-old flame-throwing righthander, Roger Clemens (24–4, with a 2.48 ERA) or the Mets' twenty-year-old flame-throwing righthander, Dwight Gooden (17–6 with a 2.84 ERA and 24–4 the season before with a 1.53 ERA). Fifteen years later, Roger Clemens has become the American League's all-time strikeout leader and Dwight Gooden, unable to land a major league contract, retired.

Drugs, injuries, and immaturity took their toll. As Gooden told me in an interview for *The Village Voice* before the 1996 World Series, "I wasn't ready for that kind of attention at nineteen; no teenager is. To be honest, I'm not sure I'm ready for it now." The list of Gooden's accomplishments before the old voting age of twenty-one is jaw-dropping. He was the youngest player ever to be named Rookie of the Year, and the youngest to lead the league in strikeouts. And that was just by age nineteen! By age twenty-one, he was already 58–19, had struck out an average of 215 batters a year for three season, and had posted three straight seasons of ERA under 2.50. Roger Clemens is considered by many, including myself, as the greatest starting pitcher in baseball history. By the time Clemens had won 58 games, he was twenty-five years old and had already lost 22.

What of the Mets other first-line Hall of Fame candidates? Well, how about a man who was, arguably, the best first baseman of the decade? Keith Hernandez was a bona fide star well before '86. Playing for the Cardinals, he had won the NL batting crown in 1979 with a .344 average, also winning the MVP award while leading the league in runs scored, doubles, and on-base average and winning a Gold Glove at first base. 1986 was his seventh season over .300, and he also led the league in walks and fielding average. He was just thirty-three, and the Mets' World Series win had gone a long way toward allowing sportswriters to forget the ugly drug-selling stories that surfaced when he left St. Louis. But Hernandez faded quickly after that; he played just four more seasons in the big leagues, and 1987, in which he hit .290, was the last in which he played more than 95 games. His last two seasons pulled his career batting average under .300, but that shouldn't have dimmed his reputation as perhaps the finest-fielding first baseman in baseball history, with 11 Gold Gloves and a record six times leading the NL in double plays. Still, the memory of his drug problems (despite the donation of 10 percent of his salary to drug rehab programs in 1985) rankles, particularly in his old town of St. Louis. I don't think Keith will ever make it to the Hall, but in 1986 he certainly was on the way.

But as good as Strawberry and Hernandez were, the heart of the Mets, or at least what was supposed to make them the team of the '80s, was their pitching staff, particularly the starting rotation. Some called it the league's best rotation *without* Gooden. The fans' (especially the female fans') favorite was Ron Darling, who, while pitching for Yale University, epitomized Commissioner (and former Yale president) Bart Giamatti's ideal of the scholar-athlete. I don't know that Darling would have been a real Hall of Fame candidate, but in 1986 the notion didn't at all seem unrealistic. Darling went 15–6 with a 2.81 ERA—the second season in a row he was under 3.00—and pitched 18 consecutive scoreless innings in the World Series against Boston. By the end of '86, he was 44–24 for three full major league seasons and part of a fourth, and who knew what the limits were? Through '87 and '88, Ron Darling continued to look like a long-term winner—by then his carrer record was 73–41—and even when he had his first nonwinning season in '89 (14–14, but with an ERA of 3.52) the future seemed bright. He was, after all, just twenty-nine in 1989. But something, an addiction to the high-life, as it was whispered in New York papers, took his fastball away. After two seasons of ineffectiveness, he was off to Montreal and, it seemed, to oblivion, until rallying for a brief comeback with Oakland in '92 where his 15–10 record helped the A's win the West. But after three more mostly frustrating seasons, he was gone from the majors, retired before his thirty-sixth birthday.

Sid Fernandez's addiction was of a different kind. For most of his career he pitched at about 30 to 40 pounds overweight, and the strain it put on his arm and shoulder left him largely ineffective after 1992. At his best, Sid was actually more unhittable than Dwight: three times he held NL hitters to the lowest batting average in the league. How great is that? Well, the greatest lefthander in New York baseball history, Whitey Ford, never did that once. In fact, for his sixteen-year career, Ford was hit for a .235 batting average by opponents. How good is that? Well, Warren Spahn, who won 363 games in his twenty-one-year career, was hit for a .244 average. Even Walter Johnson, who won 417 games, many of them in the low-average, dead ball era, was hit for a .227 average. Sid Fernandez pitched for fifteen seasons and opponents hit just .209 off him. Think about that for a moment. Nobody could get a hit off this guy, and he pitched in his youth—he was just twenty-four when the Mets won it all in '86—and, yet, after fifteen seasons, most of them with the winningest team in the game, he managed to post just a 114–96 record for a .543 won-lost percentage, scarcely better than the teams he pitched for. What was wrong?

In 1986, Sid Fernandez was 16–6. From '86 through '89, he was 54–29, and over those four years, he averaged about 7 strikeouts for every 3 walks. Why in the world didn't he become one of the greats, or at least one of the best pitchers of his time? I can think of no other reason than his horrible conditioning. From 1990 through 1997 he was 45–51 and drawing mostly snickers when he would appear (and probably devouring Snickers when he was in the clubhouse). But not giving up many hits: in his last three seasons, pitching for the Phillies and Astros, Fernandez threw just 132 innings but never allowed a batting average above .215. He stands, or sits, today, as one of the biggest puzzles, and certainly the heaviest, in recent baseball.

Two other pitchers should be remembered here. Bobby Ojeda wasn't great, not even potentially great the way Darling and Fernandez were. But in '86, at age twenty-nine, he led the World Champions in wins (18) and the league in won-lost percentage (.783). In other words, he was very, very good. In 1988, at age thirty-one, he lost part of a finger in an accident after a hard-luck season in which he went just 10–13 but posted the second best ERA (after his '86 mark of 2.57) of his career. He was just 40–36 for the rest of his career.

Then, there was Jesse Orosco. Orosco has probably inspired more butt-ugly jokes than any player this side of Randy Johnson, and the phrase "Geez, is he still around?" has probably been said about him more times than about any player in baseball history. But at the end of the '86 season, Jesse Orosco was no laughing matter: he was on the way to being one of the great relievers the game has ever seen. From '79 through '86, Orosco won 44 games and saved 91 more; his five-year ERAs were 2.72, 1.47, 2.59, 2.73, and 2.33. He made two NL All Star teams. He was just twenty-nine at the start of the '87 season. He was just 40–37 through the 2000 season, and only once more would he have more than 9 saves. If you ask me what went wrong with him, I'd say that he starred on the '86 Mets.

Were there any other legitimate candidates? I'd say there were three. Lenny Dykstra hit .295 in 1986 with 8 home runs and 31 stolen bases in just 431 at bats. He was just twenty-three years old, and it was obvious that he was a bundle of talent and speed with a great future. And yet, due to a combination of injuries and the Mets' inability to make a commitment to him, the next three seasons just seemed to slip away. Despite batting averages of .285, .270, and .270 and 70 stolen bases, he never quite took off. A third of the way through the '89 season, he was traded to the Phillies for Juan Samuel in one of the ugliest deals the Mets ever made. In 1990, he rebounded to hit .325, lead the league in hits, steal 33 bases, and make the All Star team. He seemed on his way, at twenty-seven, to fulfilling his potential. Then, more injuries struck, and he played in just 148 games over the next two seasons, though performing brilliantly when he played, hitting .297 and .301 and stealing 33 and 24 bases. In 1993, he had the greatest season of his career, batting .301, hitting a career-high 19 home runs, and leading the league in hits, walks, and runs while stealing 37 bases. He was clearly the major reason the Phillies went to the World Series that year, and he very nearly beat out Barry Bonds for the MVP award. He was just thirty, and had officially replaced Rickey Henderson as the best leadoff hitter in the game. Seven years later, Henderson was still assaulting major records, while a back injury had forced Dykstra out of the game.

How much did Lenny Dykstra lose to injuries? 1993 was the only season in his twelve-year career in which he played in more than 149 games. The numbers were all in place: he was a career .285 hitter with fine power for a leadoff hitter; his career slugging average of .419 was almost the same as Rickey Henderson's, and he stole 285 bases in 357 tries for a superb 80% average. He was an outstanding centerfielder who twice led the league in put-outs. He played the equivalent of just eight full seasons. He was an '86 Met.

So was Kevin Mitchell, who was part of that amazing bench strength that, along with the pitching, distinguished the '86 Mets. Mitchell, filling in in the outfield, at short, and at third, batted .277 with 12 home runs and 22 doubles in just 108 games. Two years later he was dealt to San Diego for Kevin McReynolds amid swirls of rumors that he was a "bad influence" on certain Mets players, leaving fans to speculate on how much of his street gang past he had left behind him. At age twenty-seven, with the Giants, he found a home, and won an MVP award for hitting 47 home runs, driving in 125 runs, and leading the league in slugging while pulling the Giants into the World Series. The next year, despite some injuries, he hit 35 home runs and drove in 93 runs. He was just twenty-eight. He played seven more season in the major leagues, and only once more would appear in more than 100 games. '86 Mets.

If power and speed signified potential greats, we are still waiting to find the reason that Howard Johnson vanished. Johnson arrived in Shea Stadium with a World Series ring; he had made a solid contribution to the Detroit Tigers' great 1984 team with 12 home runs and 50 RBI in just 355 at-bats, and proceeded to play a similar role for the '86 Mets, hitting 10 homers in 88 games for the '86 team while filling in at third and short. He was twenty-six. For the next five seasons, he put on a power-speed exhibition that few third basemen in baseball history have ever approached. Only two players in baseball history have had at least four seasons with at least 30 home runs and 30 stolen bases: Howard Johnson and Barry Bonds. Johnson averaged over 30 HR and 95 RBI *and 33 stolen bases per season*. Go back over those numbers again. How many guys with that kind of all-around talent *don't* develop into major stars? In 1989, he hit 36 home runs, drove in 101 runs, and stole 41 bases. I can't remember the last third baseman to put up a home run–stolen base total like that; I'm going to go ahead and say that I don't think it's ever been done, and if I'm wrong, write me care of my publisher and shock me. Johnson was never a good third baseman, ranking well below the league average in both assists and fielding average, and the reason why remains unclear. Why couldn't a player with his all-around ability—he was also a switch-hitter and could play shortstop and centerfield as well—find a natural defensive position? Whatever the reason, Johnson, who had 197 homers and 191 stolen bases after the 1991 season—he had led the league in home runs and RBI that year—simply fell off the face of the earth. He played just four more years, hit a ridiculous total of just 31 more home runs, and was out of the major leagues by age thirty-five. Thirty-five! In his last season, playing for the Cubs and hitting in one of the two or three best hitter's parks in baseball, he hit just .195. If only he'd reached the Mets two years later and missed that '86 team all together.

Okay, I'm being a little dishonest here. I'm leaving out the one Met who most deserves the Hall of Fame. Gary Carter is one of the four or five best catchers in National League history, and one of the top ten—maybe one of the top seven or eight—best ever. He was a ten-time All Star, had nine seasons with 20 or more home runs, and seven seasons with more than 80 RBI. Behind the plate, he led the league in assists four times, double plays five times, and total chances a record high eight times. There is no rational reason why Gary Carter should not be in the Hall of Fame right now, though he may well be by the time you read this book. But he isn't as I write this.

Everyone knows Roger Kahn's great title from perhaps the greatest of all baseball books, *The Boys of Summer*, about the Jackie Robinson–era Brooklyn Dodgers. Kahn used the first half of the line from Thomas's poem. The whole line, which sounds as if it was written for the '86 Mets, is "I see the boys of summer in their ruin."

"Who will remember?" Kahn asked toward the end of the book as he looked at the plaque where Ebbetts Field once stood. Well, who, I wonder, will remember the 1986 New York Mets, quite possibly the greatest collection of baseball talent ever assembled, and how will they remember them? As a great and dominant championship team? Because they were not that, despite the 108 victories during the regular season. Unfair as it might seem, the '86 Mets are the only championship team that will be remembered with a tinge of regret, for what they might have been. This was the team with Dwight Gooden, Ron Darling, Sid Fernandez, Bobby Ojeda, Jesse Orosco, Gary Carter, Keith Hernandez, Howard Johnson, Kevin Mitchell, Lenny Dykstra, and Darryl Strawberry, and all it produced was a single champion and, as of the 2002 season, not a single Hall of Famer.

11

Grove, Koufax, and Clemens:
A Comparison Across Time

Who is the greatest pitcher of all time? Or, at least, of the last century? There is absolutely no question that on paper Babe Ruth has the best statistics of any hitter—that is to say, if you define greatest hitter as the man who produces the most runs while using up the fewest outs—and if your intention is to win baseball games, I don't know how you could define it any other way. I have some reservations about awarding the all-time title to Ruth, but those are in another chapter. The point for now is that Ruth has *the best record of any hitter ever,* and that's making all the allowances you wish for the era in which he played—park effects, rule changes, styles, equipment, diet, physics, metaphysics, never metaphysics, whatever. But does he have an equal among pitchers?

Roger vs. Lefty and the Big Train

He does, and his name is Robert Moses "Lefty" Grove. Grove was a contemporary of Ruth's, pitching in the bigs from 1925 to 1941—in other words, beginning at precisely the time in which the Ruthian revolution changed pitching and pitching statistics forever. His peak years coincided with the peak of the lively ball era, yet Grove posted an ERA of under 3.00 nine times. In fact, he *led the league in ERA nine times,* and in just seventeen seasons. Roger Clemens is second with six, Sandy Koufax and Greg Maddux are next with five, in the modern game, while Walter Johnson, Christy Mathewson, and Grover Cleveland Alexander, among the old-timers, led their league five times.

"The Big Train," Walter Johnson, pitched from 1907 to 1927, won more games than Grove, 417 to 300, and had a lower ERA, 2.17 to 3.06, but the difference in those numbers is deceptive. Johnson pitched most of his career in the dead ball era when run scoring was much tougher than in Grove's time. Johnson also pitched his home games in a ballpark in Washington that was recorded as a pitcher's park, whereas Grove's home parks in Philadelphia and Boston were very good for hitters. Let's look at their ERAs in their ten peak seasons in relation to the league's. I've eliminated Grove's injury plagued 1934 season, and included 1926, when he was only 13–13, since he did lead the league in ERA that season.

JOHNSON (1910–1919)

Year	ERA	AL ERA	Diff
1910	1.36	2.52	1.16
1911	1.90	3.34	1.44
1912	1.39*	3.34	1.95

GROVE (1926–33, 1935–36)

Year	ERA	AL ERA	Diff
1926	2.51*	4.02	1.51
1927	3.19	4.14	0.95
1928	2.58	4.04	1.46

JOHNSON (1910–1919)

Year	ERA	AL ERA	Diff
1913	1.14*	2.93	1.79
1914	1.72	2.73	1.01
1915	1.55	2.93	1.38
1916	1.90	2.82	0.92
1917	2.21	2.66	0.45
1918	1.27*	2.77	1.50
1919	1.49*	3.22	1.73

GROVE (1926–33, 1935–36)

Year	ERA	AL ERA	Diff
1929	2.81*	4.24	1.43
1930	2.54*	4.65	2.11
1931	2.06*	4.38	2.32
1932	2.84*	4.48	1.64
1933	3.20	4.28	1.08
1935	2.70*	4.46	1.76
1936	2.81*	5.04	2.23

In 1920, the hitting revolution that had begun in 1919 was starting to affect Johnson. The AL's ERA went up from 3.22 the season before to 3.79 in 1920, and Johnson's went up, too, from 1.49 to 3.13. In fact, he was never under 2.72 again (though he led the league at 2.72 in 1924).

Anyway, no matter how you interpret the ERA numbers, Grove is at the least the equal of and apparently the superior of Johnson. The .89 difference between them in career ERA (Johnson's 2.17 to Grove's 3.06) is mostly the difference in the increase in the *league's* ERA, and in their peak years Grove led the league in ERA seven times to Johnson's four (and, once more, nine times to five in their entire careers).

I assume this settles the question of who was the greatest pitcher at least of the first half of the twentieth century, and if it doesn't for you, will you at least trust me when I tell you that Walter Johnson is the only pre-1950s pitcher that needs to be compared to Lefty Grove? I'm not going to tell you that Christy Mathewson, who won 373 games in just 17 seasons from 1900 to 1916, and who, like Johnson, led his league in ERA five times, wasn't a great pitcher. But either trust me or do the math yourself when I tell you Johnson was a greater pitcher than Mathewson. And that goes double for Grove and Cy Young, whose career began in 1890. I'm not denying Cy Young's greatness, but this book is about the twentieth century, and Young pitched for half of his career in the nineteenth.

And even if you don't believe me, you must see from a quick flip through the record book that Lefty Grove was *more dominant in his own time* than Young, Mathewson, and Johnson were in theirs. How dominant was Grove? Well, Babe Ruth had seventeen full seasons as a regular player and led the league in runs scored *eight* times; Grove pitched for seventeen and led the league in *preventing runs* per 9 innings *nine* times.

The question is: is there any pitcher in *modern* baseball who can compare to Lefty Grove? Let me toss someone at you. Here are the totals for Grove alongside the first seventeen seasons of "The Rocket" Roger Clemens:

	Lefty Grove (1925–41)	Roger Clemens (1984–00)
Seasons	17	17
Starts	459	511
Innings Pitched	3941	3661
Hits Allowed	3849	3101
Strikeouts	2266	3504
Bases on Balls	1187	1186
Won-Lost	300–141	260–142
W-L Pct	.680	.647
ERA	3.06	3.06
ERA Titles	9	6

It always surprises me when I see such striking similarities in two players whose careers were more than half a century apart and whose records are compiled under such different circumstances. After seventeen major league seasons, Grove and Clemens had exactly the same ERA, and were separated in walks by just one, 1,187 for Grove to 1,186 for Clemens. Clemens lost 142 games to Grove's 141. Grove won 40 more games, 300, and had a .680 won-lost percentage—almost tops among Hall of Fame starters—to Clemens's .647. But I'll get to that in a minute. In fact, I think that about all the stats in the chart—the starts, 459 for Grove to 511 for Clemens, the innings pitched, 3,941 for Grove to 3,661 for Clemens, the hits allowed, 3,849 for Grove to 3,101 for Clemens, the strikeouts, 2,266 for Grove to 3,504 for Clemens—are similar when looked at in the right way. In fact, I think what we're looking at in the seventeen-year records of Grove and Clemens are two strikingly similar pitchers whose differences on paper really reflect the differences in the times in which they played.

The starts and innings pitched, for instance. Grove averaged 8.62 innings for his 457 starts, Clemens just 7.17. Grove completed a remarkable 298 games, for a completion rate of .652. Clemens completed only 116 of 511 for a rate of .227. This means that Grove was the more durable pitcher, right? Well, no, it doesn't. I've been using "just" and "only" to describe Clemens's complete games and "completion average," but, in truth, Clemens, at of the end of the 2000 season, lead all active pitchers in complete games and innings pitched. Should we simply assume that for some inexplicable reason pitchers over the last thirty years have become less durable than pitchers in the first seven decades of the century, or is there perhaps something else going on here?

Look at the charts again. Grove pitched 3,941 innings, walking 1,187 batters, allowing 3,849 hits, and fanning 2,266. Let's do a little common arithmetic. It takes at least 4 pitches to walk a batter, 3 to strike him out, and just 1 to allow a hit. How many pitches did each man throw in allowing all those walks, strikeouts, and hits? Let's try another chart:

Clearing the Bases

	BB	K	H	Total
	(pitches × 4)	(pitches × 3)	(pitches × 1)	
Grove	4748	6858	3849	15,455
Clemens	4744	10,512	3101	18,357

If we assume that the number of hit batters and foul balls evened out, then we know that Clemens threw at least 2,902 more pitches than Grove in the same number of seasons, an average of almost 170 more per season. I think if you could add the number of foul balls and hit batters to the total, it would prove that Clemens pitched the equivalent of 2 and maybe 3 more complete games per year than Grove. This means that beyond the number of ground balls and fly ball outs, hit batters, and foul balls, that Grove, who pitched 3,941 innings, threw at least 3.92 pitches per inning, while Clemens, who pitched 3,661 innings, threw at least 5.0 pitches per inning in compiling his walks, strikeouts, and hits allowed. Since we don't have complete pitch counts for Clemens's career and none at all for Grove, we can't make any precise comparisons. But I think the above chart supports the commonsense conclusion that baseball fans and analysts have been coming around to for the last decade or so—namely, that there are a lot more pitches thrown in games today than in the '60s, '50s, '40s, '30s, and the '20s, and certainly more than in the dead ball era. What I'm saying, simply, is that pitchers have not "lost" the ability in the '90s to go 9 innings and throw complete games; it's just that nowadays they have thrown more pitches by the seventh and eighth innings than the old-timers threw in completing 9. I'm saying that Lefty Grove was *not* more durable than Roger Clemens, he just pitched in an era that required far fewer pitches to complete a game. If Clemens is the most durable pitcher of his era, then chances are he'd be the most durable, or at least one of the most durable, of any era, Grove's included.

Conversely, Clemens's superiority in strikeouts—he had 1,238 more in 280 fewer innings—might also be an illusion caused by the difference in eras. Grove was the consummate power-pitcher of his time, leading the American League in strikeouts from his rookie season in 1925 through 1931. Walter Johnson led the AL in strikeouts twelve times, and Bob Feller, like Grove, led the league in strikeouts seven times and probably would have made it eight or more if not for WWII, which cost him 1943, '44, and most of '45. But you have to wonder, too, what Grove might have done had he not lost five years in the major league baseball record book to service with Baltimore in the International League before Oriole owner Jack Dunn sold his contract to Connie Mack's Philadelphia A's. If Lefty Grove isn't the most overpowering pitcher of all time, he's certainly one of the top few.

But so is Roger Clemens. Set beside Walter Johnson's, Lefty Grove's, and Bob Feller's his record on paper doesn't seem so impressive, but let's take a closer look. Clemens has led the league in strikeouts five times, but he has had a great deal more competition for those titles than Johnson, Grove, and Feller. Teams in Johnson's and Grove's day didn't always use precise rotations, and even regular starters like Grove were expected to pitch several games in relief. But surely there were no more than four pitchers on each team worthy of being regular starters. Which means that for the most part, Johnson, Grove, and Feller were usually competing with about four pitchers on seven other teams and, probably, three more on their own, for any strikeout (or ERA) title. That's an average of about thirty, maybe thirty-one or thirty-two pitchers a year to beat out. The league Roger Clemens has pitched in his whole career has never had less than fourteen teams, each one of them using a five-man rotation. That's about sixty-nine pitchers you have to be better than in order to win something. Simply put, Roger Clemens had about twice as many pitchers to compete with for any title than did Walter Johnson, Lefty Grove, and Bob Feller.

Strikeouts, of course, are not in and of themselves indications of greatness. In making the case for Lefty Grove as "the greatest pitcher of all time, period," Bill James, in his 1985 *Historical Baseball Abstract*, used two main criteria, earned run average (meaning how often a pitcher led the league) and won-lost percentage. Those sound fine to me. Let's compare, starting with each man's ERA against the rest of the league's.

GROVE

Year	ERA	League ERA	Diff
1925	4.75	4.39	+0.36
1926	*2.51	4.02	-1.51
1927	3.19	4.14	-0.95
1928	2.58	4.04	-1.46
1929	*2.81	4.24	-1.43
1930	*2.54	4.65	-2.11
1931	*2.06	4.38	-2.32
1932	*2.84	4.48	-1.64
1933	3.20	4.28	-1.08
1934	6.50	4.50	+2.00
1935	*2.70	4.46	-1.76
1936	*2.81	5.04	-2.23
1937	3.02	4.62	-1.60
1938	*3.08	4.79	-1.71
1939	*2.54	4.62	-1.08
1940	3.99	4.38	-0.39
1941	4.37	4.15	+0.22

*denotes led league

CLEMENS

Year	ERA	League ERA	Diff
1984	4.32	3.99	+0.33
1985	3.29	4.15	-0.86
1986	*2.48	4.18	-1.60
1987	2.97	4.46	-1.49
1988	2.93	3.97	-1.04
1989	3.13	3.88	-0.75
1990	*1.93	3.91	-1.98
1991	*2.62	4.09	-1.47
1992	*2.41	3.94	-1.45
1993	4.46	4.32	+0.14
1994	2.85	4.80	-1.95
1995	4.18	4.71	-0.53
1996	3.63	4.99	-1.36
1997	*2.05	4.56	-2.51
1998	*2.65	4.65	-2.00
1999	4.60	4.86	-0.26
2000	3.70	4.91	-1.21

In seventeen seasons, Lefty Grove was better than the league ERA fourteen times, and the three seasons when he finished higher than the league were his rookie year, his final year, and 1934, when he had arm trouble almost certainly caused by Connie Mack's eccentric habit of using him so often in relief roles. Clemens finished *better* than the league *fifteen* times in seventeen years, only failing twice; one of them his rookie season, the other in 1993 when, after seven straight years of 228+ innings, he developed a little arm trouble. Look at those charts carefully; not only are they both remarkable, they're remarkably similar. Both men pitched seventeen seasons in the heart of the greatest hitting spans in baseball history. And both men dominated the hitters in their league to almost exactly the same degree. Even the number of times they led the league in ERA (again, Grove nine, Clemens six), sort of evens out when you consider that Clemens was competing against many more pitchers than Grove.

By the way, though I promised to avoid sabermetrics as much as possible, I can't resist tossing in that *Total Baseball*'s adjusted earned run average (created by normalizing ERAs to the league average, which is done by dividing the league ERA by the individual ERA and then factoring in the home park) ranks them almost the same—Clemens is number one at 151, Grove is number two at 148, on the all-time list. (They are, of course, ranked first in ERA in their eras—Grove's being 1920–41, Clemens is listed as 1977–99.)

So, what of the other great indicator, won-lost percentage? Grove, at .680, is fourth on the all-time list after Dave Foutz (.690), Whitey Ford (.690), and Bob Caruthers (.688), while Clemens, heading into the 2001 season, is sixteenth at .647. But Foutz, Caruthers, and three others in the top sixteen, Larry Corcoran (7), Sam Leever (9), and John Clarkson (16), pitched

Clearing the Bases

all or most of their innings before 1900 and so are not relevant to this discussion. This adjustment makes Grove's record behind Ford, and moves Clemens to twelfth. Let's compare Grove with Clemens on a year-by-year basis in relation to their team's won-lost percentage: (This last column is the difference between the pitcher's won-lost percentage and his team's).

GROVE

Season	W-L	Pct	Team	W-L	Pct	Diff
1925	10–12	.455	Phila	88–64	.579	−.124
1926	13–13	.500	Phila	83–67	.553	−.053
1927	20–13	.608	Phila	91–63	.591	+.017
1928	24–8	.750	Phila	98–55	.641	+.109
1929	20–6*	.769	Phila	104–46	.693	+.077
1930	28–5*	.848	Phila	102–52	.662	+.186
1931	31–4*	.886	Phila	107–45	.704	+.182
1932	25–10	.714	Phila	94–60	.610	+.104
1933	24–8*	.750	Phila	79–72	.523	+.227
1934	8–8	.500	Bost	76–76	.500	.0
1935	20–12	.625	Bost	78–75	.510	+.115
1936	17–12	.586	Bost	74–80	.481	+.105
1937	17–9	.654	Bost	80–72	.526	+.128
1938	14–4	.778	Bost	88–61	.591	+.187
1939	15–4	.789	Bost	89–62	.589	+.200
1940	7–6	.538	Bost	82–72	.532	+.006
1941	7–7	.500	Bost	84–70	.546	−.046
Totals		.680		1497–1092	.578	+.102

CLEMENS

Season	W-L	Pct	Team	W-L	Pct	Diff
1984	9–4	.692	Bost	89–73	.549	+.143
1985	7–5	.583	Bost	81–81	.500	+.083

CLEMENS

Season	W-L	Pct	Team	W-L	Pct	Diff
1986	24–4	.857*	Bost	95–66	.590	+.167
1987	20–9	.690	Bost	78–84	.481	+.209
1988	18–12	.600	Bost	89–73	.549	+.051
1989	17–11	.607	Bost	83–79	.512	+.095
1990	21–6	.778	Bost	88–74	.543	+.235
1991	18–10	.643	Bost	84–78	.519	+.124
1992	18–11	.621	Bost	73–89	.451	+.170
1993	11–14	.440	Bost	80–82	.494	-.054
1994	9–7	.563	Bost	54–61	.470	+.093
1995	10–5	.667	Bost	86–58	.597	+.070
1996	10–13	.435	Bost	85–77	.525	-.090
1997	21–7	.750	Tor	76–86	.469	+.281
1998	20–6	.759	Tor	88–74	.543	+.216
1999	14–10	.583	NYY	98–64	.604	−.021
2000	13–8	.619	NYY	87–74	.540	+.079
Totals	260–142	.647		1414–1273	.526	+.120

Lefty Grove pitched for seventeen seasons and in fourteen of those he had a better won-lost percentage than his team's. Roger Clemens, at the time this study was made, had pitched for seventeen years and in fourteen of those had a better won-lost percentage than his team's. Grove's team won 3 pennants and 2 World Series; Clemens' teams won 3 pennants and 2 World Series. This is starting to get creepy. Is Roger Clemens a right-handed version of the spirit of Lefty Grove, reborn forty-three years later? Is this a case for baseball's X-Files?

What's even scarier is that records suggest that had they pitched for the same teams, they would have had virtually similar records. The .102 point won-lost percentage differential between Grove and his teams is extraordinary; but Clemens's

.120 point gap is the largest I have been able to find of any pitcher in baseball history with more than 150 wins. Think about that for a moment: Clemens has one of the best won-lost percentages in baseball history, *but the difference between him and his teams is the biggest of any pitcher's in baseball history.* Stated another way, Roger Clemens has outpitched the rest of his team by a greater margin than any pitcher of the century, greater than any hard-luck pitcher from Walter Johnson to Robin Roberts to Mike Mussina (who actually has 147 wins to just 81 losses by the end of the 2000 season).

I don't know that Clemens's .120 won-lost percentage differential is a greater achievement than Grove's .102 for the simple reason that it's easier for a good pitcher to do better than teams that won 53 percent of its games than for teams that were 58 percent. I mean, how *much* better can you be than win 58 percent of your team's games? Whitey Ford, at .690, is the only pitcher in the Hall of Fame with a won-lost percentage higher than Grove's, but Ford's won-lost percentage *in relation to his team's* isn't as high as Grove's. I'll assume this, since I'm not going to add it up. Grove's teams won 3 pennants in seventeen seasons, while Ford's won 11 pennants in the fourteen seasons he was a regular on the pitching staff. I can't say whether Grove's won-lost percentage of .680 and his .102 won-lost differential above his teams is a greater feat than Clemens's .643 and .120. It rather strikes me that they are remarkably similar in scope, and indicate that, allowing for a 4- or 5-point margin of error, the men who compiled them would have virtually the same records if they had pitched for the same team.

But I know whose team I'd rather have pitched for if given the chance and so do you: we'd both have chosen to pitch for Lefty Grove's teams. They were better. If you were Roger Clemens and you had pitched for Lefty Grove's teams, you'd have won more games than 260, period. Your won-lost percentage would be higher than .647. Maybe it wouldn't be .699, which is 52 points higher—52 points being the difference in won-lost percentage between Clemens's teams (.526) and Grove's (.578)—but it would be higher. How much better? I don't know, but if Clemens pitched for teams that were 52 points better than they actually were, is it likely his career won-lost record would be, say, 33 points higher? That sounds about right, and if it is then Roger Clemens and Lefty Grove, give or take a couple of points, would, after seventeen big league seasons, have virtually the same won-lost record.

So, then, who is the greater pitcher? Bill James's judgment that Grove was the greatest pitcher ever came just as Clemens's career was beginning, so I do not know how he feels now. If Lefty Grove is the greatest pitcher of the first half of the twentieth century—and I think the statistical evidence clearly indicates this—and Roger Clemens is the best pitcher in the second half of the twentieth century—and I believe the evidence clearly indicates this too—and the two of them are strikingly similar in their effectiveness . . . then who is the better pitcher? Who, if the previous premises are correct, is the greatest pitcher of all time? I'm going to go with Clemens. I think the hitters he had to face were, on the whole, considerably tougher than the ones Grove or any pitcher in the first three quarters or so of the last century faced. I don't simply mean in terms of the number of great black and Latin players, but in terms of toughness and consistency throughout the batting order.

Every baseball fan knows, or should know, how thoroughly the home run changed baseball. Everyone knows it changed the way managers and players thought about *hitting*—that is, the strategy changed from simply reaching base and moving runners along via the steal, bunt, and hit and run, to getting the whole bundle with one swing. Grove pitched at a time when one, two, or three men were the only genuine run producers in a lineup; Clemens has performed in an era when, in theory and in practice, anyone in the lineup can deliver a big blow. Let's take a look at differences in some of the teams they pitched to in terms of slugging ability. I'm going to take Grove's 1931 season, in which he was 31–4 with a 2.06 ERA and a 2.32 ERA difference between himself and the league, as his best. For Roger Clemens, I'll use 1997, when he was 21–7 with a 2.05 ERA and a 2.51 league ERA difference. For the sake of comparison, I'll use the 1931 Yankees and the 1997 Seattle Mariners, the best hitting team that Grove and Clemens had to face in those years.

	BA	SLG A	OBA	R	HR	SB	SO	BB
1931 NYY	.297	.457	.383	1067	155	138	554	748
1997 SEA	.280	.485	.358	925	264	89	1110	626

PLAYERS WITH . . .

	40+HR	30+	25+	20+	10+
1931 NYY	2	2	2	2	3
1997 SEA	2	3	4	6	9

The '31 Yankees scored a whopping 1,067 runs—92 more, by the way, than the '27 Yankees—by getting a lot of singles (they outhit the '97 Mariners by 17 points) and walks (they had 122 more than the '97 Mariners) and moved them along by making contact (almost exactly half the number of strikeouts as the '97 Mariners and stolen bases (49 more). But most of the punch came from Lou Gehrig and Babe Ruth, who accounted for 92 of the team's 155 homers and 347 RBIs—more than one-third of the team's RBI total of 990. Ben Chapman was the only other player on the team with as many as 10 home runs (he had

17) and 85 RBI (he had 122—which means that three players drove in nearly half the team's total).

In contrast, Seattle's two 40+ homer men, Ken Griffey Jr. (58) and Jay Buhner (40), accounted for 6 more homers than Gehrig and Ruth, yet they account for less than 40 percent of their team's total. (Seattle's three leading RBI producers, Griffey, Buhner, and Edgar Martinez, totaled 364 RBI, well under half of the team's total.) In contrast to the '31 Yankees, the '97 Mariners could produce an entire lineup of hitters who had 10 or more home runs.

Which lineup do you think would be more difficult to pitch to? Which lineup would put more pressure on a pitcher to use his best stuff throughout? Ray Robinson, biographer of Christy Mathewson, says that "Mathewson was a firm believer in 'pacing' yourself, in not going hard all the time." The point of his book, *Pitching in a Pinch*, is that a smart pitcher bares down in the "pinches," against the really tough hitters and learns to coast a bit against the less dangerous hitters. "Many spectators," he is quoted as saying in his book, "wonder why a pitcher does not work as hard as he can all through the game, instead of just in the pinches." One wonders how Mathewson might pitch in today's game. In the year of Mathewson's best season, 1908—he was 37–11, by the way, with 34 complete games and led the league with 259 strikeouts and a 1.43 ERA—only two players, the Dodgers' Tim Jordan (12), and the Pirates' Honus Wagner (10) hit more than 9 home runs.

I'm not disputing that Matty would have been great in any era. What I *am* saying is that pitching in today's game, where most of the regular players in either league hit at least 10 home runs, he'd be bearing down a great deal more that he was before WWI. He certainly wouldn't be completing 34 games.

And so it is with all the fabulous totals of all the early great pitchers, from Cy Young's record 511 victories to Walter Johnson's 110 career shutouts. As the game has evolved, pitchers have had to work harder against increasingly dangerous lineups and throw more pitches to get complete games. Pitching hasn't declined over the last thirty years: hitting has gotten better, or at least the hitters have gotten bigger and stronger. One might argue that it's only in the last few decades that pitching has evolved into an art, that only in that period did it need to. And the greatest pitcher in the toughest era for pitchers has been Roger Clemens.

Sandy Versus the Rocket

While writing this chapter, I got into an email debate with a friend of mine, Jim Patton, author of the delightful cult-favorite, *Rookie—When Michael Jordan Came to the Minor Leagues.* Jim, like most people I discussed this subject with, was fully willing to accept Roger Clemens as better than Walter Johnson or Lefty Grove or anyone else from baseball's dark ages but simply couldn't believe that Clemens could be as good or better than the greatest pitcher of his youth, Sandy Koufax.

I understand Jim's disbelief: Sandy Koufax wasn't merely one of the most dominating pitchers of all time, he was the first great pitcher to be dominant on national television. The memory of him fanning 15 Yankees in the 1963 World Series is so strong for fans who grew up in my era—it was the game Jack Nicolson's McMurphy pretends to broadcast to the inmates in *One Flew Over the Cuckoo's Nest*—that nothing is likely to replace it. Jim's feelings were echoed by nearly everyone I talked to: "Clemens just wasn't as *dominant* as Koufax."

Well, not on paper, anyway. Here are their career lines at the end of 2000:

	Seasons	G	S	CG	IP	SO
Koufax	12 (1957–66)	397	314	137	2324	2396
Clemens	17 (1984–00)	512	511	116	3666.2	3504

	BB	H	ERA	W-L	PCT
Koufax	817	1754	2.76	165–87	.655
Clemens	1186	3101	3.07	260–142	.647

This looks pretty good for Koufax. He has a better won-lost percentage, a lower ERA, a better hits-to-innings-pitched ratio, and a slightly better strikeouts-to-walks ratio. He also completed 21 more games in twelve seasons than Clemens did in seventeen. Clemens, of course, had more of everything, but Koufax's quality numbers are clearly and indisputably better.

I don't want to get into those stupid debates about whether Sandy Koufax really merited the Hall of Fame, whether or not he pitched long enough or had enough great seasons. Koufax really only had seven good seasons from 1960, when he was 8–13, to 1966, when he was 27–9. The 8–13 doesn't sound like much, but he was pitching his home games in a bad park for him, in the LA Coliseum, which had an absurdly short left-field fence, which was disastrous for southpaws. That considered, his 3.91 ERA wasn't bad, and he had 197 strikeouts against just 100 walks while opponents hit a league-low .207 against him. It was the first of seven straight seasons he posted the league's lowest batting-average-against. Actually, he was to lead the league *eight* times in this category. In 1958, he was just 11–11 with a 4.05 ERA but the NL hitters' .220 was the lowest batting-average-against in the league. This, too, suggests that Koufax was a much better pitcher before 1961 than is generally recognized.

Anyway, the argument that Koufax didn't pitch enough to merit the Hall of Fame is ludicrous. The Hall of Fame is about greatness, and if Sandy Koufax didn't manifest greatness from 1961 through 1966, then no pitcher in baseball history ever has.

Let's compare Koufax from 1961 through 1966 with Roger Clemens's six best seasons.

Koufax	W-L	S	IP	CG	ERA	H	SO	BB
1961	18–13	42	255	15	3.52	212	*269	96
1962	14–7	28	184	11	*2.54	134	216	57
1963	*25–5	40	311	20	*1.88	214	*306	58
1964	19–5	29	223	15	*1.74	154	223	53
1965	*26–8	.41	*336	*27	*2.04	216	*382	71
1966	*27–9	41	*323	*27	*1.73	241	*317	77
Total	128–47	221	1632	115		1171	1713	412

*-led league

Clemens	W-L	S	IP	CG	ERA	H	SO	BB
1986	*24–4	33	254	10	*2.46	179	238	67
1987	*20–9	36	281.2	*18	2.97	248	256	83
1990	21–6	31	228.1	7	*1.93	193	*241	65
1992	18–11	32	246.2	11	*2.41	219	208	62
1997	*21–7	34	*264	*9	*2.05	204	*292	68
1998	*20–6	33	234.2	5	*2.65	169	*271	68
Total	124–43	199	1509.1	59		1212	1506	413

*-led league

In truth, Clemens, in his six best seasons, was quite comparable to Koufax at his peak, though, to be fair, Koufax might have another 10–12 wins and at least another 100 innings if not for arthritic problems at the end of the '62 and '64 seasons. And, to be equally fair, Clemens lost many starts due to injury in what might have been peak years, 1993 through 1997. At any rate, Koufax, from 1961 through 1966, had a few more starts, nearly 123 more innings pitched, and nearly twice the number of complete games than Clemens in his six best years. He also gave up 41 fewer hits than Clemens despite pitching more and he struck out nearly 200 more batters, averaging about 10 per 9 innings while Clemens averaged just exactly 9. Their walk totals are nearly identical, though Koufax's walks-to-innings pitched and walks-to-strikeout averages are slightly higher. Koufax's ERA is consistently lower. But despite all this—and here's where Clemens greatness begins to jump out—Clemens's won-lost percentage is higher, even though he pitched on teams that were markedly inferior to Koufax's Dodgers.

Many fans would have a hard time accepting that last statement. The Dodgers of Koufax's era are remembered today as a collection of banjo hitters who scratched out runs and left Sandy with a lot of close games to gut himself out of. This isn't entirely true: two of Sandy's Dodgers team hit very well, better than any teams Clemens pitched for. Let's look at each man's contribution to his team's wins during their six best seasons, as well as the team's scoring in relation to the league. (By "Team's W-L," I mean the total of all decisions that did not involve Koufax or Clemens; the "Pct" means the team's won-lost record in all other games when Koufax or Clemens didn't get the decision.)

Koufax	W-L	Team's W-L	Pct	Runs Scored	Leage Rank
1961	18–13	71–52	.577	735	2
1962	14–7	88–56	.611	842	2
1963	25–5	74–58	.538	747	6

Koufax	W-L	Team's W-L	Pct	Runs Scored	League Rank
1964	19–5	61–77	.442	614	8
1965	26–8	71–57	.555	608	8
1966	27–9	68–58	.540	606	8
Total	128–47				

Clemens	W-L	Team's W-L	Pct	Runs Scored	League Rank
1986	24–4	71–62	.534	794	5
1987	20–9	58–75	.436	842	4
1990	21–6	77–68	.531	679	7
1992	18–11	55–78	.414	599	13
1997	21–7	55–79	.410	654	14
1998	20–6	68–68	.500	816	7
Total	124–43				

The runs scored comparison isn't scientific, as Koufax's National league had only ten teams and no designated hitter, which adds, on the average, about 60 runs a year to team's total. But it doesn't really have to be. The point is obvious: the teams Roger Clemens pitched for (the Boston Red Sox from 1986 through 1992 and the Toronto Blue Jays from 1997 and 1998) in his six best seasons hit no better and mostly a little worse than the Dodger teams that Koufax pitched for in his best years. And Koufax's Dodgers were better than the Red Sox and Blue Jays Clemens pitched for.

Koufax's earned run average at his peak was awesome, but was it really better than Clemens's? Here's their ERAs relative to the league for those six peak seasons.

KOUFAX

Year	ERA	League ERA	Diff
1961	3.52	4.03	−0.51
1962	2.54	3.94	−1.40

KOUFAX

Year	ERA	League ERA	Diff
1963	1.88	3.29	−1.41
1964	1.74	3.54	−1.80
1965	2.04	3.54	−1.50
1966	1.73	3.61	−1.88

CLEMENS

Year	ERA	League ERA	Diff
1986	2.46	4.18	−1.72
1987	2.97	4.46	−1.49
1990	1.93	3.91	−1.98
1992	2.41	4.09	−1.68
1997	2.05	4.56	−2.51
1998	2.65	4.65	−2.00

There you have it—the relative ERAs in Clemens's six best seasons match and exceed those of Koufax's six best. Maybe that doesn't mean Clemens at his peak was better than Koufax; maybe it doesn't mean he was as good. But I'd say that if you were going to argue the case for Koufax, you'd have to come up with evidence better than any I've seen.

That the two of them were near-equals in terms of effectiveness is obvious from their stats. In their six best seasons, Koufax led his league in victories three times, Clemens four; Koufax led his league in innings pitched twice, Clemens once; Koufax led in complete games twice, Clemens twice; Koufax led in ERA five times, and so did Clemens; Koufax led in strikeouts four times, Clemens three. There would seem to be a slight dominance edge for Koufax here, but remember that Clemens had to beat out more pitchers to win his titles.

The bottom line, it seems to me, is that pitching for slightly inferior teams, Roger Clemens, at his six peak seasons, had a slightly better won-lost percentage and slightly better ERA in relation to the league. Koufax pitched a few more innings, completed substantially more games, gave up fewer hits, and struck out a few more batters, but I give Clemens the edge on won-lost percentage and ERA. Koufax's edge in the other stats, I'm convinced, is the difference between the mid-'60s and mid-'90s in the way the game is played. (Think about this: as much time has passed between Koufax's last season, 1966, and now, as passed between Grove's greatest year, 1931, and Koufax's last year. That's a lot of time for the game to change.) Why, then did Koufax *seem* more dominant? Because conditions were better for pitchers in the '60s than in the '90s. The strike zone was bigger, there were fewer power-hitters, and it was easier for pitchers to complete games. In fact, the '60s were one of the worst decades for hitters in the entire century.

Sandy Koufax at his peak, I am convinced, was as good as Lefty Grove in his. Roger Clemens, at his peak, was a little better than both of them. What I'm saying is that if all the pitchers in baseball history lined up in their prime to face the same opposition under the same conditions in the same year, Roger Clemens would end up winning more games than any of them.

12

Minnie Minoso: The New Latin Dynasty

What would you answer if asked "Who is the Latin Jackie Robinson?" Don't feel bad if you don't know; I didn't. I had to call the Hall of Fame to find out. Many fans, I think, would immediately think of Roberto Clemente, though we know very well that there were several Latin players in the major leagues before him. The reason we think of Clemente is because he was the first player to assert his Latinness, the first to make an issue of it. (C'mon, confess, didn't you feel just a little guilty owning one of those "Bob Clemente" cards when he had made it a matter of public record that he hated being called anything but Roberto?)

But isn't it odd that at a time in sports history when we are more issue-conscious than ever, no one has a clue as to who the first Latin ballplayer was? Well, anyway, I didn't have one, and I've been writing about this stuff for more than twenty years. Either I'm different from most fans in this regard, or the grumbling you sometimes hear from Latin ballplayers is legitimate.

Okay, so who is the Latin Jackie Robinson? First of all, we have to be specific about what we're asking, and after some thought I decided that there was no point in trying to track the first white Latin player, as there would have been no real issue regarding his admission to the big leagues. I'm not minimizing the bigotry even white Latinos must have endured, but there was no hard and fast barrier to break. Obviously, what we are looking for is the first black Latin player. The first dark-skinned Latin player, I was told by the Hall of Fame, was Cuban-born Saturnino Orestes Arrieta Minoso, "The Cuban Comet," better known to fans as Minnie. Minnie Minoso made his debut in 1949, two years after Jackie Robinson, playing for Bill Veeck's Cleveland Indians. Larry Doby, who also made his debut in 1947, shortly after Jackie, is recognized as the AL's first black player, but what about Minoso? What must it have been like for him, to be both black and Hispanic? There have been shelves full of material on Jackie Robinson, and in recent years baseball historians have started to catch up to Larry Doby, but who knows about Minnie Minoso?

Both Jackie Robinson and Larry Doby are in the Hall of Fame, but who has made the case for Minnie Minoso? I have done a Hall of Fame watch for *The Wall Street Journal* since 1995, and I never once thought to consider him. Nor in all that time has anyone written to try and convince me. I must have received hundreds of emails and letters on Bill Mazeroski, Phil Rizzuto, Gil Hodges, Ron Santo, Tony Perez, and many others, but I've never gotten one in support of Minnie. But after looking into his case, I can tell you that he is probably the most deserving player *not* to make the Hall of Fame, and that, if given the chance, I would take him at peak over both Mazeroski and Rizzuto.

Though he missed most of his prime, entering the big leagues at age twenty-seven, he played for seventeen seasons—well, twelve, really, as he played in just 9 games, batting just 16 times, in his 1949 debut, and in just 5 games in his last two seasons. For that matter, he played in just 30 games in 1964, his last year before his first retirement; he was brought back in 1976 for 3 games and in 1980 for 2 more to qualify for extra pension benefits and to become a "Five Decade Player" and he collected nearly 2,000 hits, driving in more than 80 runs eight times and 100 runs four times, scoring more than 90 runs ten times, leading the league in stolen bases three times, posting a .391 on-base average, and being voted to seven All Star teams.

This is all very impressive, but let's take it a bit more slowly. First, Minnie Minoso was a hugely popular player in the '50s and early '60s, first with Cleveland and then with Chicago White Sox fans. His flair and enthusiasm as well as his talent won over everyone. When told once that his English wasn't very good, he reportedly said "Ball, bat, glove—she no speak English." If more Cleveland and Chicago fans don't know he was the first black Latin player, it might be because he scarcely made an impression in his first season, getting 3 hits in 16 at-bats, and not getting a chance to play regularly until 1951. That's when most fans date his career from—he finished second to Gil McDougald of the Yankees in the Rookie of the Year balloting—and I'll bet a lot of people who look at that date just assume that there were several Latin players in the bigs by then. Anyway, everything about those early years is a bit odd. First off, though he was playing for a Bill Veeck team in 1949, Minoso was scarcely given a look by the Indians. He had just 19 plate appearances and had 3 hits, one a home run, and 2 walks, and, really, how much more can a rookie be expected to do when not given a chance? He was also hit by 2 pitches, which might have given someone a clue as to how good he was at that: he would go on to lead the American League in HBP a record ten times, 189 in all, a then-record and a total that, for a mere 1,835 games, may well last for all time. So his on-base average for 9 games was .350; not bad, but somehow he wound up back in the minors. Minoso spent the next year in Cuba, thus losing more than nine tenths of what are considered a ballplayers' prime seasons to the minor leagues. By the time he got a chance to play full time in 1951, he was twenty-nine—a twenty-nine-year-old rookie. We rightfully mourn Jackie Robinson's lost years, but Minnie Minoso was a year older than Jackie Robinson when he was officially a rookie.

And what of that Rookie of the Year Award? Gil McDougald was a fine player, but in 1951 he hit .263 with 14 home runs and 63 RBI and 72 runs in 131 games; Minoso hit .326 with 10 home runs, 76 RBI, and 112 runs. He led the league in stolen bases with 31 (McDougald had 14) and triples with 14 (Gil had 4). His on-base average was .422 and his slugging average, .500; McDougald was, respectively, .396 and .488. Gil McDougald was a fine rookie; Minnie Minoso was an outstanding one. His 1951 season taught a lesson to Latin players for the next forty-odd years: you will have to do better than the non-Latin player just to be noticed, and far better to win an award.

Let me make this case a bit more forcefully: Minnie Minoso was a better ballplayer than several white players of his time who are in the Hall of Fame. He was also better than the *Black* players from his era that are in the Hall of Fame. Consider the following:

	Full Seasons	G	HR	RBI	R	SB	OBA	SLGA
Player A	12	1796	185	1013	1122	201	.389	.459
Player B	10	1533	253	970	960	47	.386	.490
Player C	15	2380	169	1304	1247	64	.382	.453

Quickly, for purposes of moving my argument along, I'll define full season as 100 or more games, and I'll skip batting average in favor of OBA (see Chapter 14, "On-Base Averages"). As caught stealing information is incomplete, I'll throw in stolen bases as a category only for what it might indicate, namely speed on the basepaths, particularly as it might be valuable going from first to third and second to home.

Okay, then: who, judging from those stats, would you say was the best player? Yes, there are other things you'd want to know, such as defensive capability (player B, trust me or check yourself after I give you their names, would edge out the other two as he was the only one with a range factor higher than the league average). On the whole, though, these numbers give you an excellent idea of each man's power, speed, and consistency. My vote is for player A, who has the highest OBA, the second best SLG A, and more stolen bases than B and C combined.

Player A is Minnie Minoso, player B is Larry Doby, and player C is Enos Slaughter. Doby, the first black player in the American League and Minoso's teammate in 1949, played for only thirteen seasons from 1947 to 1959, ten of them full, and drove in 100 or more in five. Slaughter played for nineteen seasons from 1938 to 1959, fifteen of them for 100 or more games. His HOF credentials are slim; he hit over .300 ten times, drove in more than 100 runs three times, and scored over 100 three times. He is the only one of the three to finish with a batting average of .300 or better—actually, .300 exactly—and voters like round numbers like that. But he was a hustler on the field and was very popular among fans and a large segment of writers. Both Doby and Slaughter were very good players but what I would rate as borderline Hall of Fame candidates. Both had a lot of people pulling for them and pleading special case arguments; Doby had virtually all the writers who had backed the first Negro Leaguers, and Slaughter had fans such as Tom Wicker, who wrote a chapter advocating his HOF candidacy for Dan Okrent's *The Ultimate Baseball Book*.

It was often said in Slaughter's defense that he lost four prime years to World War II. I think this is a fair point, but it should be also pointed out that he did get to play from age twenty-three to twenty-six before entering the service. Doby, on the other hand, lost no seasons to military service and probably none to bigotry, as he entered the league at age twenty-three in 1947. Minoso, though, sure got shafted by someone. He didn't get a crack at the show till age twenty-seven in '49, and he wasn't officially a rookie till he was twenty-nine in '51. If you look closely at that A-B-C chart for Minoso, Doby, and Slaughter, one of the things you'd want to know is: to what extent do the quality stats such as OBA and SLG reflect their ability in their declining years, or, stated another way, did Slaughter's last few seasons pull down his overall averages? And the answer is, yes, in four of Slaughter's last six seasons, injury and age forced him to play fewer than 100 games. Age, injury, and stress took a similar toll on Doby, but earlier in his career: at age thirty-five and thirty-six, he began to slip badly and failed to play 100 games. But to a large extent the stats of Slaughter and Doby reflect their ability in their prime seasons.

But Minnie Minoso never had a prime. At the same age when Minoso got a chance to play full time, twenty-nine, Larry Doby had only seven seasons left to play and would lead the league in just two important batting categories, home runs and RBI, both in 1954. At age twenty-nine, Enos Slaughter still had fourteen years of big league ball left but would never lead the league in any category but triples (in 1949). From age twenty-nine on, Minnie Minoso led the league in hits once, doubles once, triples three times, total bases once, and stolen bases three times. From age twenty-nine on, Larry Doby never hit .300; from age twenty-nine on, Enos Slaughter hit .300 six times; and from age twenty-nine on, Minnie Minoso hit over .300 eight times.

If Larry Doby and Enos Slaughter deserve to be in Cooperstown, doesn't Minnie Minoso also deserve to be? And if Enos Slaughter was cut a little slack for his military service, and Larry Doby for the immense burden of being the league's first black player, how about cutting Minnie Minoso a little for beginning his career at a point when most players are at the halfway mark?

As I write this, Minnie Minoso's HOF candidacy doesn't really exist. When the changes regarding the HOF Veterans Committee voting were made last August, Ron Santo and Ken Boyer and others were mentioned, but not Minoso. He remains the Invisible Hall of Famer, and in this respect his career set a pattern for Latin stars that have followed. Latin ballplayers, white, black, or of mixed parentage, are still baseball's invisible men. Of the twenty players chosen to start the 2001 All Star game, eight were Latinos. If Pedro Martinez wasn't injured, that would have been nine of twenty; if Roberto Alomar—nine seasons over .300, six seasons with 100-plus runs scored, nearly 450 stolen bases at an 81 percent success rate—was chosen to play second base for the AL, as he certainly should have been, then exactly half of this year's starting All Star teams would be Latin. (Pick a DH and it would have to be Edgar Martinez.)

A quarter of the players in the major leagues in 2001 are Latin. The game's best starting pitcher, Pedro Martinez, the best reliever, Mariano Rivera, the best second baseman, Roberto Alomar—the best AL second baseman since WW II, perhaps of all time?—the two best shortstops, Alex Rodriguez and Nomar Garciaparra, the best catcher, Ivan Rodriguez—the

best all-around catcher in baseball history?—and the most prolific home run hitters and RBI producers over the last four seasons, outfielders Sammy Sosa and Manny Ramirez, are Latin.
The best all-around player in the game—Alex Rodriguez—is
Latin.

If pressed to pick the single biggest difference between the
game before 1950 and the game as it is played now, I'd have to
cite the dominance of Latin players.

13

Competitive Balance Through the Century

PARITY THROUGH THE AGES

Year	# Teams	Teams (over .600)	Teams (under .400)	High	Low
1901	16	2	5	.647 (Pitt)	.358 (Milw)
1902	16	2	3	.741 (Pitt)	.353 (NY-N)
1909	16	5	4	.724 (Pitt)	.276 (Wash)
1911	16	2	2	.669 (Phil-A)	.291 (Bost-N)
1919	16	4	3	.686 (Cin)	.257 (Phil-N)
1921	16	3	2	.641 (NY-A)	.331 (Phil-N)
1927	16	3	3	.714 (NYY)	.331 (Phil-N, Bost-A)
1930	16	2	3	.662 (Phil-A)	.338 (Phil-N, Bost-A)
1931	16	3	3	.704 (Phil-A)	.366 (Chi-A)
1936	16	3	3	.702 (NY-A)	.271 (StL-A)
1941	16	3	1	.656 (NYY)	.279 (Phil-N)
1946	16	3	3	.675 (Bost-A)	.318 (Phil-N)
1948	16	3	3	.626 (Cleve)	.336 (Chi-A)

Clearing the Bases

Year	# Teams	Teams (over .600)	Teams (under .400)	High	Low
1951	16	4	1	.636 (NYY)	.338 (StL-A)
1955	16	3	3	.641 (Bklyn)	.344 (Wash)
1957	16	2	2	.636 (NYY)	.357 (Wash)
1959	16	3	3	.641 (Bklyn)	.344 (Wash)
1960	16	2	3	.630 (NYY)	.377 (KC)
1961	18	3	3	.673 (NYY)	.305 (Phil)
1962	20	3	3	.624 (SF)	.250 (NYM)
1968	20	1	0	.636 (Det)	.404 (Wash)
1969	24	2	4	.673 (Balt)	.321 (Mont, SD)
1976	24	3	2	.630 (Cin)	.340 (Mont)
1977	26	6	5	.630 (KC)	.335 (Tor)
1978	26	2	2	.618 (NYY)	.350 (Sea)
1980	26	2	2	.636 (NYY)	.364 (Sea)
1986	26	1	1	.667 (NYM)	.395 (Pitt)
1993	28	0	3	.599 (Phil)	.364 (NYM)
1994	28	2	1	.649 (Mon)	.395 (Cal)
1998	30	2	2	.704 (NYY)	.334 (Fla)
2000	30	0	0	.599 (SF)	.401 (Chi-N, Phil)

In November of 2000, in front of the Senate Judiciary Committee's hearing on competitive balance in baseball, Commissioner Bud Selig voiced this lament, which since has been taken up by scores of would-be reformers. "An increasing number of our clubs," he said, "have become unable to successfully complete for their respective division championships . . . At the start of spring training, there no longer exists hope and faith for the fans of more than half of our thirty clubs." In one sense, the commissioner was right: the more teams you have, the more fans are going to be disappointed at the end of the season. That's a mathematical certainty.

In another sense, the commissioner was verifiably wrong. Strange as it may seem, the undeniable trend in baseball over the previous one hundred years, and particularly over the last twenty-odd seasons, has been toward the greatest level of competitiveness the game has ever seen.

One of the themes I've been stressing in this book is that modern players in the modern game are the best ever due to much greater competitive balance. Translated into players' terms, I think there's a very good chance that the domination of batting statistics by Mike Schmidt in the fully integrated mid-'70s, when there were twenty-four teams, to 1977 through 1987, when there were twenty-six, is at least comparable to Babe Ruth's domination in the 1920s when there were only sixteen all-white teams. Simply put, the notion that expansion "thinned out" talent is nonsense; expansion took advantage of, and in some cases spurred on, the development of new talent. In Ruth's day, almost all players were white and from the Northeast, the Deep South, and Midwest; by Schmidt's time the population had doubled and the talent pool included black, Latin, and white players from the Far West. Increasingly in the decades after Jackie Robinson, the game has seen better training at the high school and college level and better scouting, and the result is a major league level of play that has become sharper and more competitive as it has expanded.

In 2000, for the first time in baseball history, or at least for the first time since the National and American Leagues began to compete against each other, not a single team finished above the .600 mark in won-lost percentage or below .400 in won-lost percentage. And this was not a fluke; as the numbers show, this was the inevitable result of a trend. On our chart we have thirty-one teams from the beginning of the twentieth century to the end of last season that represent several landmarks in baseball history.

From 1901 to 1960, there were just sixteen teams in the American and National Leagues, yet in every year we looked—including the Honus Wagner Pirates, the 1919 "Black Sox," the '27 Ruth-Gehrig Yankees, the 1941 DiMaggio Yankees, the 1951 season capped by Bobby Thomson's home run, the '55 "Next Year" for the Brooklyn Dodgers, and the 1960 season (the last with sixteen teams)—there were never less than a total of four teams that finished above .600 or below .400. In fact, the average combined number of teams finishing above .600 and below .400 in those eight seasons is six per year.

Then, a strange thing happened. As the leagues expanded, the teams moved closer to the center. In 1961, for the first time in a century, there were more than sixteen major leagues teams. This was supposed to cause a major disruption in the balance of power, and in a sense it did: the Yankees got better and won easily. But overall, expansion scarcely caused a blip as far as the two leagues were concerned, with a combined total of six teams, one-third of the two leagues' number, finishing over .600 or below .400. And the next year the NL expanded, which gave the majors twenty teams, but the number finishing above .600 or below .400 did not change.

In 1969, baseball expanded again, bringing more dire predictions of thinned-out talent. But nothing of the kind showed on the field, where just two teams finished above .600 and four below .400. In other words, after expanding to twenty-four teams, baseball had a lower percentage of big winners and losers than when it expanded to twenty. In 1977, we do have a major disruption: the combination of expansion and free agency produces an all-time high (though not an all-time high percentage) of teams finishing above .600 or below .400 with eleven. Then, look what happens the next season: as teams adjust to free agency, the total swings back to four (two above, two below). In 1993, the major leagues expand to twenty-eight teams, but no one finishes above .600 and just three teams finish below .400. The next season, they expand again, to the current number of thirty, but the number of over-unders is the same as in 1941, when there was just sixteen teams.

What exactly is happening here? How can baseball be moving toward greater competitiveness at a time when there has never been a greater disparity between the revenues of the so-called large-market and small-market teams? And if baseball's coming financial crisis is being caused by the increasingly large salaries of the players, why has the competition on the field become keener than ever? The answer is that whatever free agency does to disrupt the financial structure of baseball, it simply does not have the effect on the field that its critics say it does. Either that, or much of what we think we know about the financial resources of the teams and their revenues is simply wrong.

Whatever the answer, one thing is becoming apparent: not only is baseball at the major league level more competitive than ever, it is the only major sport that truly is competitive (basketball, football, and hockey maintain that illusion only because of a bogus playoff system that rewards undeserving teams with playoff spots). Next time you see a baseball team swing a blockbuster deal to get that superstar player and ask yourself why, remember the answer: because he can make the difference. One player can't make a team, but he could make up the difference between a won-lost percentage of .400 and a shot at the division title.

I didn't use any scientific method to select the teams on the chart, I simply flipped through *Total Baseball* looking for seasons that were considered landmarks for various reasons, and also spaced just far enough apart so that every trend or important change over the last one hundred years was represented.

Some random notes

- The first nine years of the century are dominated by the great Pittsburgh teams of Honus Wagner. 1901, with seven teams above and below, seems like an aberration with nearly half the teams finishing either above .600 or below .400, and a historian might conclude that this is because the American League had been a minor league just the year before. But, in fact, it was the National League that had the team with the highest won-lost percentage and three teams below .400. By 1909, it gets worse, with the good getting better and the lousy getting lousier. In 1911, perhaps Ty Cobb's best season (he hit .420 and lead the AL in batting, runs, hits, RBIs, stolen bases, and slugging and trailed Joe Jackson by 1 point in on-base average), a rules change results in a surge of hitting—the NL ERA goes from 3.03 to 3.40, while the AL jumps from 2.52 to 3.34. But only two teams (neither of them, curiously, Cobb's Detroit Tigers) finish above .600, and only two finish below .400. In 1919, the year of the betting scandal, the number goes up again to four and three, with the highest number, .686, going *not* to the White Sox, who you would think, with all those should-have-been Hall of Famers, but to their World Series opponent, the supposedly patsy-ish Cincinnati Reds. (Time for an historical reevaluation, perhaps?)

- In 1921, the era of the big hitters begins, led by, but by no means confined to, Babe Ruth. In fact, despite Ruth, the NL ERA actually jumps more, from 3.14 to 3.78, than the American League's, 3.79 to 4.29. From there till the end of the eight-team leagues in 1960, the number of over .600s and under .400s fluctuates between four and six, never quite reaching the extremes of the first decade of the century.

And for the most part, these are all hitters' decades. Most of the seasons, when they are singled out, the 1927 Yankees of Ruth and Gehrig, 1930, when ERA's soared to 4.98 in the National League and 4.65 in the American League, to Connie Mack's greatest-ever A's team of 1931 to Ted Williams's rookie season of 1939 (when four great hitters, Jimmie Foxx, Joe DiMaggio, Hank Greenberg, and Williams dominated SLOB), to 1941, when Williams became the last batter in the century to hit over .400 and DiMaggio had his 56-game hitting streak, are famous for hitting achievements.

This stays more or less true through 1946, the first season after the war disruption, 1948, the year Jackie Robinson broke the color barrier, 1951, the year of the great Giants-Dodgers pennant race, 1955, the year of the Brooklyn Dodgers' only World Series victory, to the end of the eight-team leagues in 1960. The number of overs-unders fluctuates between four and six, with the usual number being six. What the chart doesn't show, though, is that by the end of the '50s, baseball was headed for a greater level of competitive balance than at any time in the previous sixty years, and the National League was there first. From 1952 through 1956, there was exactly one team in the NL each year that finished above .600 and below .400, and in '57 there was just one above .600 and none below .400. Things were quite different in the AL, where in the six seasons between '52 and '57 there were ten teams finishing over .600—guess who finished over .600 the most times?—and thirteen teams finishing below .400. I really can't see much mystery as to what happened: the NL began to tapping the great pool of black and then Latin talent first, thus creating a greater all-around competitiveness. Then, in '58, the AL began to catch up, with no one over .600 that year, and only one team below, and in '59 going the other way. In the National League, *not a single team finished above .600 or below .400 for 1958 and 1959.* Had the AL sped up the process of integration, near-complete parity and, quite possibly, the downfall of the Yankees, would have been achieved by 1960.

In any event, it wasn't long in coming. In 1961, when the AL expanded by two teams and the next season, when the NL increased by two, we start to see some blips on the screen, but only for a while. We see the same number of overs-unders as before, six, but among more teams, so the percentage of very good and very bad teams was actually shrinking. Then, in 1963, rules were changed to favor pitching, and, as the number of runs scored dropped, the number of great and small teams almost disappeared. In 1968, with Bob Gibson posting a fabulous ERA of 1.12 and Don Drysdale pitching a then-record 56⅔ consecutive scoreless innings and Denny McLain winning 31 games, just one team, the Detroit Tigers with a mark of .636, kept baseball from a season with no +.600 and −.400 teams.

- 1969 brought expansion to twenty-four teams, and with it a slip blip on the screen of two teams above and four below but that was still just twenty-five percent of the teams. The first real irruption in years comes in 1978, caused partly by expansion but mostly by free agency. The Rich, we were warned, would buy up all the best players, creating a major league above and minor league below, and for a moment it looked as if that would happen: eleven teams, six above and five below, give baseball its biggest total of high-lows in years—though with twenty-six teams, the percentage is only slightly higher than when there were six teams finishing above and below in a sixteen-team league. In any event, it didn't last long: by the following season, owners have learned to handle free agency, and the number of above-belows dropped to two-two.

- In the 1980s and then the '90s, the major leagues inched toward total competitive balance. In 1980, the Philadelphia Philles finally won a World Series; there were two teams above .600 or below .400 that season (the Phillies, by the way, were not one of the .600 teams). In 1993, the year before the strike, there were no teams above .600 and only three below .400, and that's out of twenty-eight teams. The next year, before action was halted, there were only two teams of twenty-eight above .600 and none below .400. And by 1998, with an all-time high of thirty teams, there are only two aboves and one below. (That the Yankees could have achieved a percentage of .704 at a time when competition was so relatively even marks them as the greatest team in baseball history.) And then, finally, there were none.

When I wrote a short piece to this effect in April 2001, I received a call first from Richard Levin, former president of Yale and member of the commissioner's blue ribbon panel. Then, three days later, I got a call from Bud Selig himself. Both took respectful issue with my conclusion that baseball was reaching a new era of competitiveness, reminding me that the biggest-market team, the Yankees, had just won their third World Series in a row. I reminded them, in turn, that nine teams, nearly a third of baseball, finished the 2000 season with better records than the Yankees and that two small-market teams, Oakland and Seattle, had come within a wisp of keeping the Yankees out of the Series. But debating large and small markets and the necessity of revenue sharing is really not my point. The point is that no matter what it costs to compete in today's game, the difference between the best and worst in baseball has never been closer. What has happened is that if the best team in baseball played the worst team ten times, the worst you could expect is that the best team would win ten games. I have yet to hear a single argument that has indicated to me why this is bad for baseball.

14

On-Base Averages

"Baseball," as my sometime *Journal* colleague Alan Schwarz once wrote, "is often referred to as the only major sport without a clock, the only game whose results unfold without the cuticle-fraying countdown of time. This makes for good poetry, but it isn't quite true. Baseball has a clock. It simply doesn't measure its time in minutes and seconds. Its unit is outs." He might have added that the team that keeps those outs ticking away the slowest has the best chance to win. This makes on-base average—or on-base percentage, if you will—baseball's most underappreciated statistic and one of its most important hitting stats.

OBP or OBA, as I prefer it, the rate at which a player gets on base via a hit, walk, or hit-by-pitch, was largely the discovery of Branch Rickey, who did as much for the popularization of usable baseball statistics as any man in baseball history. More than half a century later, though, it has yet to catch on with the average fan. But though it doesn't have the flash of slugging percentage or the cozy familiarity of batting average, it is a quieter and more trustworthy method of measuring run-scoring potential. Those of you who spend a lot of time poring over baseball stats may find this chapter unnecessary—"Doesn't everyone already know this?" you might ask. The answer is: when was the last time you heard a TV announcer mention it? Or heard on-base average brought up in a discussion of MVP candidates? More to the point, how many times do you hear OBA mentioned compared to batting average?

All baseball people *ought* to know about on-base average but surprisingly few actually do. Former Baltimore Orioles manager Earl Weaver knew it: his classic formula for winning was "pitching, fundamentals, and 3-run homers." Like all managers and coaches, he stressed defense first, but when it came to naming his favorite offense he didn't say homers, he said 3-run homers. Got to have two men on base for a 3-run homer.

There are baseball men who are still learning about on-base average. Texas Rangers General Manager Doug Melvin says, "It's something we don't look at enough. You can't win the game without moving the pieces on the board. It's all about capturing bases." Not about stealing bases; it's surprisingly easy to find guys at the major league level who can steal bases. The hard part is finding hitters at the major league level who can consistently *reach* base. Fans, writers, and a surprising number of managers are enamored of fleet-footed leadoff hitters who can steal 30 to 50 bases a year but who accumulate even fewer walks than stolen bases. Simple baseball math (and common sense) tells them that they'd score more runs with a slower hitter with less power who knows how to work pitchers for 90 to 100 walks a season.

Of course, you get a guy who can work pitchers for the walks and also has either speed or power and you've got Hall of Fame timber. OBA is the answer to many of baseball's most intriguing questions; in fact, it's the answer to many of the questions that readers ask me about baseball. For instance, "Why do the Yankees score so many runs when they don't even lead the league in home runs?" The answer is that the patient Yankee hitters have, from 1995 through the 1999 season, the highest on-base average in baseball. (Do you also need to know that the Yankees have the major's best won-lost percentage over that period?) Remember Weaver and the 3-run homer? Observe how many times the Yankees, when they do pop one, get at least 2 or 3 runs for the effort.

A year or so ago in *The Wall Street Journal*, after Joe DiMaggio's death, I asked the question "Who is the Greatest Living Ballplayer?" Some readers scoffed at my suggestion that it might be third-baseman Mike Schmidt. "I remember," one reader sniffed, "a time when a hitter with a lifetime average of .267 couldn't get a starting job." Well, the .267-hitting Mike Schmidt reached base more frequently than Hall of Fame third-base great Pie Traynor, by an OBA of .384 to .362, even though Traynor's lifetime batting average is 53 *points higher than Schmidt's*. Forget for a moment that Schmidt has nine times as many home runs as Traynor; based on OBA, which hitter would you want in your lineup?

OBA is the answer to the question of why Joe Morgan is in the discussion of baseball's greatest living player—and excluded baseball's all-time hits leader, Pete Rose, whose lifetime batting average is 32 points higher than Morgan's. The answer is that in addition to having more power and speed than Rose, Morgan also had a higher OBA, .395 to .377. OBA also is the answer to the question of how we can say Mickey Mantle was a more effective hitter than Willie Mays, even though Mays had a slightly higher batting average (.302 to .298) and identical slugging percentage, .557. Mantle's career OBA was 36 points higher (.423 to .387) than Mays's. Simply put, Mantle used up far fewer puts to accumulate a greater number of bases.

OBA also answers the question of how, home runs aside, I can still call Mark McGwire a better hitter than Tony Gwynn. McGwire's OBA is actually 10 points higher (.402 to .392) than Gwynn's.

Speaking of Tony Gwynn, he's the only modern player who cracks the top fifteen in career batting average, the statistic that is always cited by purists when making comparisons between current stars and old-timers. But what if on-base average had been used from the start as a method for rating hitters? How would the top twenty-five batters list look then? Let's take a look:

THE TOP 20 IN ON-BASE AVERAGE, 1900–2000
(FROM *TOTAL BASEBALL*, 7TH ED)

Player	OBA	BA	Player	OBA	BA
1. Ted Williams	.483	.344	15. Jeff Bagwell	.422	.305
2. Babe Ruth	.474	.342	16. Wade Boggs	.419	.328
3. Lou Gehrig	.447	.340	17. Mickey Cochrane	.419	.320
4. Frank Thomas	.446	.321	18. Stan Musial	.418	.331
5. Rogers Hornsby	.434	.358	19. Barry Bonds	.415	.289
6. Ty Cobb	.433	.366	20. Mel Ott	.414	.304
7. Edgar Martinez	.429	.320	21. Roy Thomas	.413	.333
8. Jimmie Foxx	.428	.325	22. Jim Thome	.413	.284
9. Tris Speaker	.428	.345	23. Hank Greenberg	.412	.313
10. Ferris Fain	.425	.290	24. Harry Heilmann	.410	.342
11. Eddie Collins	.424	.333	25. Charlie Keller	.410	.286
12. Max Bishop	.423	.271	26. Jackie Robinson	.410	.311
13. Joe Jackson	.423	.356	27. Eddie Stanky	.410	.268
14. Mickey Mantle	.423	.298			

I've left out all the players who are in *Total Baseball* that played primarily in the nineteenth century. (Roy Thomas played only one season in the previous century). Old-timers still dominate—there's no way batting averages are ever going to be as high as they were from 1915 to the mid-1930s—but the moderns make a respectable show with five players in the top twenty and seven in the top twenty-five, all of them beginning their careers *after* 1980. And who thought Edgar Martinez was that good?

15

Baseball's Greatest SLOBs

In 1972, I was a student at the University of Alabama in Birmingham and editing the school paper, the *Kaleidoscope*. This meant I could choose anyone I liked for sports columnist, so I chose myself. Even in Alabama, when Paul "Bear" Bryant and the Alabama football team ruled the headlines, you quickly found that you got most of your responses from writing about baseball. The reason was simple: opinion on who the best players in other sports were just opinion, but arguments in baseball invariably settled around statistics and everyone—students, administration, faculty—knew what the best statistics were and didn't hesitate to fuel debates by citing stats.

One of the faculty actually did know. His name was George Ignatin, and he was an economics professor at UAB. He began sending me letters correcting my errors in thinking that Bob Gibson was a better pitcher than Juan Marichal, or that Pete Rose produced more runs than Willie McCovey, or that Reggie

Jackson was a better hitter than Mike Schmidt to send up when you were a run behind in the ninth. We started writing articles together for the school paper, moved on to a local sports weekly, and finally, a column, "By the Numbers," in *The Village Voice*, features in *Inside Sports*, two books (*Football by the Numbers* for Prentice Hall), and several columns for *The Wall Street Journal*.

George had a wonderful ability to keep his eye on the ball. He always started with the winning teams and looked for the numbers that best correlated with them. In baseball, for instance, we would spend hours at the UAB library pouring over newspaper and baseball record books. Every time I thought I had something, he'd say, "Interesting. How does it correlate with winning?" This kind of singlemindedness eventually produced results, and we soon found the hitting statistics that best correlated with scoring runs: on-base average and slugging average.

This was before the Internet, so what we didn't know was that many others had also figured this out. Not that the idea of the value of on-base average was all that new; for nearly twenty years, Branch Rickey had been telling people that on-base average should replace batting average. What was new for us was the idea that perhaps on-base and slugging could be combined into a single ultimate hitting stat. This was years before Bill James began to publish his *Baseball Abstract*, and John Thorn and Pete Palmer *The Hidden Game of Baseball*, so a lot of fans and researchers were out of the growing loop: we didn't know others had been ranking hitters by doing just that. Just add on-base average (OBA) and slugging percentage, and the hitter with the highest number is probably the best. We liked OBA + SLG, but George took it one step further: he found that *multiplying* the two correlated amazingly with actual team scoring. George liked user-friendly stats, and for that it always helped to have a catchy nickname. Slugging average times on-base average became "SLOB"—a name for a statistic that is not quickly forgotten.

Batter run average may not be so catchy, but Dick Cramer may have got there first. In 1972, Cramer, a Philadelphia area research scientist, developed BRA. This is the formula:

(hits + walks + hit by pitch) divided by (at-bats + walks + hit by pitch) multiplied by (totals bases divided by at-bats)

In other words, on-base average (or percentage, as some have it) multiplied by slugging percentage. Cramer found that BRA correlated with actual team scoring better than any other statistic, and that the team that led the league in SLOB—oops, BRA—was bound to lead the league in scoring. And the resulting statistic is gloriously easy to understand: Babe Ruth's career BRA, or SLOB, of 32.70 means that he contributed a fraction under a third of a run for every time at bat, or, if you prefer, 32 runs for every 100 at-bats.

Which makes it the ultimate hitting statistic, right? Of course not. Even assuming that an "ultimate" statistic is possible (and one should always be wary of anything marked "ultimate"), there are always ways to fine-tune it and make it better. It might be more accurate to call it the best *simple* statistic, the best simple yardstick for offensive effectiveness that there is. (In 1984, it received more validation when John Thorn and Pete Palmer did their landmark study of baseball statistics, *The Hidden Game of Baseball*. They ranked BRA as the most accurate "simple" statistic for measuring offensive effectiveness.)

One thing BRA can't do, or hasn't been able to find a way to do it, is to figure out what to do about stolen bases; but then, most baseball analysts agree that stolen bases have little to do with scoring. What BRA *does* do is offer an easy-to-apply yard-stick for measuring all kinds of hitters from high-average singles hitters to big-whiffs, big power men. Two stats, one that measures a hitter's ability to reach base, the other that measures the run-scoring potential of a batter's hits. Why multiply? Well, as George used to tell me, "the effect of one upon the other is multiplistic," and though I've never found the word in a dictionary, I think I understood what he meant. One increases the value of the other beyond what a simple addition of accumulated bases might imply. A single, which gives a batter a perfect 1.000 on-base average, has more run-scoring potential than a walk, which also gives a batter a perfect 1.000 on-base average. So, the value of the hit is more than just the base it accumulates for the batter.

From here on in I'm going to refer to on-base average times slugging average as George did: SLOB, as homage to George (who, for all I knew, did come up with the stat first). I've referred to it several times in the course of this book, but first I thought we'd stop and see how baseball history would look if we applied it to the best hitters of the previous hundred years. Let's look at a list of the all-time leaders in batting, on-base, slugging, and then SLOB, for this past century (through the 2000 season).

I've left off players on the *Total Baseball* Top 100 Batting Average list who played most of their games before 1900; for those such as Honus Wagner and Nap Lajoie, who played a fraction of their games before 1900, I let their numbers stand.

BA		OBA	
1. Ty Cobb	.367	1. Ted Williams	.483
2. Rogers Hornsby	.358	2. Babe Ruth	.474
3. Joe Jackson	.356	3. Lou Gehrig	.447

BA		OBA	
4. Tris Speaker	.345	4. Frank Thomas	.446
5. Ted Williams	.344	5. Rogers Hornsby	.434
6. Babe Ruth	.342	6. Ty Cobb	.433
7. Harry Heilmann	.342	7. Edgar Martinez	.429
8. Bill Terry	.341	8. Jimmie Foxx	.428
9. George Sisler	.340	9. Tris Speaker	.428
10. Lou Gehrig	.340	10. Ferris Fain	.425
11. Tony Gwynn	.338	11. Eddie Collins	.424
12. Nap Lajoie	.338	12. Max Bishop	.423
13. Riggs Stephenson	.336	13. Joe Jackson	.423
14. Al Simmons	.334	14. Mickey Mantle	.423
15. Paul Waner	.333	15. Jeff Bagwell	.422
16. Eddie Collins	.333	16. Wade Boggs	.419
17. Mike Donlin	.333	17. Mickey Cochrane	.419
18. Stan Musial	.331	18. Stan Musial	.418
19. Heine Manush	.330	19. Barry Bonds	.415
20. Mike Piazza	.328	20. Mel Ott	.414
21. Wade Boggs	.328	21. Roy Thomas	.413
22. Rod Carew	.328	22. Jim Thome	.413
23. Honus Wagner	.328	23. Hank Greenberg	.412
24. Bob Fothergill	.325	24. Harry Heilmann	.410
25. Jimmie Foxx	.325	25. Charlie Keller	.410
26. Earle Combs	.325	26. Jackie Robinson	.410
27. Joe DiMaggio	.325	27. Eddie Stanky	.410

SLG A		SLOB	
1. Babe Ruth	.690	1. Babe Ruth	32.70
2. Ted Williams	.634	2. Ted Williams	30.64
3. Lou Gehrig	.632	3. Lou Gehrig	28.25
4. Jimmie Foxx	.609	4. Jimmie Foxx	26.06
5. Hank Greenberg	.605	5. Frank Thomas	25.82

	SLG A			SLOB
6. Mark McGwire	.593		6. Rogers Hornsby	25.04
7. Mike Piazza	.580		7. Hank Greenberg	24.92
8. Joe DiMaggio	.579		8. Mark McGwire	23.83
9. Frank Thomas	.579		9. Mickey Mantle	23.56
10. Rogers Hornsby	.577		10. Barry Bonds	23.53
11. Ken Griffey Jr.	.568		11. Stan Musial	23.36
12. Barry Bonds	.567		12. Jeff Bagwell	23.29
13. Juan Gonzalez	.566		13. Joe DiMaggio	23.04
14. Albert Belle	.564		14. Mike Piazza	22.91
15. Larry Walker	.563		15. Edgar Martinez	22.69
16. Johnny Mize	.562		16. Jim Thome	22.50
17. Stan Musial	.559		17. Johnny Mize	22.31
18. Willie Mays	.557		18. Larry Walker	22.18
19. Mickey Mantle	.557		19. Ty Cobb	22.16
20. Hank Aaron	.555		20. Mel Ott	22.06
21. Jeff Bagwell	.552		21. Joe Jackson	21.86
22. Ralph Kiner	.548		22. Ken Griffey Jr.	21.81
23. Jim Thome	.545		23. Ralph Kiner	21.81
24. Hack Wilson	.545		24. Willie Mays	21.55
25. Chuck Klein	.543		25. Hack Wilson	21.52

(By the way, when I have two or more players with the same three-digit stat under the same numeral—for instance, Roy Thomas and Jim Thome are tied for twenty-first in on-base-average—or four players with the same stat listed singly—Bob Fothergill, Jimmie Foxx, Earle Combs, and Joe DiMaggio are twenty-fourth, twenty-fifth, twenty-sixth, and twenty-seventh in batting average—it's because that's the way the official major league record book lists it.)

The first list, batting average, lists only two contemporary players, Tony Gwynn (No. 11, at .338) and Mike Piazza (No. 20, at .328). The second list, on-base average, has five contemporary players, Frank Thomas (No. 5, at .446), Edgar Martinez (No. 7, at .429), Jeff Bagwell (No. 15, at .422), Barry Bonds (No. 19, .415), and Jim Thome (No. 21, .413), which indicates the increasing use of the walk as a offensive weapon in the modern game. In the third, slugging average, we have *ten* current players—well, you count 'em. SLOB has nine.

SLOB isn't perfect because the stats it's derived from aren't perfect. I don't really believe Mel Ott (No. 20) was a more productive hitter than Willie Mays (No. 24). I just think hitting was a great deal easier in Ott's day than in Mays's. I really don't think Larry Walker is more productive than Ty Cobb; Cobb didn't play in a slugger's era, and no ballpark in Cobb's time boosted hitters the way Walker's home park does today. (And I simply refuse to believe that baseball ever produced thirty-three hitters more productive than Mike Schmidt at 20.23.) SLOB can't make allowances for the era or for the manner in which some ballparks distort batting statistics, but for what it is, a quick, easy measure of a hitter's approximate value, it's as good as any stat around and better than most.

16

Why Can't They Go 9 Anymore?

Year	G	Comp. Games	ERA	BA	H PG	BB PG	SO PG	HR PG
1901	549	937	3.67	.277	19.2	5.06	4.98	0.41
1920	617	701	3.79	.284	19.2	6.17	5.92	0.59
1930	616	560	4.65	.288	20.0	6.45	6.63	1.09
1941	622	569	4.15	.267	18.4	7.62	7.14	1.18
1951	617	479	4.13	.263	17.9	7.92	7.44	1.35
1961	811	417	4.03	.256	17.3	7.27	10.27	1.89
1968	812	426	2.98	.231	15.2	6.01	11.87	1.35
1976	967	590	3.52	.256	17.3	6.33	9.45	1.16
1986	1134	355	4.18	.262	17.8	6.76	11.51	2.01
2000	1132	107	4.92	.276	19.1	7.51	12.37	2.37

Here are some American League seasons from 1901 to 2000 that help define the ways in which pitching has changed (I chose the AL because the designated hitter usually allows the AL to have a few more complete games than the NL: you don't have to put in a pinch-hitter if, say, the game is tied 2–2 in the eighth). In 1920, the hitting boom is on, led by Babe Ruth and his 54 home runs, but the overall average is little more than half a homer per game. By 1930 everything: the strike zone, the small ballparks, the lack of pitching sophistication, all favor the hitter and an ERA is posted that won't be bettered till the end of the century. By 1941, the year of Ted Williams and Joe DiMaggio, things have leveled off a bit, but home runs per game continue to climb and as a result, so do walks and strikeouts per game.

1951 looks very much like '41, but it's deceptive: night baseball has shaved several points off the average. Hits drop, but walks, strikeouts, and home runs continue to climb. The only sharp drop is in complete games. By 1961, pitching actually seems to making a comeback—so much for the theory that expansion watered things down—but strikeouts and home runs are up sharply. In 1968, the year Denny McLain wins 31 games in the AL and Bob Gibson posts an amazing 1.12 ERA, things are completely reversed from 1930: the ballparks, the strike zone, and the high mounds all tilt the edge to pitchers.

By 1976, thanks largely to strike zone changes, hitters are getting some of it back. By 1986, hitters are in control again, and home runs jump to 2 per game and complete games take a nose dive. By 2000, the pitchers are being beaten to a pulp: walks go up, strikeouts take a huge boost, and home runs are at an all-time high. But look carefully: batting averages and hits allowed are virtually the same. The difference is that a century later, batters are six times as likely to hit home runs and two and a half times more likely to strike out, as well as much more likely to walk. How's a pitcher supposed to go 9 innings when he's thrown all those extra pitches—not to mention a couple of home run balls—by the sixth or seventh inning?

"What's the matter with pitching today?" "Why can't these guys go 9 innings anymore?" "What ever happened to the 300-game winners? Why can't guys today win 20 games a year?" You can't have a discussion on baseball today without these questions being at the forefront, and you can't make a case for the superiority of today's players—as I am constantly doing—without being put on the defensive about the quality of today's pitching.

I get more mail on this topic than on all other baseball topics combined. I can't answer those questions in this chapter, but I think I can offer the beginnings of an explanation. Starting with the second question, "Why can't these guys go 9 innings anymore?" the answer favored by everyone from George Will to Ted Williams is that they can—its just that we coddle them too much today. As Will phrased it in a TV interview, "There is no rational reason why a pitcher of thirty-five years ago"—I assume he means Sandy Koufax, Juan Marichal, and Bob Gibson, starters who regularly finished 20 to 25 games—"could go 9 innings while a pitcher of today can't go more than 7." And Will is correct: there *is* no rational reason. As I intimated in the chapter on Lefty Grove and Roger Clemens, if today's most durable pitchers—again, let's name Roger Clemens, who leads current pitchers in complete games (116 before the start of the 2001 season) or Arizona's Curt Schilling (who has the highest percentage of completed starts—about 27 percent) were pitching in the time of Sandy Koufax in the mid-'60s or Lefty Grove in the early '30s or of Cy Young around the turn of the century, then they, too, would be completing 20 or 25 or 30 games, depending on the norm at the time.

Okay, I don't really know that, do I? I can't prove that scientifically. All I can do is state the premises of my argument and

appeal to what I believe is common sense. What has changed
from eighty years ago to now? Or, more to the point, what has
changed from just thirty-five years ago till now? Many things,
but as the chart indicates, modern pitchers have to throw far
more pitches to get to the ninth inning than they did in times
past. Pitching effectiveness changes radically from decade to
decade depending on the ballparks and the rules; in Koufax's
prime, for instance, the strike zone was much more generous
and the pitcher's mounds were generally higher, which gave
them a substantial advantage over hitters. I'm not saying that
Koufax's amazing record was in any way deceiving; if he was the
best in his era, it must be assumed that he would be a likely candidate for the title of "The Best" in any era. But the best in
another era wouldn't necessarily have 27 wins (because he
wouldn't get so many starts) and he wouldn't complete as many
games (because he would have reached his natural pitch count
by the seventh inning instead of the ninth). I'm not going to
jump into a detailed discussion of how the strike zone change
and the flatter mounds influenced things because, first, you can
see it in the simple jump in earned run averages from 1968 (2.98
in the American League, where Denny McLain won 31 games,
and 2.99 in the National, where Bob Gibson posted a micro-
scopic 1.12 ERA and Don Drysdale pitched a then-record of
56⅔ consecutive scoreless innings) through 1969 (up to 3.60 in
the NL and 3.60 in the AL) and 1970, when hitting crept back
into a dominant position (4.05 in the National and 3.72 in the
American).

After that, for the next two decades hitting and pitching bat-
tled for supremacy as batting and earned run averages fluctu-
ated according to new ballparks and the occasional rules
change, but one thing became apparent: the game is more and
more dominated by the home run and the fact that nearly every

batter in the lineup is capable of hitting one, and so, increasingly, pitching has become a game of walks and strikeouts, as pitchers try every means of working around the strike zone rather than challenging the hitter. Which means more pitches per inning.

Let's look at it this way: by the end of the twentieth century, hitters had virtually the same batting average and same number of hits per game they had at the start of it. The huge difference was in frequency of home runs, and, thus, in the number of walks and strikeouts per game. By last season, there were, on average, twice as many combined walks and strikeouts in a major league game as there were a hundred years earlier. And though I can't prove it, I would bet that the number of foul balls per game has quadrupled over the course of the last one hundred years as hitters evolved the art of flicking the bat out to protect the strike zone. After all, in a game with far fewer strikeouts, wouldn't there likely be far fewer 2-strike situations? So that's my argument as to why pitchers can't go 9 innings today, because they have reached the 120-odd pitch limit about 2 innings earlier than pitchers did years ago when they were completing games.

As to why they can't win 300 games in a career or 20 during a season, the reasons are more subtle. First, the obvious: with fewer pitchers going 9 innings, more and more decisions are picked up by relief pitchers. I think giving either wins or losses to relief pitchers is silly, since wins and losses tell us virtually nothing about relievers. If I told you than reliever No. 1 was 6–3 while reliever No. 2 was 3–6, would that information really give you the slightest clue as to which reliever was better? I think all decisions should go to starters and that the resulting number would be a much fairer assessment of a starter's effectiveness than the current won-lost records.

But that's another story. The point I'm getting at is that as the number of complete games goes down, the number of wins and losses in a pitcher's record goes down as well. That fact and the fewer starts a pitcher gets in the era of five-man rotations as opposed to the old four are going to keep a modern ace at about 18 victories per season and a career top of about 250 or 260 wins where he might have had 20 or 22 in decades past and topped 300 for a career.

But there's another more difficult-to-detect reason why starters don't get as many wins today: competition is tighter. As I've pointed out in another chapter, there was a definite tendency as the twentieth century went on for competition to get tighter and for the won-lost percentages of the winning teams to be less sensational. And so, essentially, you have teams that are closer in talent than in years past and starting pitchers with fewer opportunities to get wins. The combination of the two has probably made the 300-game winner a virtually extinct animal.

Finally, the big question of "What's wrong with pitching today?" can be answered: nothing is wrong with pitching today. Pitchers today don't give up hits with any greater frequency than they did a century ago. It's just that the hits go much farther today than they did a century ago, which is something the pitcher cannot control. When you look at Roger Clemens or Greg Maddux or Randy Johnson or Kevin Brown or especially Pedro Martinez, you should assume that you're looking at someone who, had he pitched in the time of Koufax, Grove, or Cy Young would have pitched at least as many innings and won at least as many games.

A final word. In May 2001 I wrote a couple of hundred words on this subject for *The Wall Street Journal*. A few days later I received a call from the office of George Will. I was flattered but a bit apprehensive and braced myself for a debate, but to my surprise Mr. Will had called to concede his argument about modern pitchers being "coddled." All I can say is now that I know that people are taking some of these arguments seriously, I promise to start thinking them through more carefully.

17

Ranking Don Shula

Where will Don Shula's reputation among NFL coaches finally settle? Is he, as a *USA Today* columnist phrased it after Shula's retirement, "second only to Vince Lombardi over the last forty years"? The answer to that question is decidedly "no." Lombardi won five championships, Shula won two. But before we can assess Shula's place in relation to his more recent contemporaries such as Tom Landry, Bill Walsh, Joe Gibbs, and Bill Parcells—and the fact that Shula's list of contemporaries goes from Vince Lombardi to these guys might be the real measure of Shula's achievement— I think we have to address the most obvious argument against Shula's greatness. I am referring to his record as a big game coach.

"Don Shula," wrote Ken Blanchard in his 1995 inspirational best-seller *Everyone's a Coach*, "doesn't believe in holding to a game plan that isn't working. . . . Shula is always asking 'What if?' so that when a change occurs neither he nor his players will be caught flatfooted."

Bubba Smith, for one, might take issue with that. In his 1983 autobiography, *Kill, Bubba, Kill,* Smith says he approached Shula, then the Baltimore Colts coach, during halftime of the 1969 Colts–New York Jets Super Bowl. " 'Let me line up over the center so I can change their blocking scheme,' " Smith wrote. "And he [Shula] said, 'Just play your position.' "

Which of those quotes does Shula's record reflect, Blanchard's or Bubba's? First, some facts. Don Shula's coaching career covered thirty-two years and eight Presidents—but Richard Nixon was the only President to telephone Shula with post-Super Bowl congratulations. Shula wound up 319–149–6 in the regular season—the winningest coach in the National Football League. How good does that indicate Shula was? Bill Walsh, thought by many, including myself, to be the best coach in recent history, was 92–59–1, for a winning percentage of .609. Shula's is .679.

Clearly, Shula was one of the greatest, but his career was also one of the strangest. Let's review.

In the 1964 championship game, Shula's 12–2 Colts were 9-point picks over the 10–3–1 Cleveland Browns. This is a huge point spread for a championship game in the '60s, but in this case it seemed to be justified; the Colts, after all, had Johnny Unitas at quarterback while the Browns were led by the relatively unknown Frank Ryan. In the game, though, the Colts lost the ball four times, and, in what would become a big-game Shula trademark, they sputtered in the first half, which was 0–0, and then shut down in the second half, 27–0 (the final score).

This was one of the biggest upsets in modern NFL history before the NFL-AFL merger; it may actually be the biggest. We don't really know how good the AFL teams were until they beat the NFL in the '69 and '70 Super Bowls. But in the National Football League of 1964, nearly everyone played everyone else, and by the time the Eastern and Western Conferences squared off in the championship game, there wasn't much doubt about who the best team was. And, to go by the evidence of the regular season when the Colts outscored their opponents 428–225 to the Browns' 415–293, the '64 Colts *were* better than the '64 Browns, and the Browns stuffed them in the title game.

In the 1969 Super Bowl . . . well, if you watch the Classic Sports Network, you know all about the '69 Super Bowl. Recall only that the Colts were favored by 17 to 20 points, that Shula's team lost the ball five times, and that the Colts failed to adjust in the second half. Bubba was right.

The memory of Shula's two great teams, the '72 and '73 Miami Dolphins, particularly the perfect record established by the latter, has obscured the fact that these were the only champions Shula ever coached. Also forgotten is that Shula took virtually the same Miami roster into the Super Bowl at the end of the '71 season and was thrashed 24–3 by the Dallas Cowboys. That game displayed a pattern we can recognize: the Dolphins suffered 3 turnovers, sputtered in the first half, and were shut out in the second.

The '64 and '68 Colts were big play teams while the '70s Dolphins were grind-it-out ball control teams (albeit, one with capacity for the big play in Bob Greise and wideout Paul Warfield). But the inability of Shula's teams to adjust in big games is characteristic, no matter what the team's style. The famed 1982 "Killer Bees" were a defense-oriented, ball-control team; in that year's Super Bowl, they were shut out in the second half by the *underdog*—again we see that word—Washington Redskins and lost, 27–17. In 1984 the Dolphins were radically reoriented around quarterback Dan Marino and had one of the most potent offenses ever; it was stopped cold in the second half of the Super Bowl and lost, 38–16, to Walsh's San Francisco '49ers. This was the fourth time in seven NFL championship games that a Don Shula team had been *shut out* in the second half.

Shula's teams were 2–5 in championships and were outscored in those seven games, 142–81. More significantly, they were outscored in the second half, 91–14. And in the five losses, Shula's teams have been shut out in four and outscored, 77–7.

Now, think about that for a moment. This wasn't Bud Grant with a Vikings team that really shouldn't have been in the championship games in the first place, or even Marv Levy's Buffalo Bills or Dan Reeves's Broncos, teams that might have won a Super Bowl or two with luck but deserved, on the basis of seasonal performance, to lose *all* their Super Bowls. These are teams that were either heavy favorites or judged to be extremely competitive, coached by the winningest regular season coach in NFL history.

If you would call Don Shula the greatest coach, or even *one* of the greatest coaches, in pro football history, you must ask yourself if your definition of a great coach is someone who knows how to coach well and make adjustments in the big games. And then ask yourself if you'd want Don Shula to coach the big game for you.

CHART

Shula's team vs.	Year	2nd half	Final
Balt vs. Cleve	1964*	0–27	0–27
Balt vs. NY Jets	1969	7–9	7–16
Mia vs. Dallas	1972	0–14	3–24
Mia vs. Wash	1973	0–7	14–7
Mia vs. Minn	1974	7–7	24–7
Mia vs. Wash	1983	0–17	17–27
Mia vs. SF	1985	0–10	16–38

*NFL championship

What is remarkable about Shula's championship game record is not just that it was poor—2–5—but how absolutely *uncompetitive* his teams were in tough games and in tough situations. The only two championships he won were the '73 and '74 Dolphins, and in the first he took a team that was 10–3–1 and coached them into a rout against a Dallas team at 11–3 that was just a half a game better during the season. The next year, coaching an unbeaten Miami team, he was unable to put enough distance between the Dolphins and Redskins that a blocked punt or kick return might have tied the game.

18

Pro Football's Greatest Quarterback

Is the "best" quarterback the one you want playing for *your* team in the big game? If it is, then the end-of-century polls have got it all wrong: the best quarterback in pro football history isn't Joe Montana or Johnny Unitas or Otto Graham or John Elway. The best, and he has the rings to prove it, is Bart Starr. If you regard the late '50s and '60s as pro football's Golden Era—and this is the time that produced the running back, Jim Brown, and the defensive player, Dick Butkus, who ranked highest in most end-of-the-century polls—then Bart Starr is the guy you should want under your center in the conference title game or the Super Bowl.

Unlike the generation that was to follow, sixties quarterbacks weren't automatons, mere "snap-takers" acting out the orders of sideline brain trusts. Quarterbacks were expected to help conceive and carry out game plans, and change them on the spot when necessary. And these things Bart Starr did better than any quarterback he played against and perhaps better than anyone ever. Starting with the last 4 games of the 1959 season through a handful of injury-riddled appearances in 1969, Starr posted a standard of clutch performances in big games that is unmatched in NFL history.

To appreciate Starr's greatness—and to fully appreciate why the Packers dominated the '60s—it's necessary to look beyond the popular measurements for quarterbacks. Early in 1974, while previewing the Miami Dolphins—Minnesota Vikings Super Bowl, pioneer football analyst Bud Goode revealed that yards per pass attempt—just plain yards gained passing divided by the number of attempts—was pro football's premier statistic, the one that correlated best with winning. Goode quipped that he wanted the inscription on his headstone to read "Here lies Bud Goode—He told the world about yards per attempt."

A quarter of a century later, the football world has yet to fully absorb Goode's wisdom but, in fact, great NFL coaches have always instinctively known it: over four decades, from Johnny Unitas's sudden-death victory over the New York Giants to last year's Super Bowl, only one team, Bill Parcells's 1996 New England Patriots, has played for the NFL championship while failing to average more yards per throw on offense than it gave up on defense. Over the last twenty years, the team that averaged the highest yards per throw in a game has won more than 80 percent of the time. And interception percentage, the ratio of interceptions per 100 passes, ranked just slightly behind yards per throw as an indicator of offensive strength. (Pass-completion percentage was relatively unimportant; 1-of-3 completed for 10 yards beats 2-of-3 for 9 yards every time.) Bart Starr dominated these passing stats in the 1960s. His career interception percentage is the lowest of any passer in the decade, and his yards-per-pass mark of 7.85 is better than that of a score of quarterbacks who are generally regarded as among the best in history, including Dan Marino (7.37), Joe Montana (7.52), Roger Staubach (7.67), Dan Fouts (7.68), Sonny Jurgensen (7.56), Fran Tarkenton (7.27), Y. A. Tittle (7.52), Terry Bradshaw (7.17), and Joe Namath (7.35) (Bud Goode included sacks in "pass attempts," but pass attempts is more of a team stat. Yards per *throw* can be attributed more to the individual passer's ability). In the NFL's passer rating system, yards per throw is simply one more statistic thrown into the mix. In any event, Starr was the leading passer in the league three times during the '60s ranked by the NFL's method.

In 1960, the Western Conference Green Bay Packers lost to the Eastern leader, the Philadelphia Eagles, in the NFL championship game, 17–13. It was to be the first and last big game Bart Starr ever lost.

In 1961 and again in 1962, the Packers faced the New York Giants in consecutive championship games. Both team's rosters were littered with All-Pros, many of them future Hall of Famers. The most prominent Giant, of course, was the balding veteran quarterback Y. A. Tittle, who was enjoying the first two years of an amazing three-season run in which he would throw 86 touchdown passes in 41 games. No one thought the difference between the two teams would come down to the difference in the performance of Tittle and Starr, who threw far less often than Tittle. But in frozen Green Bay on New Year's Eve in 1961 and then the following year on December 30, in an even more frozen Yankee Stadium, Starr was 19 of 38 for 249 yards, nearly 6.5 yards per pass while Tittle was able to complete just 24 of 61 passes for 262 yards, just a little over 5 yards a throw. In the 2 games, Tittle failed to throw a touchdown pass in either game and was picked off 5 times; Starr had 3 touchdown passes with no interceptions. The Packers won both games by a combined score of 53–7.

The totals don't seem impressive by today's standards, but

championship games in Starr's era weren't played under domes or in palm tree country. It's difficult for today's fans to appreciate the hardship quarterbacks faced trying to put together an offensive attack on sheets of ice or frozen slush. Many of Starr's great performances came under conditions so horrendous that other fine passers were completely nullified. For instance, in the NFL championship game on January 2, 1966, on a Green Bay field covered with snow and mud, Cleveland quarterback Frank Ryan, who had riddled the Baltimore Colts with 3 touchdown passes in the previous year's championship game, was limited to just 115 yards on 18 throws, 2 of them interceptions. Starr also threw 18 times but gained 147 yards, with just 1 interception as the Packers won easily, 23–12. Two years later, in the most famous pro football game of the decade, Don Meredith was completely ineffective in Green Bay's subzero temperature, gaining just 59 yards on 25 passes. Starr threw 24 times for 191 yards as the Packers won their third straight title and fifth in seven years.

The totals for those four championship games are startling: Tittle (twice), Ryan, and Meredith, were a combined 42 for 104 and 436 yards, just 4.2 yards a throw, with just 1 touchdown and 8 interceptions. Starr was 43 of 80 for 587 yards, 7.3 a toss, with 6 touchdowns and only 1 interception. The 7.3 yards per pass average is good for most passers at most times; the TD-to-interception ratio is remarkable under *any* conditions.

Of course, Starr didn't need bad weather in order to shine. In his five other postseason appearances, he was 87 for 134—a remarkable 64.7 per cent for 1,174 yards—that's for an even more remarkable 8.76 yards per throw—and 9 TDs against just 3 interceptions. That's an astonishing virtuoso display of clutch passing. In 9 postseason games against the best defenses in the National Football League—and at the cap of the 1966 and '67 seasons, the American Football League—*Starr bettered his career averages in yards per throw and interception rate.* The question, then, is why Bart's star isn't higher on the list of all those fans and writers who voted in these All-Century polls? Because under Vince Lombardi's system, passers didn't rack up big totals in yardage and scoring passes. The Packers' philosophy was to strike early with the pass, then mix in runs, more as the game went on, to keep the clock moving. In other words, and contrary to popular belief, the Lombardi Packers didn't so much win because of their rushing yards as they accumulated rushing yards because they won.

Starr finished his career throwing nearly 2,000 fewer passes than his great rival, Johnny Unitas, and thus gaining just 24,718 yards to Unitas's 40,234 (their career yards-per-pass average was identical, 7.8). Yet, a glance at the Packers' strategy in big games shows how much they depended on Starr's passing. From 1965 through 1967, Starr and the Packers won 6 consecutive postseason games en route to three championships, and in 5 of those the first Green Bay touchdown came on a pass from Starr. Green Bay's image as a running team, exemplified by the title of Lombardi's book with W. C. Heinz, *Run to Daylight*, was so strong that it outlined reality. In both 1961 and 1962, the Packers, paced by fullback Jim Taylor and halfback Paul Hornung, led the league in both rushing yards and yards per carry, and Starr's gaudy passing stats—he had 28 touchdown passes in two seasons against just 8 interceptions—were widely regarded as the side product of that rushing dominance. And yet, by the mid '60s, the Packers running game had faded badly—in '65, Green Bay was eleventh among fourteen teams in yards per rush, and in '66, they were next to last—and *Starr's passing statistics got better*. In 1966, his best season, he threw for 14 touchdowns against just 3 interceptions and averaged an amazing 9 yards per throw.

Clearing the Bases

The quarterback whom Starr was most often compared to is Unitas, which is understandable. From 1958 to 1968, eleven seasons, either the Green Bay Packers or Baltimore Colts went to the NFL championship game in every season but one, 1963. (That year the Giants played the Chicago Bears, who beat out the Packers for the Western conference title by half a game, 11–1–2 to 11–2–1. Starr missed the second Packers-Bears game with an injury.) In five of the nine years that both men threw enough passes to qualify, Starr was ranked higher than Unitas by the NFL's system, and in five of those nine seasons, Starr had a higher yards-per-pass average than Unitas. There is a tendency among football writers and historians to write off Starr's domination of Unitas as evidence of the Packers' superiority, but, in fact from 1960 to 1969, Starr's last season as a starter, the Packers were 96–37–5 to the Colts' 92–42–4— exactly the edge the Packers held over the Colts in head-to-head competition.

Even when Johnny Unitas and the Colts were good, Bart Starr and the packers were better. In 1967, Unitas was the NFL's Player of the Year, and the 11–0–2 Colts played the 10–1–2 Los Angeles Rams for their division's playoff spot; the Rams, with their great defensive line, "The Fearsome Foursome," crushed Unitas and the Colts, 34–10. Shortly afterward, in the first round of the playoffs, Starr quarterbacked a masterpiece, completing 17 of 23 passes for 222 yards as the Packers trounced those same Rams, 28–7, going from there to beat Dallas and then Oakland in the Super Bowl. Bart Starr won on the field, but Unitas has now won the polls. No matter—all the polls in the world can't take those rings away.

BART STARR AND JOHNNY UNITAS IN THE POSTSEASON

	Comp	Pass	Pct	Yds	Yds/Pass	TD-INT	Int Pct
Unitas	103	196	52.6	1541	7.8	5–10	5.1
Starr	130	214	60.7	1751	8.2	15–4	1.9

In addition to dominating Johnny Unitas in head-to-head competition, Bart Starr was by far the greater postseason passer, bettering Unitas in virtually every relevant statistic. Moreover, Starr's edge over Unitas after 1959 is even more eye-opening. Following Unitas's victory over the New York Giants in the '59 title game, his postseason passing numbers were a dismal 65 of 127—51 percent—for 915 yards (7.2 per throw) with 3 TDs and 9 interceptions. In fact, though the Colts won nearly as many games as the Packers in the '60s, Unitas was able to lead his team to just one championship game, after the 1964 season against the Cleveland Browns, and was shut out, 27–0.

19

The Great Forgotten
Running Back of the NFL

A few years ago, a well-respected sports magazine printed a feature in which various writers compared NFL teams from different eras. One of them, in a position-by-position breakdown comparing the 1971–'72–'73 Dolphins with the 1960–'61–'62 Packers, commented: "Of course, [Larry] Csonka was better than [Jim] Taylor or any other fullback the Packers ever had." I've waited a long time to say this, and now I'd like to reply. Sez who?

I don't want to get into any debates right now about teams from different eras, and the ten years separating those Packers from those Dolphins does constitute an era in terms of how radically different playing styles were—but no matter how you want to look at it, there has never been a back in football history so good that he can easily dismiss comparison with Jim Taylor.

Jim Taylor has been curiously forgotten by a new generation of football fans and writers. Almost all the other great stars of

that time—Unitas, Starr, Jim Brown, Y. A. Tittle, Paul Hor-
nung, Sam Huff, Rosey Grier, Alex Karras, Raymond Berry, Ray
Nitschke, Bobby Mitchell, Lance Alworth, Frank Gifford, Gino
Marchetti, Lenny Moore, Forrest Gregg, Willie Davis, Herb
Adderly, Sonny Jurgenson, and perhaps half a dozen others—
are still in the public eye to some degree, or at least the subject
of occasional sports-special flashbacks. Most of the above,
including most of his Packer teammates, were inducted into the
Pro Football Hall of Fame within six to nine years of retiring:
Taylor had to wait ten.

Despite the flood of great tailbacks that began pouring into
the NFL right around the time he retired, Taylor was still number eight on the all-time rushing chart going into the '86 season.
For what such comparisons are worth, he played only ten seasons to Csonka's eleven. He is, and always will be, slightly ahead
of Csonka in yards gained, yards per carry, and touchdowns. He
was a tremendous big-game player, starring in Green Bay's consecutive title game victories over the New York Giants in the '61
and '62 games, and outrushing Jim Brown, 96 to 50, in the 1965
championship game, played in the mud and slush of Green Bay.
It's true that Taylor had outstanding support: four of the offensive linemen who played in front of him—center Jim Ringo,
guards Jerry Kramer and Fuzzy Thurston, and tackle Forrest
Gregg—were perennial All-Pros. But most of the great runners
have had good blockers in front of them; even O. J. Simpson,
starring for an otherwise mediocre Buffalo team, had the Elec-
tric Company ("They Turn on the Juice"—remember the ban-
ners on "Monday Night Football"?) opening his holes. Taylor
also had the advantage of playing with a Hall of Fame halfback,
Paul Hornung, and quarterback, Bart Starr. But Hornung didn't
make the Hall until this year, and the irony of Taylor's selection
coming after Starr's is that for several years, Taylor was a Pro

Bowler and Starr wasn't, and the usual reason offered as an explanation was that, well, who couldn't be a great quarterback handing off to backs like Taylor and Hornung?

No matter how much Taylor's stats owe to his teammates' talents, there is no doubt that from 1960–64 they were awesome. In three of those five seasons, his yards per carry was higher than Jim Brown's. In all of these seasons he gained over 1,000 yards, the first man ever to do so for five straight seasons. This in a time when the NFL season was only fourteen games. In 1960, 1961, and 1962, when the Packers won three straight Western Conference titles (there were only two conferences then, East and West), Taylor averaged 5.2 yards a try and scored 45 touchdowns in 38 regular-season games. Over the course of the '61 and '62 championship seasons, at the height of Jim Brown's career, Taylor was the two-year rushing leader of the NFL, a workhorse who averaged almost 100 yards a game and 5.4 yards a carry. No running back in modern NFL history—not Brown, not Tony Dorsett, not Franco Harris, not John Riggins, not Walter Payton—ever had better seasonal stats for a championship team. To whatever degree his numbers largely reflected his own skill, the dominance of the Packer line, or the versatility of his teammates, there can be absolutely no doubt that the power of the early Lombardi Packers, offensively at least, was reflected in Jim Taylor's stats.

I'm not sure just when Taylor's rep started to decline, but I do know he was never very popular with the people in and out of football. He was very, very conscious of his rivalry with Jim Brown—or, rather, he made each Green Bay–Cleveland game (as I recall, they played four times during the regular and post-season between 1961 and 1965) into a personal rivalry, and since Taylor was a white Southerner, there always reporters willing to take his offhand remarks the wrong way. Or, perhaps some of them knew him after all and took them the right way. If Brown ever took any public notice of Taylor, I'm not aware of it.

Whatever, I'm sure that some of his teammates resented his obsession with his own stats. His most famous blocker, Jerry Kramer, went out of his way to malign Taylor in his last book, which, because it was reprinted in part in *Playboy*, went a long way toward trashing what was left of Taylor's memory. You can get away with that kind of obsessive stat-gathering in baseball, where reporters choose to see their own boyish dreams reflected in Pete Rose's selfishness, but in football, where five guys who don't get their turn at-bat are getting their brains knocked in, it's not so charming.

But Jim Taylor probably wasn't even as nice a guy as Pete Rose. If you had to pick someone from baseball to compare him to, it would probably by Ty Cobb. Watching him carry the ball 25 times a game was one of the genuinely thrilling, guilty pleasures in sports. He kicked, bit, gouged, squirmed, elbowed, cursed (well, you knew he was cursing), and spat before and after the whistle; he never hesitated to take cheap shots at men 60 or 70 pounds bigger than himself. I swear there were times when it looked like he had a clear path to run and would swerve yards out of this way just to hit someone one-to-one, in the open field. He ran, someone said, like a Sidewinder missile. He didn't seem to be looking for holes; he seemed to be on a seek-and-destroy mission looking for targets.

No ball carrier—no player—that I have ever watched seemed to take such sheer, unadulterated joy in the physical contact of the game. (I heard that after he left the NFL, he still played regularly in semi-pro just because he enjoyed the hitting so much.) My most vivid memories of him are the 1961 Packers-Browns game in which he carried—I'm relying on memory now, as I've no way to check them—31 times for 156 yards and 4 TDs while Jim Brown was held to about 72. Taylor was positively gleeful, smashing, sliding, driving his stumpy body (he was about 5' 11" and 212, small for a running back in the NFL and very small for a fullback, looking like a Rocky Marciano who spent an hour a day in the weight room) through and over fallen Cleveland defenders. I remember reading that he had to be revived several times with smelling salts; he was hitting people so hard, the reporter said, he was almost knocking himself out.

I also remember his famous clash with Sam Huff on the frozen turf of Yankee Stadium in the 1962 championship game with the Giants. Huff wasn't exactly a pacifist either, and I hated the Giants back then, but it was obvious to me that whatever his role was in escalating the conflict, it was clearly Taylor's intention to have it out that day. The ultimate Jim Taylor photographs are from that game and show him seated on the sidelines with a hood practically covering his crew cut, his face spattered with blood and mud, spitting blood, gazing toward the field with a crazy, crooked half smile, just itching to get back into that game. Thirty years later I saw another face like it when Vernon Wells's Wez, the most brutish of the Mohawk-coiffed bikers confronted by Mel Gibson's Mad Max in *The Road Warrior*, squirms in ecstasy while pulling out a crossbow bolt that had been shot through his bicep.

Football is one of the most brutal sports in the world, almost certainly the most brutal team sport. If there is some way of measuring it, I'm sure it would prove more brutal than boxing, whose serious injuries are due in large part to lack of any kind of regulation or authority to protect fighters. Public moralists have recently grown fond of saying that boxing is the only sport where there is intent to cause physical harm to the opponent. Bullshit. The job of most players on a football field is to do just that, and quite often to do it to someone who is engaged in an activity like passing or catching or kicking a football and are thus in no position to defend themselves—which makes football a hell of a lot less fair than boxing, where, in theory at least, the first rule is always to protect yourself. The flag that's thrown two or three times a game for unnecessary roughness is a reminder that what happens on the field the other 120 or so times a game is supposed to be necessary roughness. Yet, when a young boxer is hurt or killed, we're subjected to a spate of editorials urging the abolition of boxing, whereas something similar in football is made to look like the spectacle I saw in Birmingham several years ago: a former player for TCU, paralyzed from the waist down from an injury incurred against Alabama, praised the game for all it had taught him about "character" and said that if given the choice, he'd do it all over again. His audience wept and applauded.

The key here, I think, is that unlike the boxer, the football player was felt to have made a sacrifice for his team, his school, and I have no doubt he really felt that he had done that. But whatever one's feelings on the subjects of boxing and football, it's easy to forget that the color and pageantry, the emphasis on teamwork and the sophistication of preparation, can easily obscure the primal nature of the game, the fact that no matter what else attracts us to it—and there is obviously much else to attract us to it or we'd all be watching the roller derby instead—the basis of the game's appeal is still men who must smash into other men hard enough to kill most ordinary men and then not feel so bad about it that they can't get right up and do it again.

Watching men like Jim Taylor play football made you remember this, made you realize things about yourself you didn't want to admit to or wanted to forget you had in you—or knew you had and were ashamed of. For ten years, even after the '63 season, when a bout with hepatitis left him weakened and probably took between 1,200 and 2,000 yards off his lifetime total, Jim Taylor was one of the most unrelenting forces pro football ever saw, the most reliable short-yardage ball carrier of his time, a superb short-pass receiver and a savage blocker who probably ended more than one career prematurely with a twisted kneecap. (That's where he undoubtedly did have it over Brown; Brown couldn't, or wouldn't block. There was nothing Taylor would have rather done than block, except, of course, carry the ball.) You can ignore a lot of the violence that happens in football because the action of the play often moves away from it. But you couldn't ignore the violence of players like Jim Taylor, because they carry it with them. He deserves to be remembered today as a reminder of the best and worst that the game of football brings out in men. He was one of the ten best backs—maybe one of the best five or six—ever to play the game.

Running backs have a short life span, shorter than most football players at other positions (and football players have the shortest life span, on and off the field, of any pro athletes). Jim Taylor's was shorter than most. Though he seemed indestructible at his peak, hepatitis took him during what looked like his peak season, 1963, and reduced him to merely good. (He averaged just 4.1 yards a carry after 5.4 for the previous two seasons.) He rebounded a bit in 1964 (gaining 5.0) but was never the same again, and played just three more seasons.

I decided to add up his four best seasons along with those of several other great running backs from the last half century and found some surprises. For one thing, though I hadn't realized it,

Clearing the Bases

Jim Brown and Jim Taylor were really the first great "work-horse" running backs of the NFL. I was going to include Marion Motley, the great running back from the Cleveland Browns and one of the first black players in pro football, but to my surprise I found he played just four seasons (1946–49) and gained just 3,024 yards. I also meant to include the famed fullback from the '50s Colts, Alan "the Horse" Ameche, and found he had played just six seasons and gained just 4,045 yards in his entire career.

Of course, to say "just" 3,024 yards or 4,045 yards is grossly unfair. That was the way the game was played back then. Why didn't the best runner get the ball more often? My guess is that it was a hangover from the era of "one platoon" football when everyone had to put in some time on both sides of the ball. As coaches pushed the rules more and more to two-platoon ball, the era of specialists was ushered in. Until the coming of Jim Brown, they probably didn't know that a guy *could* carry the ball that often.

Starting with Joe Perry, the closest thing to a "workhorse" that the '50s produced before Brown and Taylor, here's what some of the greats looked like at their four-year peaks:

Player, Years	G	CAR	YDS	YDS/CAR	YDS/G	TD
Joe Perry, 1952–54, '58	48	648	3550	5.47	73.9	30
Jim Taylor, 1960–62, '64	54	980	5051	5.15	93.5	57
Jim Brown, 1958, '63–65	54	1117	6380	5.71	118.1	53
OJ Simpson, 1972, '73, '75, '76	56	1243	6574	5.28	117.3	42
Larry Csonka, 1970–73	56	820	4045	4.93	72.2	24
Franco Harris, 1975–77, '79	57	1118	4722	4.22	83.7	46
Walter Payton, 1977, '79, '84, '85	62	1408	6697	4.75	108.0	48
Eric Dickerson, 1983, '84, '86, '88	64	1561	7393	4.73	115.5	57
Barry Sanders, 1991, '94, '96, '97	57	1315	7037	5.35	111.6	45
Emmitt Smith, 1991–93, '95	62	1398	6535	4.67	105.4	64

Some observations: first, it's hard to say that greater statistics indicate genuine superiority, partly because of the different styles of football that are played in every era but also because the way a back is used depends very much his team. For instance, discounting Joe Perry, who is a product of the '50s, the three backs here with the lowest number of carries—Jim Taylor, Larry Csonka, and Franco Harris—all played for winning teams. (Their teams won eleven championships among them. Emmitt Smith is the only recent back to play on winning teams and still get over 6,000 yards.)

On the whole, modern runners get more carries than old-timers, and not just because the number of games has increased. But though they get more carries than the old guys, their yards-per-rush average has gone down: the first four on the list (which goes to the 1976 season) also average over 5 yards per carry; five of the next six are under 5. But look at Barry Sanders! His yards per carry at peak is perhaps his best argument as the best of all time: he was getting 5+ yards at a time when no one else was getting 5.0 (see chapter 20 on Barry Sanders).

20

Barry Sanders: Pro Football's Greatest Runner

If Barry Sanders's retirement wasn't a ploy to get the Detroit Lions to deal him to a playoff-level team, then it should have been. God knows he certainly earned the right to play for a contender. Sadly, though, it wouldn't matter much if the Lions did want to trade him, thanks to the economics of professional football. When strikes and lockouts interrupt the action, a great many fans and sports writers are quick to support the owners' contention that salary caps are needed: what they are less quick to acknowledge are the injustices that caps do to players such as Sanders. The simple fact is that with spending limits firmly in place, most contending teams simply can't afford to pay Sanders, the greatest running back in pro-football history, what he is worth.

Did I say the greatest running back in National Football League history? I did, and though such judgments can never be more than subjective, I'd say there's plenty of evidence to back up the claim. First, if Sanders were to play this season and perform at close to his usual level, he would pass Walter Payton as No. 1 on the NFL's all-time rushing-yards-gained list (he's only 1,457 yards shy of Payton's career record of 16,726). Sanders, who is now 33 years old, also would have passed the 16,500-yard mark two years earlier than Payton did, and in at least 30 fewer games. Sanders averaged more than half-a-yard per carry more than Payton, and nearly 12 yards more per game. So much for the Walter Payton argument.

So much, in fact, for the argument for every other running back of the modern era. O. J. Simpson, Eric Dickerson, Emmitt Smith, and anyone else you care to name—Sanders was at least their equal in durability and their superior in elusiveness. You have to go back to Jim Brown to find Sanders's equal. Smith may well pass Sanders and Payton in total yardage—my guess is he'll do it by the end of the 2001 season—but could anyone deny that Smith also had much more support from the Dallas Cowboys' offensive line and passing game?

Not everyone, least of all Jim Brown himself, would concede that Barry Sanders has displayed "equal" durability. This is certainly understandable. Brown is one of the handful of truly dominating team athletes this century—eight rushing titles in nine seasons is all the evidence needed to back this up. But considering that the NFL has grown from fourteen teams in Jim Brown's day to twenty-eight teams, and that Sanders has twice as many competitors for the rushing title as Jim Brown did, Sanders's four titles in ten seasons is pretty impressive.

Consider, too, that rushing defenses are simply better now than they were when Brown played in the '50s and '60s. Rosters now are bigger, with most of the spots going to defensive specialists, which is one reason why the yards-per-rush average in the NFL, from '58 through his last season, '65, the league's yards-per-rush average was never below 4 yards a try, and three times it stood at 4.2 or better. From Barry Sanders's rookie year in '89 to last season, the league average reached 4.1 just once, and in five of ten seasons it dipped to 3.9 or lower.

Also, in the early part of Brown's career the league schedule was just 12 games; in '61 it went to 14. Sanders, on the other hand, played a 16-game schedule his whole career. Give Sanders a point for durability; in his best season he carried the ball 44 more times than Brown did in his best season. Who had more "quality" carries? Well, in his three best seasons, Brown averaged more yards per rush than Sanders did in his three best. But the game in Brown's day was more run-oriented, and the league's overall average was higher. In terms of *relative* yards per rush, that is, the runner's average vs. the league's, Sanders and Brown were, at their respective peaks, about dead even. But if you take the argument that the best defenses in league history were to appear in the 16-game era, then you must concede that Barry Sanders is the best ever.

And if you don't, what the hell, I'm really not going to the barricades to argue *against* Jim Brown. I'm here to argue *for* Barry Sanders, not *against* Jim Brown. Personally, I'm not sure I believe the entire argument myself, but if it doesn't succeed in putting Sanders over Brown, it does put a little daylight between Sanders and his contemporaries and near contemporaries.

SIX OF THE TOP RUNNERS IN MODERN PRO FOOTBALL

	G	Yds	Yds/Rush	Yds/G	TDs
Jim Brown (1957–65)	118	12312	5.2	104.3	106
O. J. Simpson (1969–79)	135	11236	4.7	83.2	61
Walter Payton (1975–87)	190	16726	4.4	88.0	110
Eric Dickerson (1983–93)	146	13529	4.4	90.8	90
Barry Sanders (1989–98)	153	15269	5.0	99.8	99
Emmitt Smith (1990–98)	140	12566	4.3	89.7	125

Clearing the Bases

BARRY SANDERS VS. JIM BROWN—THEIR THREE BEST SEASONS

SANDERS

Year	G	Rushes-Yds	Yds/Rush	Leag Avg	Diff
1997	16	335-2053	6.1	4.0	2.1
1994	16	331-1883	5.7	3.7	2.0
1989	15	280-1470	5.3	4.0	1.3

BROWN

Year	G	Rushes-Yds	Yds/Rush	Leag Avg	Diff
1963	14	291-1863	6.4	4.1	2.3
1958	12	257-1527	5.9	4.2	1.7
1960	12	215-1257	5.8	4.1	1.7

It could be argued, I suppose, that Barry Sanders *ought* to have more yards than Jim Brown because he got to play at least 2 extra games a season, but really, it's *carries* that matter, not games, and from that standpoint, Sanders, who was 5'9" and about 205 at his peak, was at least as durable as Brown, who was 6'2" and usually played about 228. By the way, if Brown had played longer, it's likely that that gaudy 5.2 yards-per-rush average would have dropped a little as it did with all other great backs who played after age thirty.

21

Walter Payton: Pro Football's Greatest Player

When Walter Payton passed Jim Brown to become pro football's all-time rushing leader in 1984, the Bears' hometown announcer beamed, "That's the equivalent of Henry Aaron passing up Babe Ruth." Yes and no. In terms of dominance, Jim Brown was very nearly Babe Ruth but not quite. For one thing, Brown had a remarkably short career, just nine National Football League seasons. Had he played 190 games, as Payton did, it's doubtful anyone would have approached his career-rushing total.

But the Payton-Aaron comparison is startlingly apt. Both had amazingly long careers—Payton's thirteen seasons as an NFL running back is about the equivalent of Aaron's twenty-three years as a major-league ballplayer—years that were largely injury-free for both of them. Both Payton and Aaron were versatile players, but they are best known for establishing career records for power: Aaron for home runs, Payton for the most

yards rushing. Both were known for a high quality of performance over a long period. Both spent most of their careers with
bad to mediocre teams and managed to walk away with one
championship ring.

Neither Payton nor Aaron was ever quite regarded as the
best—or at least, the best ever—at his position. Still, both Aaron
and Payton were so good on the field—and so well respected off
it—that any kind of qualification of their records almost sounds
like criticism.

The numbers make an irrefutable argument that Walter
Payton was one of the four, or even three, best running backs
ever, but beyond that it's a value judgment. Football statistics
are less sophisticated than baseball stats—that's often a disadvantage to the football analyst because it means you have less to
work with. But in some cases, such as in this one, it is a consid-
erable advantage. Babe Ruth was the most spectacular home-
run hitter in baseball history, period. Aaron had to bat more
than 3,000 more times to pass him up. Based simply on the
numbers, without considering any mitigating factors, Ruth was
clearly the greater slugger. End of that argument. Now I could
make a case that any mitigating factors work in Aaron's favor in
such a comparison, but that is another argument for another
time. No similar arguments can be made, however, when it
comes to comparing the great modern NFL running backs.
Football has been fully integrated since the early '60s, the rules
and tactics have remained substantially the same over that
period, and such innovations as night games have had little
impact on football compared with baseball. So it is possible to
make at least approximate comparisons.

In the Barry Sanders chapter, I made a comparison of the six
modern (since 1960) running backs who are acknowledged as
the best. Of those, Eric Dickerson, a contemporary of Payton's

who was considered as good as or better than "Sweetness" in several seasons, had the same yards-per-carry average and nearly 3 more yards per game, but 3,197 fewer yards gained. Virtually everyone who knew them would have preferred to have Payton on their team, as Dickerson was perceived as a selfish, one-dimensional player (check out the gap in receptions and passing yards), while Payton was considered a team leader. O. J. Simpson was the equal of or superior to Payton in most stats but faded much more quickly. While it may not be fair to blame Simpson for being injured, one must nonetheless give Payton big points for his durability. Advantage, Walter Payton.

Of course, one man who stacks up well against Payton is Brown. But while there weren't many changes in NFL football between Brown's time (1957–65) and Payton's, those changes all work to Payton's disadvantage. He had to play at least 2 more regular season games per year than Brown, which gives you more rushing opportunities but takes a greater physical toll. Speaking of which, Payton played numerous games on artificial turf, which, no matter what the management-produced statistics indicate, the players simply do not like. Also, rosters increased from Brown's era to Payton's, and opposing defenses had more specialists to put in key situations. This is an area where the fans must make their choices based on intuition because the stats can't tell you who accomplished the most. Here's one item I'd add to Payton's side of the ledger: though he was smaller, he was a much better blocker than Brown, who was notorious for not wanting to block.

The modern back whose record comes closest to Payton's is Barry Sanders and here the debate goes all Sanders's way. Sanders had a higher yards per rush, more yards per game, and if he'd played another season he might have surpassed Payton's career rushing total (he certainly would have passed him if he had played two more seasons). I can't see how this argument can be tilted toward Payton. The only nod that goes to Payton here is for durability, but then Sanders missed just 7 games.

For all that, Payton was both a better blocker and receiver than Sanders. So if I can't call Walter Payton the best running back in NFL history, maybe we'll have to settle for another title; my award for the best football player in NFL history.

Did I mention he filled in at quarterback in 1984?

RANKED BY RUSHING YARDS

	G	Yds	Yds Rush	Yds G	TDS
Walter Payton (1975–87)	190	16726	4.4	88.0	108
Barry Sanders (1989–98)	153	15269	5.0	99.8	99
Eric Dickerson (1983–93)	146	13529	4.4	90.8	90
Emmitt Smith (1990–99)*	147	13174	4.3	89.5	126
Jim Brown (1957–65)	118	12312	5.2	104.3	106
O. J. Simpson (1969–79)	135	11236	4.7	83.2	61

RANKED BY RECEPTIONS

	Recpts	Yds	Yds Catch	TDS
Walter Payton	492	4538	9.2	15
Emmitt Smith*	362	2236	6.2	8
Barry Sanders	281	2327	8.3	4
Eric Dickerson	281	2137	7.6	6
Jim Brown	262	2499	9.5	20
O. J. Simpson	203	2142	10.5	14

°Includes 7 games of 1999

Payton's Place

Someone argued that there was little difference between a pitchout to Payton and a pass to him, and judging from the huge difference in the number of career receptions between Walter Payton and most of his contemporaries, that's probably true. The only one of the great running backs with a chance to approach Payton in total catches is Emmitt Smith, and look at the whopping difference in yards per catch! Considering that for several seasons the Bears' only real passing threat was short passes to Payton—not safety-valve dropoffs but plays intended to swing the ball out to Walter and designed realistically to pick up no more than 5 or 6 yards—you have to wonder if about 150 of those tosses (and, say, maybe 1,000 of the yards gained on them) shouldn't be attached to his *rushing* totals. And then you have to wonder what his yards-per-catch average would look like if they were. You'd have the most prolific runner in NFL history with the receiving stats of a wide receiver.

22

Wilt vs. Russell:
A Reassessment

They were individually bigger than the game. In fact, to a large portion of the sports public in the '60s that only paid attention to pro basketball when the championships came around, they *were* the game. It wasn't Boston vs. Philly or, later, Boston vs. L.A.; it was Wilt vs. Russell. You have to realize that the dunk as we know it—the macho, crowd-pleasing power play—started with Chamberlain. And the shot-blocking specialist, the man capable of stopping the dunk—was Russell.

It goes without saying that Bill Russell is one of the greatest NBA players of all time, being voted the league's MVP by his fellow players no less than five times. But because Russell and the Celtics dominated pro ball, it's widely assumed that Russell outplayed Chamberlain in their many duels. In fact, it's almost a b-ball commonplace that the Celtics won primarily because Russell stopped Chamberlain. But though Russell was the greatest *winner* in NBA history, there's plenty of evidence to suggest that he wasn't the greatest *player*.

The Russell/Chamberlain debate usually tips in Russell's favor because Big Bill played for a team that won eleven NBA titles in thirteen seasons—more than any player in history. That's a pretty good reason. But as a result, a significant part of the press and public labeled Russell a winner—rightly so—and labeled his rival, Wilt, a loser/choker, an unfair tag that colored the way Chamberlain is viewed in basketball history.

Some of this, no doubt, had to do with resentment. Wilt Chamberlain, quite simply, was the most imposing physical specimen ever to step on a basketball court. Since his day, NBA players, because of weight training and diet, have grown by an average of nearly 30 pounds a man. But the game has yet to produce another Wilt. He stood over 7 feet and weighed around 300 muscled pounds. There had been other seven-footers before him (Bob Kurland and Walter Dukes were the best), but Wilt was stronger than just about all of them, and those who came close to matching his muscle couldn't match his quickness. Wilt dominated long before big, strong, and agile seven-footers like Jabbar, Walton, Ewing, Robinson, and O'Neal ever laced up a pair of high-tops, and he may have been the greatest athlete of them all. Because of his size and athletic prowess, no player in NBA history had more expectations placed on his huge shoulders than the Big Dipper. He could run and jump like a small forward—he ran the 440-yard dash and high-jumped in high school and college—and he was capable of breaking the arm of anyone who tried to block his dunk. His proposed bout with Muhammad Ali—the photo of them each extending their jabs toward each other highlighted Wilt's absurd advantage in reach—was largely a public relations stunt.

But Wilt was so powerful that there were sportswriters who gave Wilt a puncher's chance. Jim Murray, writing in the January 21, 1964, edition of the *Los Angeles Times*, glibly characterized Wilt's larger-than-life aura this way: "He was put together in a laboratory by a mad doctor with a pair of pliers, a screwdriver and a Bunsen burner." And Wilt's scoring and rebounding totals were otherworldly. He was a statistical Paul Bunyan—basketball's version of Babe Ruth—his scoring and rebounding numbers exceeding his peers' as the Babe's did his. In our own time, Dennis Rodman has been called "the best rebounder in NBA history." This is nonsense; Chamberlain (and for that matter Russell) was a much better rebounder, and on offense Chamberlain was a greater scorer than Michael Jordan.

On defense, Russell was cut from a similar mold. He was a rebounding and shot-blocking machine. In fact, he made shot-blocking and intimidation an art form, altering shots with a feint, keeping blocked balls in play instead of swatting them out of bounds—a play that usually triggered a Cousy-led fast break. Russell's catlike quickness and help-out defense allowed his teammates, especially K. C. Jones, the best defensive guard of his day, to gamble defensively. If Cousy or Jones went for a steal and missed, old number 6 was there to help out. Leonard Koppett, former *New York Times* columnist, in *24 Seconds to Shoot: An Informal History of the National Basketball Association* (Macmillan, 1968), wrote that former NBA All-Star Jack Twyman said: "Russell couldn't throw the ball in the ocean, but he allowed his teammates to press and gamble. You knew that if you got by Cousy or Heinsohn, that SOB Russell was back there waiting to block your shot." And Russell's defensive rebounding ferocity allowed his teammates to concentrate on offense. As Tommy Heinsohn said in Nelson George's *Elevating the Game* (HarperCollins, 1992), "We began crashing the offensive boards with abandon, which meant we were now taking more shots than ever, and our fast break became truly devastating."

The slender Russell was strong, but compared to Chamberlain, he looked like a mere mortal. At 6'9" and 225 lithe pounds, he was big enough to give Chamberlain a battle but small enough to *appear* like an underdog. And when the underdog's team won consistently, it maybe the bigger dog seem like a loser.

Actually, this winner/loser tag predated their first meeting in an NBA game. At the University of San Francisco, Russell and future Celtic teammate K. C. Jones won NCAA titles in 1954–55 and 1955–56 (winning 55 straight at one point). After his senior season, Russell turned down Abe Saperstein's offer to play for the Globetrotters and teamed with K. C. to help lead the 1956 Olympic team to a gold medal. The next season Chamberlain carried the Kansas Jayhawks to the NCAA title game (beating a Russell-less San Francisco squad in the semis). Kansas faced the University of North Carolina in the 1957 final. Wilt played well, scoring 23 points and grabbing 14 rebounds, but no other Jayhawk could find the basket with any consistency. In the first two overtimes, Chamberlain's teammates missed free throws and turned the ball over.

Two plays at the end of the game would come to symbolize other heartbreaking losses Wilt endured in his future NBA career. The first happened with thirty-two seconds left in the third OT when Tommy Kearns drove the middle against Wilt. Chamberlain blocked the shot, but Joe Quigg, trailing the play, grabbed the ball and was fouled. Quigg hit both free throws to put UNC up 54–53. The final play was supposed to be an alley-oop to Wilt, but the Tarheels surrounded him and the inbounds pass came in low and was batted away to preserve the win. It was the longest game in NCAA Final history. Afterward Tarheel coach Frank McGuire said, "We had a better team. We beat Kansas, not him. We put five guys on him and he still scored, but we won. But that wasn't Wilt's fault." No matter. Young Wilt took the fall.

Even before they faced off, the critics said, "The unselfish Russell won two NCAA titles while the selfish Chamberlain didn't win one." After the 1956 Olympics, Russell signed with Boston for $22,000. He led the league in rebounding (19.6) and helped Boston beat Bob Pettit and the St. Louis Hawks in the 1957 NBA finals, 4 games to 3. While Russell was winning his first crown, Chamberlain, who left Kansas after his junior year, joined the Globetrotters, signing for the then-lofty sum of $65,000. The line, after that, was "Russell is a proud warrior who wants to play against the best; Chamberlain the clown takes the money and runs." The Chamberlain vs. Russell debate became a morality play that colored people's views of the two players' abilities.

Too often the debate on their various merits would end with the question "Who has the most rings?" A fairer question might have been "What would have happened had Wilt played with Russell's Boston teams?"; or "How many titles would Russell have won with Wilt's supporting casts?" And in truth not everyone assumed that Russell was superior. As Leonard Koppett wrote in *24 Seconds to Shoot*, "The reason Wilt's teams were taking Russell's teams to seventh games in the playoffs was because of Wilt and his incredible ability. It is absolute nonsense to say that Wilt dragged his teams down."

Clearing the Bases

What do the numbers say? From 1959 to 1969, Russell and Chamberlain faced each other 162 times. Russell's team won 88, Chamberlain's 74. Not nearly as great a disparity as many would have guessed. Chamberlain averaged 28.8 points and 28.7 rebounds in those games compared to 23.7 and 14.5 rebounds for Russell. Wilt had a 62-point game on January 14, 1962, in Boston, and had six other games of at least 50 points against Russell. The most Russell ever scored against Wilt was 37 points, and he had only two other 30-point games. Chamberlain grabbed an NBA-record 55 rebounds against Russell on November 24, 1960, and had six other games of at least 40 rebounds against Russell. Russell's best rebounding night against Chamberlain was 40 on February 12, 1961. But Chamberlain's teams lost all four seventh games they played against Russell's Celtics; the margins of defeat in those games totaled 9 points.

Here's a more detailed look at Wilt's and Russell's statistics during the ten years their careers overlapped.

WILT CHAMBERLAIN

Year	Reb	Reb/Avg	FG%	Pts	Avg
1959–60	1941	26.9	.461	2707	37.6
1960–61	2149	27.2	.509	3033	38.4
1961–62	2052	25.6	.506	4029	50.4
1962–63	1946	24.3	.528	3586	44.8
1963–64	1787	22.3	.524	2948	36.9
1964–65	1673	22.9	.510	2534	34.7
1965–66	1943	24.6	.540	2649	33.5
1966–67	1957	24.1	.683	1956	24.1
1967–68	1952	23.8	.595	1992	24.3
1968–69	1712	21.1	.583	1664	20.5
10 years	19112	24.2	.543	27098	34.5

BILL RUSSELL

Year	Reb	Reb/Avg	FG%	Pts	Avg
1959–60	1778	24.0	.467	1350	18.2
1960–61	1868	23.9	.426	1322	16.9
1961–62	1891	24.8	.457	1436	18.9
1962–63	1843	23.6	.432	1309	16.8
1963–64	1930	24.7	.433	1168	15.0
1964–65	1878	24.0	.438	1102	14.1
1965–66	1779	22.8	.415	1005	12.9
1966–67	1700	20.9	.454	1075	13.3
1967–68	1451	18.6	.425	977	12.5
1968–69	1484	19.2	.433	762	9.9
10 years	17602	22.6	.438	11506	14.8

Why, you may ask, didn't I rank them by the same Max Points formula I use in *The Wall Street Journal?* And the reason is simple: several of the stats needed for Max Points such as blocked shots and steals weren't kept back then. In fact, it was the play of these two that caused these stats to be kept. Anyway, when you compare the numbers, it's obvious that Wilt was the most prodigious scorer who ever played. He led the NBA in scoring in his first seven seasons. And in 1961–62 he *averaged* 50.4 points per game on 50 percent field goal shooting. The field goal percentage is the key; not only did Chamberlain outscore Russell by a wide margin, which would probably be expected given the dependence of Wilt's team on him, but his shooting percentage is more than 100 points higher than Russell's. Wilt's superiority wasn't simply a question of scoring opportunities. During the Russell years, Chamberlain averaged 34.5 points per game against the league; against Russell he scored 28.7 points per game—5.8 points below his league-leading average. That, of course, shows how much better defensively Russell was than the other centers around the league. Still, Wilt did average 28.7 points against perhaps the greatest defensive center who ever played and poured 40 points or more against Russell twenty-six times. Russell, on the other hand, averaged a modest 14.8 points per game during that ten-year span against the rest of the league. (He averaged 15.1 points during his thirteen-year career.) Against Wilt, he scored 23.7 points per game, 8.9 points *higher* than his regular season average. That shows you how adaptable and talented Russell was; it's also an indication that Russell could have scored more points if the Celtics had needed him to. He scored more against Wilt because he felt he had to. Against the rest of the league he didn't need to score for the Celtics to win. Still Wilt averaged 5 points per game more than Russell during their head-to-head meetings and he had a higher field goal percentage during the ten year span they faced each other every year except Wilt's rookie season. Scoring advantage: Wilt.

Rebounding? Bill Russell is regarded by many as the greatest rebounder to ever play, and he was an octopus under the boards, averaging 22.5 a game for his career. *But Wilt averaged more rebounds in eight of the ten seasons they both played in the league. And against Chamberlain, Russell averaged just 14.8 rebounds per game.* Wilt's career rebounding average was 22 per game. Against Russell, he averaged 28.7, 4.5 more than he pulled down against the rest of the league. Rebounding edge: Wilt.

Blocked shots? Again, back then, the NBA didn't keep blocked-shot stats. But it's generally acknowledged that Russell and Chamberlain were the greatest shot-blockers of their time. Referee Earl Storm, who worked countless games between the two, said, "Wilt and Russell were getting 8 to 10 blocks a game for most of their careers." But Chamberlain scored so much he didn't get as much credit for clogging the middle as Russell.

Clearly, the most telling reason Russell is considered the more dominant player is winning percentage. From 1959 to 1969, Chamberlain's teams won 62 percent of their games while Russell's Celtics won 71 percent. Russell, of course, was the main man in the greatest dynasty in NBA history. But compare the respective rosters and check the number of close playoff games the two faced off in, and it's not unreasonable to contend that Wilt's squads did more with less.

In 1960, Chamberlain's rookie season, he led the NBA with 37.6 points and 27 rebounds per game. The Celtics, who beat Wilt's Warriors in six games in the divisional finals, had seven future Hall of Famers on the roster: Russell, Cousy, Bill Sharman, Tom Heinsohn, Sam and K. C. Jones, and Frank Ramsey. Eight, if you count coach Red Auerbach.

In 1965, Chamberlain was traded in midseason from San Francisco to Philadelphia. Once again, Wilt met Russell's Celts in the Eastern Conference finals. Not only had Wilt lost to Russell in 1960, but he was edged out by Boston in the Eastern Conference finals in seven games in 1962, and in 1964 Wilt's San Francisco Warriors lost in five games to Boston in the NBA Finals. In game 7 of the 1965 Eastern Finals, Boston seemed to be in control, up 110–103 with two minutes to play. But Wilt scored 6 straight and Boston's lead was cut to 110–109 with five seconds left. All Boston had to do to win was inbound the ball. But Russell, who was throwing under his own basket, banged the ball off a guide wire that supported the basket, giving the ball back to Philly. But as frenzied Celtic announcer Johnny Most told the world that was listening on radio, the Sixers never got off a shot because

Clearing the Bases

"Johnny Havlicek Stole The Ball!" Again, the press colored the public's perception of the Wilt-Russ rivalry. "Later," wrote Terry Pluto, "one wouldn't talk about how Bill Russell messed up the inbounds pass, or how the Celtics couldn't score in the last two minutes of the game—a home game. They would not remember that Wilt had carried the Sixers back into the game with his clutch play. Some fans would insist that Chamberlain 'choked,' incorrectly saying that Wilt threw away the inbounds pass to Havlicek. . . . and naturally, like Boston announcer Johnny Most, what they remember is that Havlicek stole the ball and Boston won, 110–109." For the record, Boston beat L.A. in seven games to win their seventh straight NBA title.

In 1966–67, Wilt showed the sporting world what he could do with a competent coach, Alex Hannum, and a strong supporting cast that featured Hal Greer, Chet Walker, Luke Jackson, and supersub Billy Cunningham. (A quick note on Hannum: from 1957–69, Boston won 11 NBA titles in thirteen years. The other two belonged to Hannum-coached teams— the 1958 St. Louis Hawks and the 1967 Sixers.) Wilt averaged a then-career low 24 points per game on a career-high 68 percent shooting. (Philly was awesome, winning an NBA record 68 games.) He was also third in the league in assists with 7.8 a game. It was the first time since Wilt came into the league that he was not the NBA's leading scorer. Many critics said that Chamberlain would have won more titles earlier in his career had he scored less. As Terry Pluto mentions in *Tall Tales*, Hannum disagrees. "For the first time it wasn't necessary for Wilt to lead the league—or even his team—in scoring for us to win. He was never on a team with as much talent as we had on the 1967 Sixers. If we weren't that deep, I would have needed Wilt to score more." In his matchup against Russell in the

Eastern Conference Finals, Wilt averaged 22 points, 32 rebounds, and 10 assists—that's a triple-double for the five-game series.

In winning his first NBA crown, Chamberlain immodestly juxtaposed his success against Russell's. "What made the Celtics great was that all Bill Russell had to do was the blue-collar work—rebound and play defense. He had other great players around him to score the points. When Wilt Chamberlain was given that same luxury, the result was that the Sixers were the greatest team of all time."

Russell's greatness cannot be discussed without references to Red Auerbach. Cousy characterized Auerbach this way: "Arnold was a gutter rat out of the ghetto. His strength was motivation. During a game, he was demonstrative and emotional, up and down on the bench, yelling, wearing your ass out. Red ran training camps like Vince Lombardi, making the Celts the best-conditioned team in the NBA. And he was the master of taking a technical foul to fire up his team." Auerbach was also superb at molding talent into one cohesive unit. He ran a system that accentuated each player's strengths and hid their weaknesses. His emphasis was on the team concept—his prowess as an evaluator of talent made Boston the well-oiled machine they were. When sixth-man supersub Frank Ramsey, whom Auerbach called "the most versatile player in the NBA," slowed down, he was replaced by John Havlicek, a tireless clutch player who starred in the NBA for sixteen years. And in Satch Sanders, Boston had the best defensive forward in the NBA. When Cousy and Sharman retired, for example, Auerbach had K. C. and Sam Jones on the bench. The "Jones Boys," as they were called, were not brothers, but they complemented each other like twins. Sam was his perfect partner. Few people mention him when they talk about great scoring guards (Oscar Robertson and Jerry West may have something to do with that), but Sam was a brilliant scorer (he was famous for banking the ball off the glass) and a renowned clutch shooter. Unlike Wilt, Russell rarely took the last shot in a close game. Sam Jones did.

Leonard Koppett wrote in *24 Seconds to Shoot* that Wilt was a victim of poor management: "I call Wilt Chamberlain a very honest workman. By that, I mean he always did what his employer wanted. No star athlete has ever given his boss more for the money than Wilt did during his career. Eddie Gottlieb wanted Wilt to score like no man ever had, so Wilt did. Some of his other coaches wanted him to pass and play defense, so he did that, and he played 48 minutes a night. Those who criticized Wilt—first for his scoring, then for not scoring more—really should have criticized his employer." Or perhaps, not have criticized Chamberlain at all.

Did race play a role in the public's perception of the two players? Chamberlain has said that Russell was more popular because he played a style that fit the media's image of what a black player was then supposed to be—a blue-collar worker who was there to rebound and play defense—letting the other guys score. In Nelson George's superb *Elevating the Game*, Wilt is quoted as saying "They didn't want any black player to steal the scoring thunder from the white stars, until yours truly did it." However reluctant one is to accept this, it's true. Wilt Chamberlain was a black star who understood his worth and expressed his opinions, something blacks were not supposed to do in the 1950s and 1960s. Al Attles, a longtime friend of Wilt's, says in the same book, "Wilt drove big cars, had a lot of girlfriends and was very opinionated. This bothered some people, especially the establishment types and some of the older people in the media. So he was portrayed in a negative light, as if he were a trouble-maker. Yet he was always there for practice. He'd play every minute of every game and he was good with the fans . . . but he also knew basketball was a business and he wasn't about to let people take advantage of him when it came to his contracts."

Perhaps Wilt could have won more had he not been so preoccupied with answering the sportswriters who questioned his ability to win the big one. And certainly, his horrible foul shooting hurt his team in close games. In four seventh-game playoff losses to the Celtics (1962, 1965, 1968, and 1969), Boston won by a total of 9 points. In those four losses, Wilt missed 24 free throws. "It was as if he had an ax to grind with the press," said John Havlicek, "whereas Russell never let himself get caught up in that."

Then again, if he had had more skillful coaches or better teammates, he wouldn't have had to shoot so much and he might have won six or seven titles instead of two and thus been given his due as the most dominant center ever to play.

Again, this is not to diminish Bill Russell's accomplishments. He could reasonably be called the greatest defensive player and winner the NBA has ever known. He just wasn't the best player. Ironically, Russell's defensive greatness brought out the best in Chamberlain. Bill Cunningham told a *Philadelphia Inquirer* reporter, "When you were on the court with them, they so dominated that you'd find yourself stopping just to watch them. I've never had that feeling with any two other players."